Your Towns and Cities in

৵৵

Clacton-on-Sea and the Surrounding Coastline in the Great War

Ken Porter

Pen & Sword
MILITARY

First published in Great Britain in 2017 by

PEN & SWORD MILITARY

An imprint of
Pen & Sword Books Ltd
47 Church Street
Barnsley
South Yorkshire
S70 2AS

ISBN 978-1-47386-025-4

Typeset in Times NR MT10.5/13.5 by SRJ Info Jnana System Pvt Ltd.
Printed and bound in England
By CPI Group (UK) Ltd, Croydon, CR0 4YY

Pen & Sword Books Limited incorporates the imprints of Atlas,
Archaeology, Aviation, Discovery, Family History, Fiction, History,
Maritime, Military, Military Classics, Politics, Select, Transport, True
Crime, Air World, Frontline Publishing, Leo Cooper, Remember When,
Seaforth Publishing, The Praetorian Press, Wharncliffe Local History,
Wharncliffe Transport, Wharncliffe True Crime and White Owl.

For a complete list of Pen & Sword titles please contact
PEN & SWORD BOOKS LIMITED
47 Church Street, Barnsley, South Yorkshire, S70 2AS, England
E-mail: enquiries@pen-and-sword.co.uk
Website: www.pen-and-sword.co.uk

Contents

Acknowledgements

Writing a book of this nature requires a considerable amount of research and I could not have completed it without the help and co-operation of a large number of people and interested groups. Special thanks must, however, go to the Basildon Heritage and Laindon and District Community Archive who have helped with research and the verification of information that I have sourced, in particular Norman Bambridge and Dawn Knox, Sue Ranford, Joy and Rob Springate, and Chris Saltmarsh who has provided many postcards; Many thanks must go to Phyllis M. Hendy for allowing me to use her research concerning the men of St Osyth, and also Reverend Peter Kane and Peter Luckin, Church Warden of St James Church, Clacton, and Jo Jellis and Jean Clements for allowing me to use their research on the Parish of St James. Finally Andy Shaw for also allowing me to use his research on the men of Frinton.

I have made every effort to contact the copyright holders of images and documents and would like to thank those that have given their permission and I would like to apologise to anybody not properly acknowledged or whom I have not managed to trace.

Introduction

❧

As we were all taught at school the last time Britain was successfully invaded was by the Normans under William the Conqueror in 1066. That does not mean that there have not been numerous attempts since, however. The Spanish Armada in 1588 is one example and there are numerous beacons around the country that commemorate this event.

One of the country's biggest scares came at the time when Napoleon and his French troops were sweeping across Europe and, as we had gone to the aid of our European allies, he decided to invade England. As usual our Navy came to our rescue with Nelson defeating the combined French and Spanish fleet at the Battle of Trafalgar in 1805.

The county of Essex has possibly one of the longest coastlines in England, at over 350 miles, and with its rivers and inlets is in theory an open invitation for invasion. The coastline from Brightlingsea on the mouth of the River Colne round to the Naze at Walton, a distance of approximately twenty miles, is part of the Essex Sunshine Coast, a coastline of sandy beaches and low cliffs. No wonder it was seen as not being particular difficult to penetrate by a resolute invasion force.

For this part of Britain's east coast possibly its only saviour is the North Sea and its many dangerous sandbanks such as Dogger Bank. However, it did not deter our early visitors, the Celts, Saxons and Vikings. So it's not surprising that as the centuries passed, Essex, with the fear of possible invasion by the Spanish, Dutch and French, had become a very heavily defended county. It had many military camps scattered across it. Colchester, for example, only sixteen miles from the Clacton coast, is one of the oldest military garrisons in Britain.

In anticipation of an invasion by the French the government built a chain of fortifications known as Martello Towers between 1805 and 1812. They got their name from the tower built at Martella Point on the island of Corsica. The authorities built 103 of them from Seaford in Sussex to Aldeburgh in Suffolk. Examples were also built in Scotland, Wales and Ireland and also in its many overseas territories.

Martello Tower, Jaywick. (Author's collection)

Eleven were built in Essex: two at St Osyth, one at Jaywick, three at Clacton, three at Holland-on-Sea and one at Walton. The three on Holland marshes were demolished in 1819, one of those at St Osyth was demolished in 1967 and the one at Walton was demolished due to the eroding coast. The remaining towers are all Grade II listed.

The towers were all brick built with the walls facing the seaside 50 per cent thicker. They had three floors with the entrance at first-floor level reached by a ladder or where there was a moat with a drawbridge. The first floor was divided into three parts, one for billeting the garrison of twenty-four men, one room for the commanding officer and the other for the quartermaster's storeroom. A rack holding twenty-seven muskets ran around the central column. The basement was for storage of provisions and ammunition. The roof area was usually armed with a 24-pounder gun, two smaller carronades plus howitzers installed for short-range defence.

Soldiers mining Clacton Pier.

Once the threat of invasion had passed, they were vacated by the military and took on other functions, such as bases for the coastguards. However, many towers were re-fortified in subsequent crises until developments in weapons technology rendered them obsolete.

In the First and Second World Wars many were adopted for military use and concrete pillboxes were in some cases constructed on their roofs to house Royal Observer Corps (ROC) posts.

The Tower, Marine Parade West, Clacton-on-Sea became a coastguard lookout station in 1888 but during the Great War became a piquet station for G Company of 8th Battalion, the Essex Regiment, as was the tower at Point Clear, St Osyth. Piquet duty was where a section of men provided a first line of defence in the event of an attack. Their job was to hold up the enemy long enough for the main force to be deployed efficiently

Although the possibility of war and a German invasion was being played down in late July 1914, army reservists had been instructed to report to their stations. Clacton Pier, for example, was placed under military guard on 30 July. Armed sentries appeared along the Clacton seafront. Territorial units took up positions along the coast and the resorts of Clacton, Great Holland, Frinton and Walton were placed in a designated prohibited zone that stretched inland for up to ten miles, and presumably Brightlingsea and St Osyth fell within this zone. Restrictions were particularly severe and by September the resorts were placed under martial law regarding the illumination of streets and shops, particularly near the seafront.

The military prepared defences along the seafront with barbed wire and sandbag parapets, and trenches were dug along the cliffs where possible. Clacton Pier was mined and the seafront closed to the public at night and throughout the war troops were billeted and trained in the area and patrolled the coastline.

The following is an extract from Harold Bartholomew's memories of one of his patrols in the opening days of the war, taken down by Age Concern:

It is August 3rd 1914, I am at my home – Earls Colne – it is August Bank Holiday and there is an air of excitement and talk of war. I have my latest girlfriend with me – we decide to cycle back to Braintree in the cool of the evening. We say good night at midnight and I return to my lodgings. There on the table is a long buff envelope with my calling up papers. I hastily read it – Report 9 am the square Braintree – full marching order. I rush round to my girl's home – some pebbles on the bedroom window does the trick – we seem to have a lot to say and at 3 am I return to catch a few hours' sleep. Then at 9 am I join the rest of the boys of H Coy. 8th Essex Cyclist Battalion under our Sergeant Major and we moved off to destination unknown. Late afternoon found us dispersed in small sections along the Essex Coast and marshes from Walton on Naze to Tollesbury. E, F, and G coys were sharing the coast from Harwich to Walton and Maldon to Shoeburyness.

I could fill a book with the amusing episodes which happened during my period of patrolling the area. There was the case of the cow. I was corporal and was in charge of a section of 9 men stationed in the Martello Tower near the jetty (now demolished). We had a sentry posted on the jetty – which had the golf links and marsh land behind it. Before turning in I made a tour of duty to see if the 3 sentries were ok. The one at the jetty was a fellow named Sparrow – who had a flair for playing games and hoaxes on others, but now he seemed worried and nervous – he said he had heard someone walking about on the marshes behind the hedge – So I told him (perhaps with tongue in cheek) he knew his orders – challenge etc – fire a shot. Imagine my surprise a few

> minutes later as I was getting into my blankets to hear a shot.
> I rushed along to Sparrow – he was peering through the hedge.
> 'What's happened' I shouted. He replied 'I heard him again and
> I said halt – I could hear his breathing – halt or I shoot – and he
> coughed right in my face – so I fired and heard a thud'. We crept
> through the hedge and there laid the cow!

Amusing now but story just brings home how scared even our soldiers were.

Brightlingsea housed Australian and New Zealand engineers. Clacton's Middlesex Hospital Convalescent Home and Reckitt's Convalescent Home became military hospitals for the duration of the war. Clacton also had an airfield established.

With fear of invasion spreading local volunteer defence groups were formed but their numbers were soon depleted as the younger members enlisted. The groups were often short of equipment, for example by February 1915 Clacton's group had sixty members but only twenty-five rifles between them.

Was it then the assassination of Archduke Franz Ferdinand of Austria and his wife Sophie by a young Serbian, Gavrilo Princip, that caused the Great War? Hindsight now tells us that this, along with Russian support of Serbia, was just the final straw following a century of discontent and short ethnic conflicts amongst the nations Europe and the Balkans, along with distrust heightened by the Franco-Prussian (German) war of 1870–1 and the Balkan Wars of the early twentieth century.

There is no doubt that even if Russia had not supported Serbia in defying Austria and war at this time had been averted, sooner or later the various alliances would have made war inevitable. A commitment to defend Belgian neutrality and a promise to protect the northern coast of France if it was threatened by Germany resulted in Britain being dragged into the war, but there was no need to worry because the war would be over by Christmas.

While all the political wrangling was going on, what was the public in Britain thinking and doing? Well, Britain had given Germany an ultimatum to get out of Belgium by midnight of 3 August, this was ignored. So at 7 pm on 4 August Britain officially declared war on Germany. Crowds had been gathering outside Buckingham Palace for a few days, reaching record numbers within a short time of the

THE MILITARY IN ESSEX.

Military camp at Clacton. (Author's collection)

announcement of war. The King and Queen, accompanied by the Prince of Wales and Princess Mary, initially appeared on the balcony at 8 pm to wild, enthusiastic cheers. They reappeared following further shouts of 'We want our King' at 11.10 pm with the crowd cheering and singing the National Anthem.

Volunteers rushed to sign up for the adventure, food prices started to rise immediately but as a cricket fanatic it was interesting to see that a full programme of first-class cricket matches were to continue. However, it was only a matter of weeks before first-class cricket was cancelled. A letter from W.G. Grace to *The Sportsman*, helped to prompt the cancellation, although where possible club cricket continued throughout the war.

The progress of the previous thirty years therefore came to a grinding halt and the trade and prosperity of the seaside towns were considerably curtailed. As it turned out, the area did not see any actual fighting other than the occasional Zeppelin or aircraft raid, although there was a considerable amount of military, naval and other war activities.

An Essex infantry brigade, a Territorial unit of around 3,000 men were in their annual camp at Clacton about two and half miles from the sea front. The men were offered £1 if they stayed on for fifteen days but then instead of going home they were sent off to make up the numbers in various regiments.

Four 15-pounder field guns were soon positioned at Clacton with four more at Frinton. Up on the Naze, a brick and concrete emplacement was erected overlooking the estuary, capable of supporting a field gun. Elsewhere the areas that were susceptible to a possible invasion by the Kaiser's army were cut up by trenches and the countryside was dotted with pillboxes. Residents were also advised of the various ditches in which they might seek shelter should such a situation arose.

The 17th Battalion of the Gloucestershire Regiment (TF) spent 1917 and 1918 at Clacton, Walton-on-the-Naze and St Osyth, and we must not forget the Australians and New Zealanders who were stationed at Brightlingsea for the majority of the war or our womenfolk who took on the jobs of our men or became nurses at home and overseas.

As late as May 1918, however, the village of St Osyth experienced a nasty scare. On the night of 19 May some thirty to forty German long-range Gotha and Giant bombers made their last attack on London. They dropped twenty-nine bombs killing forty-nine people and injuring seventy-seven, but the cost to the enemy was also high with between seven and eleven aircraft failing to return to their airfields.

The attack lasted three hours; three bombers were brought down between London and the south-east coast by Sopwith Camel fighters and anti-aircraft fire. Two more crashed into the sea and one Gotha crash-landed at Parks Farm on the outskirts of St Osyth after being hit by anti-aircraft fire from Bradwell in Essex. The pilot had jettisoned his bombs in a desperate attempt to keep his aircraft airborne. Fortunately the bombs fell harmlessly on the marshes, but close enough to scare the inhabitants of an old farmhouse at Cockett Wick near Pump Hill.

The aircraft had hit a tree, killing its pilot Leutnant H. Rist and slightly injuring his two crew members. They were taken prisoner by a young soldier armed with an unloaded Lee-Enfield rifle with an 18in bayonet fixed. The dead pilot was buried with full military honours a few days later at Great Clacton Cemetery. Forty years later his remains were exhumed by the German War Graves Commission and reburied at the German Military Cemetery at Cannock Chase in Staffordshire.

While our young men were initially rushing to sign up, the remaining local inhabitants as indicated were preparing to support them, in particular our womenfolk who in addition to taking up nursing were taking over the jobs previously done by the menfolk.

In the years before the Great War the various villages and small towns that made up this section of the Sunshine Coast were still mainly agricultural, with strong connections to the sea, in particular Brightlingsea, but as has already been mentioned, all were becoming well-known seaside resorts. For example, in 1914 at Clacton-on-Sea on the August Bank Holiday weekend, which was the 2nd and 3rd, thousands flocked to the town. Presumably it was the same in the other seaside towns on this stretch of the Essex coastline. Arnold Bennett, a famous novelist of the time, reported a great crowd at Clacton on the day war was declared but a week later it was practically empty of visitors.

To win this war not only did our politicians need to stay committed but we also needed to be successful on four war fronts, the home front with its volunteers, maintain control of the sea and the air, and then win the land battle.

More than 8,000 Essex men were killed in action or died of wounds or disease during the war. Clacton and the surrounding area lost their fair share and one cannot write a book on the area without mentioning Frinton's VC hero from the Boer War, Captain John Norwood, and Walton's VC hero, Herbert Columbine.

Many of the battles described are not necessarily in chronological order but before looking at our local heroes and the battles they were involved in, let's have a brief look at the history of the area over the decades/centuries prior to the Great War: Brightlingsea, St Osyth, Clacton-on-Sea, Frinton-on-Sea, Walton-on-the-Naze and the Holland area.

CHAPTER 1

Our Towns

࿇

Brightlingsea

Our first port of call is Brightlingsea, and being on the mouth of
the River Colne with access to the North Sea it was as you would
expect an ancient maritime town. Its traditional industries other than
agriculture were boat building and fisheries (it was famous for its
oysters).

The *Chelmsford Chronicle* reported on 27 February 1914 that the
Brightlingsea sprat season had reached its end and though the fish
arrived late, four firms exported to Germany 82,000 bushels with the
fishermen obtaining good prices; a little surprising considering the
political rumblings on the Continent at the time. Even a month after
the war had commenced we find that the Brightlingsea fishermen
were still sending large quantities of oysters to the Continent. Also the
Colne Oyster Fishery Company offered 10,000 oysters for wounded
soldiers.

Brightlingsea is also famous for its connection with the Cinque
Ports of Kent and Sussex. The ports, five in all, were established well
over 1,000 years ago to maintain and supply the King with ships and
men. Years later it was found necessary to have a number of subsidiary
ports call 'Limbs' and Brightlingsea became the limb of Sandwich,
Kent, the only port outside Kent and Sussex. Back at the time of
the Domesday survey (1086) it was still an island and the name the
Normans gave it was Brictriceseia, possibly a Norman misspelling
of the Saxon name Brickesey meaning the Brictric's island belong to
Saxon tribe called Brihllingas or Brightlings.

The harbour at Brightlingsea, 1915. (Author's collection)

Because of its yachting scene it has been favoured by a number
of visits from Royalty: King Edward VII and his son the Prince of
Wales, the Italian Duc de Areizzi, nephew of King of Italy, and Duke
Alexander of Russia, cousin of the Tsar, when he visited to purchase
the *Lady Tor Freda* from a Mr Bayard Brown.

In the centre of the town is Jacob's Hall, possibly the oldest
surviving timber-framed building in England and probably named
after its original owner. It gets its first mention in 1315. On 13 June
1938 Her Majesty Queen Mary visited the hall along with Princess
Alice, Countess of Athlone, The Earl of Athlone and Viscountess
Byng of Vimy. The Queen also went on to visit the 'Hard', possibly
one of most attractive spots of the town in its early days. The 'Hard'
with its fine causeway was constructed in 1882 and was the harbour
for the local boat industry and a place of interest for townsfolk to
gather and watch the boats arrive from the various yachts at anchor
or the sailors on their return from fishing expeditions.

The ancient parish church (Grade I listed) of All Saints' stands on
a hill at the northern edge of the town and dates from the thirteenth
century. One of its amazing features is a band of some 200-plus square
memorial tiles dating from 1872 to 1973, recording persons who had
died at sea. The tiles were idea of Reverend Arthur Pertwee following
a disaster in 1883 when nineteen Brightlingsea men were drowned off
the Dutch coast. He decided to go back to the year he was inducted
at All Saints', 1872, and record all those Brightlingsea men who lost

Jacob's Hall. (Author's collection)

their lives at sea. He was helped in his work by the churchwarden, William Stammers, and Arthur Blyth who wrote the inscriptions. Mr Stammers also donated £200 to be used for the erection and maintenance of the tiles. As far as it is known these memorial tiles are unique in English churches. Another interesting building is Bateman's Tower. It was built in 1883 by John Bateman as a folly for his daughter who was suffering from consumption. It is situated on West Marsh Point at the entrance to Brightlingsea Creek.

In 1866 the Wivenhoe and Brightlingsea Railway opened and was a branch line until it fell victim to the Beeching cuts in the 1960s. The opening of the railway was probably part of the reason that in the next thirty years the population increased by nearly 1,500 (1871 – 3,075, 1901 – 4,501). The railway also helped attract tourists to the town, the beginnings of a seaside resort. The town cinema opened on Boxing Day 1912.

Unlike the other towns, agriculture played second fiddle to the fishing and boat-building industry in the years leading up to the Great War and is no doubt the reason why so many young men from Brightlingsea ended up in the Royal and Merchant Navies.

All Saints' Church, 1912. (Author's collection)

In the later months of 1914 Brightlingsea saw the arrival of many companies of the Royal Engineers, the first from Bristol, as its natural facilities were ideal for training in pontooning, bridging and engineering work. Many of these engineers were skilled artisans, surveyors and architects who were taken into local homes and treated with great hospitality, as were the Australians and New Zealanders who came and went over the next four years.

Batemans Tower. (Author's collection)

Brightlingsea People who lost their lives as a result of the Great
War 1914-1918

Tell the dear old folks I thought of them
And that I did the best I could
And that if I had had the chance
To come back home I would,
But a Greater Power came in Between,
No more on Earth will I roam,
But tell them that the last thought of their boy,
Was of the dear old folks at home

By Sydney Lulkin Vinson

Sydney Vinson was born in Brightlingsea in 1895 to William John and Ada Vinson. The 1911 census has them living at 47 Tower Street, Brightlingsea. Sydney's occupation at the time was that of a shoemaker. His mother was widowed, his father having died in 1907. From his medal card it would appear that he embarked for France on 14 August 1915 having joined the Royal Army Medical Corps, rank private, serial number 100. However, the records show he was discharged on 4 August 1916 but unable to establish whether this was through injury or illness. He was awarded the 1914-15 Star, Victory and British Medals.

He had three other brothers, William, Gordon and Clarence, all older, so one can only assume they enlisted into the army and as they do not appear on the Brightlingsea Roll of Honour one can only assume that they like Sydney survived the war. There was a fourth brother, Kenneth, but he was only 14 when the war ended.

St Osyth

Moving eastward along the coast we come to St Osyth. It gets its name after the saint and Anglian princess 'Osyth'. Osyth was given the village by Sighere, King of Essex (664–83) to open a convent, a little surprising considering he had re-converted to paganism. To the west of the village, near the River Colne, is the village of Point Clear.

In 1121, Richard de Belmeis, Bishop of London, founded St Osyth Abbey, initially as a house for Augustinian monks. It became one of the largest monasteries in Essex. Prior to being named Osyth

Clacton Road, St Osyth. (Author's collection)

the village was called CiC (Domesday survey spelt Chicc). normally pronounced Chich (Chiche or Chick), referring to the creek and meaning bent or twisted or curved.

In 1118 Bishop Richard also founded the now Grade I listed church of St Peter and St Paul which is situated in the heart of the village and is one of the finest churches in Essex. Although a religious centre the village got caught up in the witch persecutions of the sixteenth and seventeenth centuries and in fact a total of ten local women were hanged as a result.

One of the interesting buildings that unfortunately was finally destroyed by a gale in January 1962 was the Tide Mill situated at the head of St Osyth Creek, built around 1730. Tide mills are very rare, the water for driving them being held back by an ancient embankment or causeway. This large lake of some forty acres allowed the millers to work between six and eight hours a day. It is a great pity that neglect and indifference allowed it to disappear.

Arable agriculture and sheep were the village's main industries over the centuries but with the agricultural depression of the late 1870s and the fact that the parish authorities stopped the railway from reaching the village resulted in the decrease and stagnation of the population over the next forty-odd years. The men moved to the industrial centres for work and girls went into service in London resulting in a drop in the local birth rate. With the fast and cheap railways heading for the neighbouring towns such as Clacton, much local business moved away, resulting in many parishioners finding themselves living in real need and hunger becoming the norm. For instance, orphans were sent to Australia when the workhouse could no longer cope. In 1871 the population was 1,674 but by 1881 it had dropped to 1,405 and in 1911 it still only stood at 1,391. In fact it took until 1951 for it to get back to the 1871 level. At the beginning of the First World War fifty of St Osyth's young men had volunteered. By the end of the war around 175 men had volunteered or been called up, of whom at least 70 did not return.

The village still has 112 listed buildings, the largest group of listed buildings on one site in all Essex. It is also considered to be one of the driest spots in the British Isles.

Clacton-on-Sea

Bypassing the area we know as Jaywick, our next stop is Clacton itself. Jaywick was originally fields and salt marshes separating St Osyth and Clacton.

Today it's amazing to think that Clacton-on-Sea just 140-odd years ago was an area of peaceful cornfields, sandy beaches and desolate cliffs. However inland there were the villages of Great Clacton and Little Clacton. We know that the area of Great Clacton was occupied by the Celts, probably the Catevellauni, who were later displaced by the Belgic tribe the Trinovantes (Trinobantes). Clacton's, name is derived from the Saxon meaning the village of the Clacc's people. It gets its first mention in a ships roll document of 1000 when Claccingtune were required to provide two men towards a ship's crew. (Other spellings, Claccingaton, Clackinton.) Little Clacton gets it first mention in 1286, although we know that the parish church of St James was founded by Bishop Richard de Belmeis around early 1100. It is also believed that Richard was responsible for the building of the Church of St John the Baptist at Great Clacton, initial dedication understood to have been St Nicholas. A new church of St James was built in 1913.

During the 1800s prehistoric finds were being discovered on the beach and cliffs but in 1911 amateur archaeologist Hazzledine Warren discovered a wooden spearhead that was subsequently dated to be some 400,000 years old, from a time when Britain was still joined to the continent of Europe. The settlers who reach this part of Europe

Clacton Beach, 1908. (Author's collection)

would have come up the River Thames, which at that time flowed on a more northerly route through Clacton where it met up with the River Rhine. So though Clacton was relatively unknown until the late 1800s, its history is as fascinating as anywhere else's.

The majority of the land we now know as Clacton-on-Sea belonged to the owners of Sea Side House Farm. In fact in 1809, William Howard in his will left the farm in trust to his daughter Elizabeth and her husband William Watson, not to be sold in their lifetime to ensure that it was not sold to speculators looking to buy land on the coast to develop a seaside resort. The area at the time was known as Clacton Beach. The farmhouse itself was demolished soon afterwards but further cottages were erected and in 1851, eleven families were living in the area, mainly coastguards or farm labourers. By now the beach was beginning to attract visitors in search of a few hours of relaxation. They would have come in their own carriages from as far away as Colchester, Halstead and Sudbury, and on their way home they could stop for refreshments at a little cottage known as the 'Hotel'.

Elizabeth died in 1848 and William in 1864 and their son Joseph lost no time in advertising the property for sale. Joseph was willing to sell the land in one or multiple lots. Peter Bruff, a civil engineer who was engaged on the project to build a branch line through nearby

Great Clacton. (Author's collection)

Weeley to Walton, saw the advert in the press and promptly acquired land. At the time, he was investing a great deal of money promoting Walton-on-the-Naze as a seaside resort but as soon as he acquired the land in 1865 he dropped the Walton project as Clacton appeared a more attractive prospect.

He immediately applied for Parliamentary powers to construct a railway link to Thorpe-le-Soken and to build a 300-foot pier. Although permission was obtained, against the wishes of the villagers of Great Clacton, Bluff was having cash-flow problems. The Woolwich Steam Packet Company came to his aid, however; the railway did not come to fruition under Bluff but on 18 July 1871 the SS *Queen of the Orwell* docked at the pier. Then on 27 July 1871 Clacton-on-Sea's status as a town was officially declared when the Woolwich Steam Packet Company brought 300 guests aboard the SS *Albert Edward*.

Initially there was very little to offer visitors to the new resort but within a few years businesses, hotels, lodging houses, shops, theatres, etc soon sprang up. The railway eventually arrived in July 1882 and then just before the Great War Clacton's first cinema opened. An extra boost for holiday resorts was the passing of the Bank Holidays Act of 1871 which gave the public longer weekends. By the time Bluff died in 1900 at the age of 87 Clacton-on-Sea had grown into a flourishing town and seaside resort of 7,000 people.

For many years leading up to 1900 the fields on the outskirts of the town (West Clacton) were the scene of annual training camps for the army. It was also the headquarters of a volunteer company of the Essex Regiment and of a troop of the Essex Imperial Yeomanry.

In 1898 the town witnessed a military exercise in which a foreign army was supposed to have landed. Then in September 1904 a major exercise was to come to the attention of the nation, a mock invasion at Clacton. Even the Dublin *Daily Express* reported on the exercise with the headlines:

Invasion of East Anglia
The Landing at Clacton
Stirring Scenes

Because the manoeuvres had been publicised, hundreds of sightseers descended on Clacton to watch the proceedings. It was a military and naval exercise, simulating a surprise landing on the beaches of Clacton by an enemy force of some 150,000 men. The invading force got as far as Colchester, and a mock battle followed, before they made a rapid retreat and re-embarkation from the beaches in rough seas. The exercise was applauded by the crowds that had gathered on the promenade.

As Clacton continued to grow in popularity, entertainment was at the forefront of the visitor's minds and a Professor George Webb tried to provide it by riding a bicycle the length of the pier and jumping off the end in a blazing sack. However, during the war the pier was mined so holidaymakers were less inclined to venture onto it. Although as early as April 1914, the public must have had suspicions of impending war, Clacton Council decided to provide a bathing pavilion on the East Cliff to accommodate eighty bathers at a cost of £850.

There was also some excitement at Clacton in late April 1914 which was reported in newspapers all over the country. The *Portsmouth Evening News* had this to say about the incident:

First Lord's Air Trip
Mishap to Naval Seaplane

Churchill's forced landing, April 1914. (Author's collection)

Mr Winston Churchill, First Lord of the Admiralty, arrived at Sheerness yesterday to join the Admiralty yacht *Enchantress* on an informal weekend visit.

Early in the afternoon the right hon. gentleman left the Isle of Grain Naval Air Station in Seaplane No 79 on a flight to Harwich. The machine, which was piloted by Commander Seddon, developed engine trouble a few miles from Clacton and it was found necessary to descend. The aircraft was towed on to the beach near the jetty and Mr Churchill and his pilot drove to the Royal Hotel. A message was sent in the meantime for another seaplane.

At the Hotel the First Lord was recognized by Councillor Quick, the proprietor of the 'Clacton times' who greeted him.

Mr Churchill said he would rather have remained unrecognized but added that he was impressed with the large improvements now being made to the front. Asked to perform the opening ceremony in May, he declined with a smile.

Speaking of the water plane, he said he had not been in danger but the works were running badly and he thought it best to have another machine. He thought it part of his duty to understand flying and to visit the great naval centres.

On arrival of the second water plane, Mr Churchill drove along the front in a cab and was encountered by a local suffragette, Mrs Worts, who gave him her views. He entered water plane no 19 with suffragette literature in his hand and took the driver's seat. He seemed to have difficulty in starting the new machine but finally got away amid cheers. A third water plane arrived during the afternoon in case of emergency.

There was more excitement a couple of months later on 30 July when a seaplane from Felixstowe which was patrolling the coast beached near the pier for most of the day and naturally attracted quite a large crowd.

Like the rest of the country Clacton and the surrounding district saw very little actual warfare, other than the occasional incursions by enemy aircraft or Zeppelins and the noise of the guns in Flanders. In addition to the soldiers that were stationed in the area during the war, its closest link to the front was looking after the thousands of wounded soldiers in its several convalescent homes.

There was at least one fright, however, when the 5th Battalion Essex Regiment, which was encamped at Clacton for its annual training, on 2 August 1914 received a message at half past eleven at

30 July 1914. (Author's collection)

the Territorial camp that a regiment was needed to repel a German raid on the coast by Clacton.

Colonel J.M. Welch of the 5th was given the order to take his men out at once. The troops, most being asleep, were speedily roused from their tents and within half an hour had been given twenty rounds of ball cartridge each, probably the first home Territorial Regiment to be so armed. They then marched to the coast two miles west of Clacton, where they remained for several hours. The expected raid did not materialise so back to camp they went. After arriving back at camp further message was received at 3 am that the Territorials were to break camp and return to their headquarters to await further orders. Colonel Welch recorded that the regiment behaved splendidly and were as keen as mustard and ready for anything that might have happened. It was later explained that the sudden call was due to information received on Sunday 2 August that the Germans had invaded France without declaring war and what they would do in one place they might probably attempt in another.

Little Holland – Holland-on-Sea – Great Holland

The name Holland first appears in the ship rolls of 1000 as Holande and in the Domesday survey as Hoilanda, the name meaning 'cultivated land by a hill-spur'. Since the Middle Ages it had been known as Little Holland up to the early twentieth century when it became known as Holland-on-Sea, presumably because of the attempts to turn it into a seaside resort.

Despite it being near the sea Little Holland was an agricultural rather than a maritime area. The parish, like others along the peninsula, suffered from coastal erosion and probably because of this, it was sparsely populated right up until modern times. For example, the number of households in 1428 was ten, and by 1650 it had dropped to eight. At the time of the expected Napoleonic invasion some 3,000 troops were stationed in the area amongst a local population of under sixty. Other than the farm cottages there was a small beer house, the site of which eventually became The Roaring Donkey.

Little Holland suffered continuously from coastal erosion and further east along the coast, Holland Brook ran out into the sea at the

The Hall, 2016. (Author's collection)

estuary known as Gunfleet. The name has long since been transferred to the sandbank some four miles offshore and the estuary has been worn away by the constant erosion. The village also suffered by being cut off from other villages in the area, there was only one road entering the village from Colchester and this terminated at Little Holland Hall. The Hall was once the residence of the various lords of the manor but by the middle of the eighteenth century it was no more than a farmhouse, and now it is a nursing home. Also at that time another road was built linking up Great Holland and on to Kirby and Walton.

Like Peter Bruff at Clacton, the resort entrepreneur who set out in 1900 to change the hamlet of Little Holland was David Preston. Unlike the other villages/towns along this stretch of the Essex coast it was a real struggle and in the next eight years only ten houses were built, of which one was a shop near the beer house. Preston had hoped to develop Holland-on-Sea by the coast but due to fact that he had not been able to obtain a liquor licence to build a hotel nearer to the coast the village grew up further inland, near the existing beer house which was now owned by the Greene King brewery and called The Princess Helena (now The Roaring Donkey). The population by the

Holland-on-Sea cliffs. (Author's collection)

outbreak of the First World War was still only 140. However, with war on the horizon Holland once again became the centre of military activity as soldiers returned to patrol the cliffs and dig trenches.

Further along the cliffs to the north-east we come across Great Holland, a small village and parish separated from Little Holland by marshland, marshes that for a long time had been the haunts of smugglers, who had hideouts in the cliffs. Like its neighbour Little Holland its main economy was farming. It first came to prominence in the mid- to late 1200s when a rector was appointed to the village's All Saints' Church. The village was known as either Much Holland or Holland Magna.

The Church of All Saints' was entirely rebuilt in 1866 on old foundations with the exceptions of the West Tower and in 1891 a Wesleyan Methodist chapel was built. The first shop was opened in the mid-1860s by the Crampin family and by the early twentieth century there was a bakery, dairy, butchers, confectionery shop and some light industry. The village was being served by two public houses, The Ship Inn, which is still there, and The Red Lion. Its windmill was still standing in 1912. Being approximately a mile from the coast it never took off as a seaside resort like its neighbours. The population in 1911 stood at 483.

Frinton-on-Sea

Frinton is our next stop which was just as sparsely populated as Holland-on-Sea. It gets its first mention in the Domesday survey where it appears to have been dependent upon farming. The hamlet consisted of two manors, Frietuna and Frientuna. For most of its history, Frinton's economy was based on mixed arable farming and pasture for sheep and like the Holland area does not appear to have had any maritime history. In fact as late as 1871 and 1881 the only non-agricultural occupations were that of two railway workers, a tracker and a platelayer.

Whites Directory of Essex of 1848 gives a brief view of what Frinton was like at the time:

> Frinton a small parish on the sea coast, two and a half miles South West of Walton-on-the-Naze, has only 44 inhabitants, 470 acres of land, four houses and a few cottages, though it is said to anciently had a village, which was washed away by the Ocean, at least two centuries ago and since then the sea has continued to encroach annually upon the land.

Three years later the population had jumped to fifty-four but the extension of the railway from Thorpe-le-Soken to Walton-on-the-Naze in 1864 with an unofficial halt at Frinton brought an influx of new visitors. This prompted the Great Eastern Railway to build a station at Frinton in 1888. Development was still slow and by 1891 the population had only risen to eighty-seven. Part of the problem was the lack of a viable water supply. However, Peter Bruff of Clacton fame discovered a water source at nearby Mistley and formed the Tendering Hundred Water Company which brought water to Frinton in 1888. It was not until 1893 that Sir Richard Powell-Cooper purchased the bulk of the land and started to develop the village along the lines that Bruff had envisaged. He began by laying out a golf course that opened in 1895, followed by the Grand Hotel in 1896 and the Lawn Tennis Club in 1899.

In 1903 the local council acquired the land and it was from this date that Frinton began to take its present shape and character and become the exclusive seaside resort it is today. No pier, no scenic railway, no amusement park, no funfairs and certainly no cockle

Greensward and cliffs at Frinton. (Author's collection)

stalls, though it does have beach huts and the other amenities of a seaside resort, i.e. bathing, boating and of course a sandy beach.

By 1911 Frinton had grown from an area of scattered settlements to a small town with a population of 1,510. The 1911 Whitsunday weekend saw 1,084 visitors to the town and the sea wall was completed by late 1911. Frinton had arrived as a recognized seaside resort with a difference. It also has one of the smallest churches in the country, the fourteenth-century St Mary the Virgin.

Walton-on-the-Naze

Walton is our last stop along this section of the Sunshine Coast and was becoming established as a seaside resort some fifty-odd years earlier than the other villages along this stretch of coast, the possible reason being that unlike the open sites and scattered hamlets of Clacton, Holland and Frinton-on-Sea, Walton was an ancient village with a history of over 1,000 years. To give some idea of its size compared to its neighbours the population of Walton in 1800 was 250 with Frinton having only 30.

Walton-on-the-Naze, or more properly Walton-le-Soken, had its beginnings as a seaside resort back in the 1820s when bathing was coming into vogue as a healthy exercise. In 1829 it had its first large hotel and, to put it right on the map, a short history and boarding-house guide was published. This sounds rather impressive but Walton was still only a small village and it relied on its lovely beach and pleasant situation to bring visitors in.

The following are the opening lines of a poem in one of the town's early guides:

> When pleasure you seek
> For a month or a week
> Or when your pursuit
> Is your health to recruit
> To Walton repair

The name Soken came from by the fact that the three parishes of Walton, and nearby Thorpe and Kirby, were back in the time of William the Conqueror given special privileges or 'sokes' as they were called, allowing them to administer justice within their parishes.

The meaning of the name Walton has, however, been lost in the mists of time but many believe it is derived from the Anglo-Saxon word 'Weala tun' meaning the 'Farms of Britons'. It has also been suggested that it was known as Eadolfenaesse and possibly Waltonia. The Naze is a peninsula north of the town again we believe the name comes from the Anglo-Saxon word 'Neas' meaning Ness or Nose.

The original village of Walton was well inland and as would be expected agriculture was the main industry, the land being particularly suitable for cereal crops. The Romans, however, nearer the coast collected Septaria for making cement and up to the middle of the 1800s Copperas was obtained from the London Clay in the cliffs, which when processed was used for dying, tanning and the manufacture of ink.

As previously mentioned the cliffs along this section of the Sunshine Coast were under continuous threat of erosion and the Walton area was particularly affected and in the early and mid-1700s the village was swallowed up by the sea. In 1768 the Essex historian Philip Morant (1700–70) wrote that the ancient church was half a mile from the coast: thirty years later in 1798 it had disappeared into the sea. It is believed that the old village is now nine miles out at sea. This erosion of the coastline, although a problem, has led to the discovery

The beach, Walton-on-the-Naze, 1908. (Author's collection)

of vast quantities of Neolithic stone implements – arrowheads, axe-heads, spearheads and fossils of animals confirming that the area has been inhabited by man and beast for many thousands of years.

Its heyday was during the Victorian period with visitors on excursions enjoying picnics on the secluded beaches, initially people from the local area but the building of the original pier in 1830 and the arrival of the railway in 1867 allowed travellers by boat or train from further afield to enjoy the delights of the beach and the healthy air. In the 1880s a lifeboat station was built, the current one now being at the end of the pier.

The original pier, along with the Marine Hotel, was built by John Penrice but later development of Marine Terrace, South Terrace, Clifton Baths (today Pier Hotel) and a new longer pier was begun by Peter Bruff before he left to develop Clacton. The pier was later extended and is believed to be the third, or possibly the second, longest in the British Isles.

In the 1800s John Warner and family, who owned and ran a large iron foundry in London, moved to Walton. The family built another foundry there which proved to be a major source of employment in the town from the late 1800s until the mid-1900s (closing in the

Naze Cliffs and Tower in the background. (Author's collection)

1960s), employing between 150 and 300 men. They made a variety of iron products as well as producing material for the Indian Railways and were bell-founders for Queen Victoria, King Edward VII and George V.

The Naze headland has long been dominated by the Naze Tower, built in 1721. Its original purpose was to act as a marker for ships heading for Harwich, a predecessor of lighthouses. In early 1900 radio masts were erected at the top of the tower for experiments in long-range transmission. It has also played a part in many of the wars since the 1700s. Locally it is known as the 'Landmark' and for hundreds of years it has been a symbol of Walton's history. Unfortunately every year at least two metres of the coast disappears into the sea, so at this rate the tower could disappear under the waves in twenty years if nothing is done about it.

> Look at a map to see how many Waltons there are,
> There are twenty-five, near and far,
> But our Walton-on-the-Naze excels
> With its sandy beaches and pretty shells.
> There's a Pier, candy floss, sun and fun.
> The folk are friendly and kind.
> When it's windy the cafes are
> Handy for body and mind.

Our Parish Church stands sentinel over the town.
So come to Walton and you won't wear a frown!

By Jean Barrs

There we have it: our villages/towns along this section of the Sunshine Coast, Brightlingsea, maritime village, St Osyth, sleepy village, Clacton-on-Sea, Frinton-on-Sea and Walton-on-the-Naze, all thriving seaside resorts, and the Holland area, a mixture of seaside resort and sleepy village, all having something different to offer. The question is, were they in the front line for an invasion?

Well, if you look at the local papers in the few months leading up to the war, very little is reported, life is just going on as normal, although there is no doubt the military were preparing themselves.

CHAPTER 2

If Only

᭣᭣᭣

- If only – an angry student hadn't shot Archduke Franz Ferdinand and his wife.
- If only Russia hadn't support Serbia in its argument with Austria-Hungary.
- If only Austria-Hungary hadn't declared war on Serbia and Russia.
- If only Germany hadn't declared war on both Russia and France and invaded Belgium.
- If only Great Britain hadn't declared war on Germany.
- If only we'd all known then, that the rules of civilization were about to be suspended for four, long, harrowing years.
- If only they had known, would our young men have made different choices?

Or was there a terrible inevitability which led to one of the darkest periods in human history – that god – forsaken time between August 1914 and November 1918 that we now call the First World War (Great War). All over Europe, men some so young they were hardly more than boys – left homes and loved ones and joined up ready to fight for freedom, for justice and to protect everything they held dear. Some joined up for adventure and excitement and some to escape lives that offered no future but whatever the reason, join up they did

(From the play by Dawn Knox *The Sons of Three Countries Remembered*)

The war started for the British with the following announcement from the Foreign Office that Great Britain was at war with Germany:

Opening scene from The Sons of Three Countries Remembered *(performed by Dot Productions).*

> Owing to the summary rejection by the German Government of the request made by his Majesty's Government for assurances that the neutrality of Belgium would be respected. His Majesty's Ambassador in Berlin has received his passports and his Majesty's Government has declared to the German Government that a state of war exists between Great Britain and Germany as from 11 pm on August 4.

The King held a Council at midnight to sign the proclamation declaring war and at 12.10 am the German Ambassador went to 10 Downing Street to receive his travel papers. It is understood he looked a broken man. In Germany Sir Edward Goschen, the British Ambassador, also demanded his passports.

The government had obviously been planning for the day as the state immediately took over the railways. Millions of £1 notes were to be put in circulation within days to be followed by 10s notes to protect the national gold reserves.

The War Office immediately put out appeals for doctors and motorcyclists. The following appeared in the *Daily Mail* on Wednesday, 5 August 1914:

> The War Office require immediately for service the following at the stated rates of pay:
>
> • Coppersmiths, electricians, pattern-makers, 52s, 6d

- Blacksmiths, dispensers, drivers of motor-lorries, farriers, fitters, moulders, painters, saddlers, turners, wheelers, 42s
- Bakers, butchers, clerks, cooks, hospital subordinates, tailors, 33s
- And labourers and loaders (packers), 21s

Married men must allot one-third of their pay to their families, who will also receive separation allowance at Army rates.

A bounty of £5 will be paid each man on enlistment and £5 on discharge, in addition to any war gratuity, Clothing and equipment will be free.

Clerks, labourers and mechanical transport drivers must be between 20 and 45 years of age; the age for other classes is 20 to 40 years.

Motor-cyclists are also required. Motor-cycles will be either taken over at a valuation or to be replaced by new ones. The pay will be 35s weekly.

Civilian doctors wishing to serve at home or abroad as surgeons should write to the Secretary, War Office, London. S.W. Gentlemen accepted will be granted the temporary rank of Lieutenant. They must be registered practitioners; engage for 12 months or until no longer required; pay to be 9s a day, with certain expenses, free passages to and from any country abroad and a gratuity of £10 at the end of service. Age limit is 35 years but in exceptional circumstances gentlemen up to 40 may be accepted.

What really amused me was that the next article in the *Daily Mail* report was that owing to the war, marriage licences could be obtained at any hour of the day or night at a fee of £7 for an ordinary licence and £8 for special licences, the latter allowing marriages to take place immediately in the Church of England. This was prompted by men hoping to get married before going to the Front.

So why did Britain end up on 4 August declaring war on Germany and its allies, a conflict we understand our government did not want and I am sure the British people did not want? After centuries of being involved with conflicts around the world, the last being the Boer War of 1899–1902, we as a country appear to be coming of age, an age that did not want to keep sending our young men into conflicts to be killed. We were happy with our 'splendid isolation', a period of approximately a hundred years of non-involvement in Europe's squabbles with the exception of the Crimean War of 1853–6. Being an island and the fact that Britain had not been invaded for nearly a thousand years allowed the country to adopt this policy, therefore it only had a small standing army, although it had by far the largest navy the world had known, to control and maintain its worldwide empire.

In 1908 Churchill had this to say about the so-called German menace: 'I think it is greatly to be deprecated that persons should try to spread the belief in this country that war between Great Britain and Germany is inevitable; it is all nonsense. There is no collision of primary interests – big, important interests – between Great Britain and Germany in any quarter of the globe. There is no feeling of ill-will towards Germany,' he continued, 'I say we honour the strong, patient, industrious German people.'

Were we as innocent as these statements make out or was it because the likes of France, Russia and Germany were jealous of our position in the world? For example, Britain's net overseas investment in 1913 had been twice its GDP; 42 per cent of all world's foreign investments belonged to Britain, twice as much as America and Germany combined.

Well, we could go back at least to the early 1870s to see the beginning of the landslide that led to outright war. This was the Christian uprising in Turkish-ruled Bosnia and Bulgaria, in which upwards of 15,000 men, women and children were killed by Turkish irregular forces. Russia immediately marched on Constantinople, forcing the Turks to surrender. Britain took a different view and wanted to defend the Ottoman Empire, so sent a naval force to Constantinople. A congress met in Berlin in 1878. chaired by Bismarck, the German Chancellor. The agreement reduced the territory seized by the newly-independent Bulgaria, and placed Bosnia and Herzegovina under Austrian administration, Britain gain Cyprus as a naval and military base to support the Turks against Russia.

What followed was the scramble for colonies in Africa with Britain, France, Italy and Belgium trying to outdo each other while Germany was also trying to establish an African empire, which also increased the mistrust between the various nations. During this period we had Britain taking control of Egypt to secure the Suez Canal but this meant we got involved in the neighbouring Sudan. A bigger crisis arose in 1885 with the Russian threat to Afghanistan and Britain threating to go to war. In 1898 an Anglo-Egyptian army led by General Kitchener defeated an army of Mahdist Sudanese at Omdurman. The battle received considerable publicity, since it involved one of the last full-scale cavalry charges in British history and none other than the 23-year-old Winston Churchill took part in it. We then got ourselves involved in the Boer War where we find Winston Churchill again being involved. Back to the European scene, there was the Franco/Prussian war of 1870–1 that we managed to stay out of. France was well and truly beaten within months, the outcome being the establishment of the German states into one unified empire, masterminded by Bismarck. This created, as one would expect, French resentment right up to the Great War and beyond.

As we move into the 1900s we have Germany starting to expand its navy so to compete with Britain. Britain signed a treaty with Japan in 1902 as we were concerned with Russian expansionism in China. What followed was the Russo-Japanese War of 1904–5, convincingly won by Japan. We were also concerned with Russian eyes on Afghanistan which could threaten the North-West Frontier and the plains of India. France was also concerned, so in 1904 Britain and France signed the Entente Cordiale. Then in 1907 these countries along with Russia formed the Triple Entente. Supplementary agreements with Japan and Portugal followed. These formed a considerable alliance to counter the Triple Alliance of Germany, Austria-Hungary and Italy, although Italy kept out of the war initially and in fact joined the Entente in 1915 by signing the Treaty of London.

While this political manoeuvring was going on, the Ottoman Empire, which included many of the Balkan states, was weakening as they began to assert themselves. This resulted in them becoming pawns for competing European power but they were not going to be kept quiet and in 1903 Serbia began to assert itself against its former protector Austria-Hungary, and when the Young Turks seized power in Constantinople in 1908, Austria took advantage of the confusion and annexed Bosnia.

This caused a grave European crisis and in early 1912 Russia tried to form a Balkan Alliance against Austria but the Balkan states (Serbia, Bosnia, Bulgaria and Herzegovina) took things into their own hands and attacked the Turks in what became the First Balkan War. They drove the Turks out of Europe but by the summer of 1913, Bulgaria became disillusioned and attacked its former allies in the Second Balkan War. Bulgaria was heavily defeated and it left the region even more dangerously unstable and as we know it all came to ahead with the assassination of Austrian Archduke Franz Ferdinand and his wife Sophie by the Serbian student Gavrilo Princip.

To give you a further idea of how unstable Europe was at this time you only need to look at the number of political assassinations that had taken place in the previous fourteen years:

Austria
- 1913 Franz Schuhmeier – Socialist Member of Parliament.

Bosnia & Herzegovina
- 1914 Archduke Franz Ferdinand and his wife Sophie.

Bulgaria
- 1907 Dimitar Petkov – Prime Minister of Bulgaria.

Finland
- 1904 Nikolai Ivanovich Bobrikov – Governor General of Finland.
- 1905 Eliel Soisalon-Soininen – Attorney General.
- 1911 Valde Hirvikanta – President of Turku Court of Appeal.

France
- 1914 Jean Jaurès – Politician, pacifist.

Greece
- 1905 Theodoros Deligiannis – Prime Minister of Greece.
- 1907 Marinos Antypas – Greek politician.
- 1912 Andreas Kopasis – Governor of Samos.
- 1913 George I of Greece – King of Greece.

Italy
- 1900 Umberto I of Italy – King of Italy.

Kosovo
- 1902 Haxhi Zeka – Albanian nationalist.

Ottoman Empire
- 1913 Mahmud Servet Pasha – Grand Vizier of the Ottoman Empire.

Russia
- 1902 Dmitry Sipyagin – Russian Interior Minister.
- 1904 Vyacheslav von Plehve – Russian Interior Minister.
- 1905 Grand Duke Sergei Alexandrovich Romanov – Former Governor-General of Moscow.
- 1911 Pyotr Stolypin – Russian Prime Minister.

Serbia
- 1903 Aleksendar Obrenović – King of Serbia and Draga Masin – Queen Consort.
- 1903 Dimitnije Cincar-Marković – Prime Minister.

Spain
- 1912 Jose Canalejas – Prime Minister.

It is interesting to note that Britain and Germany were free of such atrocities, with Russia and Greece topping the list.

All this resulted in four main reasons for the outbreak of the Third Balkan War, soon to be referred to as the Great War, and eventually the First World War.

- Nationalism – The various countries and states of Europe were flourishing in national pride and many ethnic groups craved independence.
- Imperialism – The major countries in Europe held many colonies abroad and new lands were being contested by them.
- Militarism – As nationalism and imperialism took hold so the need for greater military strength to defend their possessions became necessary.
- Lack of international organization – There was no international governing body to help solve the various problems. The League of Nations was not established until after the First World War.

> I said to the German Ambassador that, as long as there was only a dispute between Austria and Serbia alone, I did not feel entitled to intervene; but that, directly it was a matter between Austria and Russia, it became a question of peace of Europe, which concerned us all.
>
> Sir Edward Grey, Foreign Secretary

Though concerned with the problems in Europe and the various agreements signed in an attempt to keep the peace, Britain had one other major problem: it was party to the Treaty of London of 1839 where it had agreed to uphold Belgian neutrality. Other signatories to the agreement were France, Russia, Austria, the Netherlands and the German Confederation (led by Prussia). However, Germany ignored this 'Scrap of Paper' as they put it, so there we were – the 'war to end all wars' had started. The underlying question was whether any of the parties were ready for it. Germany probably was, France and Russia should have been. Britain certainly was not.

It all began three weeks after the shooting of Archduke Franz Ferdinand when on 23 July 1914 the Austro-Hungarian government issued its ultimatum to the Serbian government, which comprised a lengthy list of demands. In essence it was accusing the Serbian government of being implicated in the events at Sarajevo. They were given two days to respond.

The British government at this stage had not discussed the growing crisis in Europe for nearly a month, being more concerned with the problems in Ireland. However, with this latest ultimatum to Serbia the government did discuss the crisis and Sir Edward Grey commented that he had 'never before seen one State address to another independent State a document of so formidable a character'. The Serbians, with the support of Russia, conceded to practically all the Austro-Hungarian demands bar one or two minor clauses. Nonetheless, war was declared by Austria-Hungary shortly afterwards. The British government tried to organize a conference among the major European powers to resolve the dispute. France, Italy and Russia agree to participate but Germany refused.

With the unconditional support of Germany, Austria declared war on Serbia on 28 July, one month to the day after the assassination. The next day Winston Churchill wrote to his wife 'everything tends towards catastrophe and collapse' and Britain called for international mediation to resolve the worsening crisis, along with Russia urging German restraint but it was too late – the various countries were mobilizing their troops.

On 1 August Germany declared war on Russia and on 3 August declared war on France and invaded neutral Belgium, putting into action the Schlieffen Plan. This plan had been devised by the Chief of the General Staff Alfred Graf von Schlieffen in December 1905. He believed that any future European war would include France and Russia, with France being the most dangerous. He also believed that Russia would take six weeks to mobilize, sufficient time for Germany to defeat France. He also concluded that a massive and successful attack against France would put off Britain becoming involved in a European war. The plan was to use at least 90 per cent of Germany's army to go through Belgium go into northern France and take Paris.

What went wrong was that Russia mobilized in two weeks and Britain upheld its 1839 treaty with Belgium.

As we now know, Germany invaded Luxembourg on 2 August and Belgium on 3 August when they were refused free passage. Germany ignored Britain's ultimatum, resulting in Britain declaring war on 4 August. It is interesting to note that the small state of Montenegro declared war on Austria-Hungary on 5 August and Germany on 9 August. On 6 August, Austria-Hungary declared war on Russia. France declared war against Austria-Hungary on 11 August and Britain did the same the day after. Austria-Hungary on 22 August declared war on Belgium. Surprisingly on 23 August Japan declared war on Germany and two days later on Austria-Hungary. Another interesting point is the states which declared their neutrality: the Netherlands on 28 July, Italy and Denmark on 1 August, Switzerland on 3 August and the United States on 4 August. Russia mobilizing quicker than expected meant that the Germans had to move valuable troops to the Eastern Front and with the Belgians and French putting up heavy resistance and the British coming to their aid at Mons on 23 August, their progress was slowed considerably and the plan fell apart. The next phase of the campaign saw the Retreat from Mons but eventually at the Battle of the Marne the Allies stopped the advance on Paris (5–12 September) putting the final nail in the coffin of the Schlieffen Plan but there was still another four years of bitter fighting to come.

The opposing sides were made up of the Central Powers: the German Empire, the Austro-Hungarian Empire, Ottoman Empire and Bulgaria, later to be joined in 1918 by Azerbaijan and Lithuania once Russia had dropped out. And on the opposite of the fence the Allies were made up of France, Russia, the British Empire, Serbia and later USA, Romania and Italy.

> The lights are going out all over Europe; we shall not see them lit again in our lifetime.
>
> Sir Edward Grey, Foreign Secretary, 3 August 1914

CHAPTER 3

Defence of the Realm – Spies, Spies and Spies

જાજી

When war was declared on 4 August 1914 the country erupted in jubilation. However, behind the scenes, the government was terrified. Trade unions had a long history of holding employers to ransom, the suffragettes were causing unrest in their quest for equality and there was a deep mistrust of German businesses and 'spies in our midst'.

Fearing insubordination and disorder, the government rushed the Defence of the Realm Act (DORA) through Parliament. The proclamation said: 'We strictly command and enjoin our subjects to obey and conform to all instructions and regulations which may be issued by us or our Admiralty or Army Council'. It took just four days for DORA to receive Royal Assent, being published in Gazette Supplement 28869 on 11 August 1914. It proved to be an Act that would touch the lives of every British citizen over the next four years.

In a nutshell, DORA was designed to help prevent invasion and maintain morale at home. It gave the government wide-ranging powers, such as the authority to requisition buildings needed for the war effort, or by creating new criminal offences. It also ushered in a variety of measures of social control.

As the war progressed, DORA was amended and extended six times. The two main themes were press censorship and the taking of any land for government use, but there were also many restrictions on civilian life such as:

- Talking about naval and military matters in public places.
- Spreading rumours about military matters.

- Buying binoculars.
- Trespassing on railway lines.
- Melting down gold or silver.
- Lighting bonfires, fireworks or flying a kite.
- Using invisible ink when writing abroad.
- Buying brandy or whisky in railway refreshment rooms.
- The ring of church bells.

In addition to these strict rules, people were affected in other, more curious ways. They were forbidden to loiter near bridges and tunnels, and whistling for a London taxi was banned, in case it could be mistaken for an air-raid warning. DORA even intervened in British drinking habits: by the spring of 1915, pub opening hours were limited, people were banned from treating others and even the strength of alcoholic drinks was reduced. If anybody broke these rules, they could be arrested, fined, sent to prison or even executed. A total of eleven German spies were executed under the regulations.

Some of these provisions today seem rather harsh but they had their purposes. For example, flying a kite or lighting a bonfire might attract Zeppelins. There were around fifty-two Zeppelin air raids on Britain, mainly in 1915/16, which killed approximately 500 people. Limiting time in the pub helped to reduce drunkenness, resulting in increased productivity, and when rationing was introduced in 1917, banning the feeding of wild animals helped to prevent the waste of food. The censorship of reporting British troop movements, their numbers or any other operational information, helped prevent the enemy from finding out sensitive military information, which potentially saved lives.

The first person to be arrested under DORA was John Maclean, a Scottish Marxist and revolutionary. He was arrested for uttering statements that were deemed 'prejudicial to recruiting'. He was fined £5 but refused to pay. He spent five nights in prison and was dismissed from his post as a teacher by the Govan Board of Education (anybody with a criminal conviction was not allowed to teach, or practice law or medicine).

It is estimated that almost a million arrests were made under the Act and eleven men convicted of spying were executed. They were:

- Carl Lody, 34, executed 6 November 1914.
- Carl Muller, 57, executed 23 June 1915.

- Willem Roos, 33, executed 30 July 1915.
- Haicke Janssen, 30, executed 30 July 1915.
- Ernst Melin, 49, executed 10 September 1915.
- Augusto Roggin, 34, executed 17 September 1915.
- Fernando Bushman, 25, executed 19 September 1915.
- George Breeckow, 33, executed 26 October 1915.
- Irving Ries, 55, executed 27 October 1915.
- Albert Meyer, 22, executed 2 December 1915.
- Ludovico Zender, 38, executed 11 April 1916.

Carl Lody was the first person in about 150 years to be executed at the Tower of London.

In addition to the DORA, on the day that war was declared the Aliens (Restriction) Act was also passed. It required foreign nationals over the age of 16 to register with the police and if deemed necessary they could be deported or interned. Between 1914 and 1919 over 32,000 Germans and Austro-Hungarians civilians in Britain were interned. Surprisingly, many were interned for their own safety as there were many outbreaks of violence in the towns and cities of Britain with German-owned property being destroyed or looted. Civilian prisoners were entirely exempt from forced labour and at no time during the war were women or children interned. However, this did not mean they did not come under suspicion.

This all sound a little dramatic but spy-phobia had become a national obsession and any German or other person with a foreign accent was automatically suspected of being a spy and the Clacton area was going to have a number of scares.

A prohibited area under the Aliens (Restriction) Act was one where a special military presence had been established to guard against espionage, such as vulnerable coastal areas, and the Clacton area was a classic example. Police in the prohibited areas were soon expelling German and Austrians. Take Frinton for example: within three weeks of war breaking out the police expelled twelve such cases.

We have the case of Bertha Augusta Emelie Tebbutt of Wellesley Road, Clacton-on-Sea, a German married to Mr Tebbutt, an Englishman and employed in a rate collector's office. They had three children and had been married for fifteen years. Her neighbours were suspicious of her very pro-German attitude and her outspoken comments about her native country. They were also aware that she often travelled to London to meet other Germans and therefore believed her to be a spy. Eventually in January 1915 a Mrs Kimbley of Assington Street, Hyde Park, reported her to the Metropolitan Police. It would appear that the censorship authorities were also suspicious as Mrs Tebbutt had requested a recipient in Switzerland to address her letters to Mrs Wilson on the belief that her letters would therefore not be censored. After further investigations an expulsion order was made by the Military Authority on 22 June 1916, but she successfully appealed to stay in Clacton on the basis that her husband could not earn a living elsewhere because of his deafness. Then on 10 May 1916 a further recommendation for expulsion was made but it was deferred. Finally, on 24 January 1918, on the orders of the Military Authority, she left Clacton for London.

The next case also shows that letter-writing was a hazardous business. A Mr Odell, who managed the Grand Hotel, Clacton, was reported to the local police by the War Office as he appeared to post many letters inland and abroad. The police carried out discreet enquiries on 5 January 1916 and reported back that there was no evidence against Mr Odell to establish a case. His wife was French and though they lived apart it was possible that he wrote to her brothers who were serving in the French army. They concluded that as he managed a hotel his correspondence was likely to be extensive and they could not ascertain whether he wrote to any other country other than France. Finally they confirmed that Mr Odell was leaving the Grand Hotel and would be sailing via the Cape for Singapore to manage the Hotel Europe there, taking over from German managers.

On 12 December 1915 the Home Office reported to the police that a John Etty of Frinton-on-Sea had received a £2 money order from Mrs Etty in The Hague. It would appear that she had also sent other monies to various people living in the United Kingdom and they would like to know the reason for these remittances. Enquiries were made, and the police reported that John Etty had resided at Southleigh, Frinton, for some nine years and his birth certificate confirmed he was born on 14 April 1872 in Leeds. Etty informed the police that the remittance was a Christmas present from his cousin, Mrs Jane Elizabeth Etty, wife of a millionaire of Hotel-de-Zalm, The Hague, and it was her custom to send money each year. John was unaware of the reason for the other monies sent. However, some three years later, in May 1918, the War Office was asking questions about six remittances from Mrs J. Etty, now living in Arnhem, to a Miss Binnington between 1914 and 1917. It turned out that Miss Bennington was the cousin of John Etty and living with him at Southleigh, South Avenue, Frinton-on-Sea. Reports on both were sent and, as you would expect, no further action was taken.

Why be suspicious of contact with Holland? It stayed neutral throughout the war and though the British had a long history of wars with the Dutch going back as far as 1652, both countries respected each other. This situation obviously changed somewhat following the Boer Wars of the late nineteenth and early twentieth centuries (the Boers being of descendants of Dutch colonists), Dutch shipping was routinely intercepted by the British blockade during the war, and later on the British seized all the Dutch merchant ships in the foreign harbours they controlled. The result of this blockade was that the Dutch suffered almost as much as the Germans. This all meant that by the end of the war Dutch relations with the British were at a very low ebb. So maybe it was not surprising for there to be a little concern about contact with that country. It also emphasized how careful you had to be and it would appear that nobody, whatever their connections, could escape suspicion.

Charles and Florence Strauss of Marine Parade, Clacton, were looked upon by the Military Authority with some suspicion and it was considered that some restrictions should be placed on them in case of emergency arising. What is surprising is that Charles' brother Edward Anthony Strauss was currently the Member of Parliament for Southwark West and in 1916 he was a member of a deputation to the Secretary of State for War, Lord Kitchener, to press for better defences against air raids on London. Both Charles and Edward had been born in Islington, their father Joseph Strauss being a wealthy merchant from Southwark of German-Jewish background. We are, however, unaware of what the final decision was.

The following report in the *Chelmsford Chronicle* of Friday, 14 September 1917 is another case of just how careful you had to be:

> Frank Wallis of Dollis Avenue, Finchley was charged with taking photographs in a prohibited area without permission of the military authority – In a letter the defendant said he merely took

snapshots of a headland at Walton-on-the-Naze at the request of his wife, who was staying at Frinton for her health and wanted to paint a picture of the promontory. He added that he had been 30 years with his firm – Corpl. Cameron said he took possession of the defendant's camera, which bore out the defendant's reference to it as little more than a toy. – Supt. Day stated that notices warning people against taking photos on the coast-line etc had been posted up all over the district. A fine of 20s with 7s costs was imposed.

Armaug (*sic*) Deboise, a young Belgian, employed as a waiter at the Frinton Hotel was fined 5s for being an alien in a prohibited area without an identity book and without permission of the Registration Officer. PC Girt stated that the defendant had been warned by the Metropolitan Police not to come to Frinton without permission.

At the same tribunal Madame Nelly Bolli, a young Frenchwomen, wife of a munitions worker, and Alice Muller, staying at Walton-on-the-Naze, were similarly charged and were each fined 2s 6d. This was followed by Edward Nicholas, landlord of the Queen's Hotel, Walton-on-the-Naze, who was summoned on 5 August for not keeping an aliens register and for failing to require Annie Sinnett to furnish a signed statement. PC Browning said Sinnett was staying at the defendant's hotel. The bench fined the defendant 20s in each case.

William Chippindale-Aston was living at Belgrave House, Clacton-on-Sea, when an anonymous letter was received at the Home Office on 3 October 1917 stating that he had been educated in Germany and trained in the German Army. On investigation it was established that Aston, who was 49 years of age, had been born in Warwickshire, educated at a public school and was believed to have gone to Oxford. At the age of 17 he travelled to Frankfurt in Germany to finish his education, returning to London after a year and starting work in an office. He then emigrated to New Zealand, where he had a number of jobs – cattle rancher, miner, policeman and hospital orderly – before becoming a ship's officer in the employment of the Elder Dempster Line, Liverpool. He eventually settled in Clacton around 1913 and on the outbreak of war endeavoured to obtain a commission in the army but was deemed too old. He took a job in a munitions factory, Messrs Davey Paxman in Colchester, and then after a year was appointed a paid special constable for duty at Clacton-on-Sea and at the time of the letter to the Home Office was still employed as such. A report was sent to the Home Office on 6 October 1917 stating that Aston was looked upon as an Englishman of a very good type and had no pro-German sympathies.

Only a few months before the end of the war individuals were still being prosecuted for offences under the various Acts. The *Essex Newsman* reported in October 1918 that Josephine Dubourdeaux, a French governess in the employ of Lady Cadogan, was charged with having entered a prohibited area without having an identity book in her possession, she being an alien. PC Girt reported that on 13 September he examined the aliens register at the Esplanade Hotel, Frinton. He found on it the name of Josephine Dubourdeaux, described as a French subject. Subsequently, the defendant came to his house and said that she had not registered with the police as an alien and that she had lost her identity book. Lady Cadogan said she would take all responsibility but she was told she could not and that the defendant must obtain an identity book. Josephine eventually found her identity book but she was still fined £2. It would appear even our allies were under suspicion.

It was not only single individuals that came under scrutiny. On 22 October 1914 the police received information from the War Office that The General Electric Company, Frinton-on-Sea, which was an English company had been taken over by a German parent company. There was some concern as to whether it was a going concern. It was soon discovered, however, that the five men working for the company were all British and that no evidence could be found to suspect that aliens had been visiting the company. Although it was established that some of the directors had distant German heritage, the final report verified that all the directors connected with The General Electric Company were British subjects and that there were no German or Austrian subjects employed by the company. The company was actually supplying carbon etc, to the government for searchlights.

The following letter from the Home Office was sent to the various Chief Constables well after the above investigation and helps explain why local police authorities were keeping a close eye on local firms:

CONFIDENTIAL

10th June 1916

Sir,

I am directed by the Secretary of State to say that it is anticipated by the Admiralty that, as a result of the recent fighting in the North Sea, there will be attempts made by German agents to ascertain the extent of the damage to His Majesty's ships. It is not unlikely that the persons seeking information of this kind will come in the guise of Commercial Travellers connected with some sort of business which would bring them into contact with ship-building firms. Two such suspected characters have already been observed and orders for their arrest have been given. Their ostensible business was the selling of 'template board' cards which, it is understood, were offered as a substitute for template boards used in ship-yards for obtaining correct measurements.

A sharp look out should be kept by the police for any attempt to obtain such information and special inquiry should be made into the bona fides of any Commercial Travellers who are ostensibly engaged on any business connected with ship-building or which does not appear to justify engagement of Commercial Travellers and might be equally conducted by post.

All Commercial Travellers of alien origin arriving in your jurisdiction should be severely interrogated, with a view to ascertaining precise particulars as to:-

- How long they have been in business?
- What remuneration they receive?
- How long they have been with the firm which they now represent?
- Whether they are paid commission on orders received?
- From whom they have received orders?
- When such orders are to be executed?
- Where the goods are coming from and how they are to be delivered and so forth.

If necessary, reference should be made to the firms who have been visited by these men with a view to ascertaining whether any genuine business has been done. In nearly every case of enemy agents who have been arrested it has been ascertained that when they came in the guise of Commercial Travellers, as the bulk of them did, their business merely consisted in calling on firms as cover for their real business of spying and in no case could it be ascertained that any business whatever was done.

In any case in which there is reason to suspect an offence against Regulation 18 of the Defence of the Realm Regulations, the person should be detained and reference should be made to the War Office (department M.I.5.) as to the names and addresses of the firms and Continental Houses which he represents and also as to any addresses which may be found in his papers. If, in your opinion, the conduct of any alien in this connection, though suspicious, does not justify detention, you should, if possible, require him to leave the area, e.g. under Article 18B. (2) of the Aliens Restriction Order and report the circumstances to the War Office (M.I.5).

I am, Sir – Your obedient Servant

Within a month a further letter was sent out by the Home Office:

CONFIDENTIAL

Sir,

I am directed by the Secretary of State to say there is reason to believe that the German Government is endeavouring to recruit circus-riders, music-hall performers and persons on regular stage for purpose of espionage in this country. Two such persons, circus-riders, who were of German origin, have recently been detected endeavouring to come to this country and have been refused permission to land and a third, who had been touring as a music-hall performer with a Dutch passport, is believed to be a German and is now in custody. I am therefore to request that special attention may be paid to any persons belonging to these professions who may visit your area, more particularly if they appear to be in the habit of performing at important Naval centres and that if there is any reason to suspect that they are endeavouring to obtain Naval or Military information the strictest inquiry may be made as to their nationality and antecedents under the powers conferred by Regulation 53 of the Defence of the Realm Regulations.

If, as the result of such inquiry, there is such reasonable ground for suspicion as to bring the case within Regulation 55, the suspect should be detained and all papers found in his possession forwarded to the War Office (Dept, M.I.5. (g) for examination.

Where there is not sufficient ground to justify detention, full particulars should be reported to the War Office and in the event of the suspected person removing to another Police area the Chief Constable concerned should be notified and requested to keep him under observation.

It is very desirable that the War Office should see all papers in such cases in order to ascertain whether they contain any spy addresses within the meaning of Regulation 18A.

I am, Sir – Your obedient Servant.

There is no doubt these instructions were taken very seriously by the police in the Clacton area, not only because of the naval and military presence there but also because having several well-established seaside resorts it was an ideal area for travelling entertainers.

One case I initially found a little strange was that of Rosalie Schenk Abberfield, who the Military Authorities believed should have some restrictions placed on her. Rosalie had been born in 1854 in Hungary of Russian parents and had come to England thirty years previously following her marriage to Elmet Charles Abberfield, an Englishman. Unfortunately she had been widowed nineteen years previously, Elmet being killed in a hunting accident abroad. They had five children, all British-born, with two sons serving in the British Army. Rosalie had resided in Clacton for ten years and the police considered her to be a quiet, respectable women who kept largely to herself. So it seemed strange that the military considered the need for her to have restrictions placed on her in case of emergency.

Further investigation shows that the police report on this case was not that thorough. Firstly she had six children not five (three sons and three daughters) with two of the boys and one daughter being born in Germany and I have no doubt that the hunting accident took place in Germany. Individual hunting in Europe was and still is a more popular pastime than it is in the British Isles. In the 1911 census Rosalie had her occupation listed as a Boarding House Proprietor and the military tended to keep an eye on these places because of the variety of visitors they might receive. So just with this little extra information one can see why the military, if they were aware of these additional facts, were a little nervous where her sympathies might lie. However, with two of her sons, Arthur and Elmet, in the British Army you would have thought that they would have lain with the British. We have not been able to trace any more information on Arthur other than he had enlisted in the Royal Engineers – 5th Essex Regiment. He was one of the sons born in Germany. Elmet was born in Chelmsford on 31 December 1894 and had been given his father's name. The Clacton Roll of Honour has his regiment listed as 'Gen Huttons Mtd Scouts' (Motor Transport Dept.). From his damaged war records we have been able to establish that he enlisted as a private at Colchester on 4 September 1914 into a cavalry regiment (service number 20638) often referred to as 'Hussars of the Line' but he was subsequently transferred to the Army Service Corps on 23 October 1914 (service number M/398539). Then on 8 February 1915 he transferred to the Army Cyclist Corps (service number 5613). He served in France from 9 September 1915 to 14 April 1917, but unfortunately I have not been able to establish where. He was finally demobbed on 11 March 1919 being transferred to Z Class Army Reserve the day after. He appears to have put in disability claim but the records are unclear to whether he was successful but the question arises was that the reason he was transferred back home in April 1917?

The main role of the cyclist was communications and reconnaissance and the majority of cyclist battalions were based at home. They were armed like the infantry and could provide mobile firepower if required, so they therefore received the same level of pay as infantrymen. Those units that went overseas continued in these roles. However, once the war moved into the stalemate of entrenched warfare they tended to spend most of their time occupying trenches and on manual work.

There was a third son, Terrio, born in Germany in 1887 but the only record of him that can be found is that he was living with the family in Moulsham in 1911. There may have been another son, because on 24 August 1914 the *Essex Newspaper* reported the following:

'Spy' – Charge Dismissed

On Monday at Clacton Petty sessions Ernest Abberfield of 18 Station Road, Clacton was charged on remand with being suspected of having committed or being about to commit an offence under the Official Secrets Act 1911 between Wivenhoe and Aylesford, on 18 August. The evidence has been already reported. The disposition had been to the Home Office and a communication was now read from the Public Prosecutor recommending that unless there was fresh evidence the Justices be asked to discharge the prisoner.

The chairman said he understood the mother of prisoner was an Austrian. Mrs Abberfield: I am a Hungarian, my husband was an Englishman, and by marriage I took his nationality. The accused was discharged.

I just wonder what her sons thought of the military's suspicions but this is just another of the many example of how paranoid the public and authorities were becoming and the media was fuelling this paranoia. The following is a report from the *Portsmouth Evening News*:

Signals from the Coast
Are there German agents in Essex?

Mysterious flashlight signals from the wooded country between Clacton-on-Sea and Harwich (says the *Daily Express*) are seen almost every night by sentries posted along his portion of Essex Coast.

There is no doubt that German agents are still abound in the district and that by means of flashlights they are endeavouring to communicate information to enemy ships or submarines at sea. Great efforts have been made to trace the signallers but they are elusive as will-o-wisps and at night time it is extremely difficult to judge the exact spot at which the lights are seen. It is suggested by some that the spies have secret retreats in the woods stocked with provisions, where they can hide in safety for days if too closely pursued.

It is curious fact that the flashlights were especially frequent on the night following the Zeppelin raid on Maldon, when airships passed directly over Frinton-on-Sea.

All along the East Coast it is felt that the strongest measures should be taken by the authorities to remove every alien sufficiently far inland to prevent any possibilities of communications with the sea.

It therefore did not take long before suspects were being hauled before the authorities for the feeblest of reasons. The *Essex Newspaper* reported the following on 8 August 1914:

Spy Charge at Walton

Two young visitors to Walton-on-the-Naze, William Chas. Garrett and Gilbert Henry Garrett, of 32 Kensington Gardens, Ilford, were arrested at Walton-on-the-Naze on Wednesday evening and brought to Clacton where they were detained.

They were brought before Mr T Lilley, J.P. on Thursday evening, on the charge of making sketches, taking a photograph of the signal station at Walton, belonging to H.M. the King.

Supt. Mules said he had made full inquiries. He verified the names and addresses of the accused were the sons of a respectable man in Ilford. They had come to Walton for a holiday. He felt sure they had acted in ignorance. The Magistrate, being satisfied that the young men had acted in ignorance, discharged them. Supt. Mules retained the photo plate.

On the same day the paper reported a more serious incident:

Spy shot dead at Newcastle

Newcastle telegram states that just before dawn this morning a foreigner was challenged by a patrol on the high level bridge over the Tyne. He ran down the steps to the river and jumped into a boat, refusing to stop, he was shot dead.

There were a number of Zeppelin raids during April 1915 that passed over Clacton and Walton-on-the-Naze. In fact on 16 April the newspapers reported that when an airship was seen over Harwich a powerful motor car with its headlights on was reported travelling at tremendous speed in the direction of Walton-on-the-Naze. It was challenged by a military patrol but did not stop. The soldiers apparently fired on it but it continued without slowing down. Efforts were being made to trace the motor car.

Approximately a week later on Thursday, 22 April a similar incident occurred when at least two Zeppelins were seen over Walton-on-the-Naze at 11.30 pm and two London ladies, Mrs Baldwin and her daughter Miss E. Baldwin, recounted a terrifying experience in which a very heavy motor car with two very powerful lamps passed them between Maldon and Burnham, when the whirring of Zeppelins was heard overhead. Miss Baldwin expressed the opinion to the authorities that she felt sure the car and its occupants were guiding the Zeppelin. The question is, was this the same vehicle and did the authorities ever track it and its occupants down?

With regard to the last two incidents and that local police were told to look out for commercial travellers, it is not surprising that Thomas Farrow. a commercial traveller, appeared before the local Clacton court in September 1916 charged with having illegal headlights on his motor car and for carrying two electric lamps each giving a greater candlepower than a 12-watt bulb. His witness Herbert Smith, an electrical engineer, testified that he had re-arranged the lighting of the defendant's car and believed he put tissue paper in the side lamps and there were no headlights on the defendant's car. The case was dismissed. He was lucky – he could have been accused of spying.

On 5 September 1914 the *Essex Newsman* reported the following: 'What were thought by an alert cliff patrol to be mysterious flashlights signals, apparently from the window of a private residence situated on the front not many miles from Clacton caused excitement and the house was surrounded but on investigation a satisfactory explanation was forthcoming.' Surprisingly it was not until September 1914 that the Admiralty directed that all lights on the sea front and public places at Clacton and Walton-on-the-Naze be extinguished.

On 1 August 1914 Christopher Cordsen of 63 Tower Street, Brightlingsea, German by birth (born in Kappalin) but a naturalized American citizen, attended the Colchester Police Station in the hope he could stay in Brightlingsea. They registered him as an enemy alien and on 19 August he was ordered by the police to move out of the prohibited area. The following day he returned and produced a master mariner's certificate in support of his previous statement. The police were still not satisfied but gave him a permit to go to London to get further proof. On 21 August he returned to Colchester with a certificate from the American Ambassador in London stating that he was an American citizen. The certificate was forwarded to the War Office, which replied a few days later that unless there were good grounds for various sections of the Aliens Act to apply it would appear that he could remain in Brightlingsea. On 28 August the police reported that he was living quietly at Brightlingsea and there was no reason to suspect that he was doing anything detrimental to the interests of the country.

As early as 1908 the War Office had been keeping an eye on Cornelius Coblenz. a German who had served in the German Army and had come to England from New York on 25 March 1895. He moved to Clacton in 1905. It is believed that he was in the wine and tobacco trade in London, was a Freemason and associated himself with the local lodges. The authorities became suspicious because he was receiving a monthly money draft of £11.8.0 from Deutsche Bank, Berlin, and on one occasion his wife received a draft of £525. It was understood that Cornelius had fallen on hard times and the money was being sent over by his father. The police also reported that he visited Germany about once a year but did not appear to receive any visitors from there. However, the 1911 census showed that his wife Ada was also German and that staying with them at the time was his sister-in-law Paula Stake, also German. Their only son Robert had been born in England. On 6 October 1914 he reported to the Clacton police, producing his naturalization papers dated 12 August 1912. However, the public still had strong suspicions and considered him to be a spy. The police recommended his removal and on 24 October he was ordered to leave and moved to Highgate. It is not clear whether the family went with him.

Finally we have the case of Herbert Thomas Waterman, who for a short time lived at Walton-on-the-Naze and at times appears to have been a little outspoken and therefore got himself into trouble. On 24 April 1918 a letter was received by the local police from the military authorities as they were concerned about various allegations he had made against the Royal Family. On investigation by the police, it was discovered that he had moved to Walton-on-the-Naze in June 1916 and that he was living with a young women who he referred to as an Indian Princess. Although he appeared to be rather reserved, the public looked upon him with some suspicion. He finally left for Hampshire in May 1918 and it is understood that on leaving he was heard to say the Germans would blow up the place within twelve months. His nationality is unknown so it is his loose tongue that brought him to the attention of the authorities.

Another example of just how nervous people were is the experience of Herbert Reynolds:

> My first experience was not in fighting but took place at Frinton-on-Sea in 1914. I had cycled to Frinton from Kirby Cross, a village a few miles away, where I lodged with an old lady. It was evening and I had to use my cycle lamp, although kept dim.
>
> No sooner had I reached the corner of the Old Road and Connaught Avenue, when I was immediately pounced on by two armed soldiers, they then escorted me to their H.Q., where I was charged with being a German spy, signalling with my lamp to an unseen enemy.
>
> After such interrogation I was finally escorted to my lodging by a diminutive soldier, who was armed with a loaded revolver and ordered to shoot if I attempted to escape but on reaching my lodgings, the soldier was satisfied that I was okay and certainly no spy. He confessed afterwards that while he was escorting me, he feared, as I was a bit bigger than him, that I might land him the first blow. So it ended in triumphant note as I saw the Sergeant Major next day and we shook hands with a smile.

These are just a few cases of people in Clacton and the nearby towns who came under scrutiny but they show how the slightest indiscretion could have had you in trouble with the authorities.

As one would expect the situation in Germany was the same. When war broke out Germany had approximately 15,000 British and French residents. Initially they were not considered a security risk and they were merely required to observe a curfew and report once a week to their local police station. Although the public were concerned about spies and saboteurs the main reason for internment of the British in November 1914, French in December 1914, Canadians, South Africans and New Zealanders in January 1915 and Australians in February 1915 was the internment of German nationals in those countries.

Following mobilization, women, children and men over military age were allowed to leave Germany. The measures then adopted in November saw over 4,000 British men being interned at a former racecourse at Ruhleben, near Berlin. Most of them would not be released from the camp until the end of the war, but as usual the British spirit shone through and somehow they managed to maintain a unique way of life for the four years of their unwelcome internment. Other than arranging sporting contests, there was a camp newspaper and an entertainment group which arranged for many songs to be written and performed:

The Ruhleben Song

FIRST VERSE

Oh we're roused up in the morning, when the day is gently dawning,
And we're put to bed before the night's begun,
And for many months on end, we have never seen a friend,
And we've lost the job our energy had won.
Yes, we've waited in the frost, for a parcel that got lost,
Or a letter that the postman never brings,
And it isn't beer and skittles, doing work on scanty victuals,
Yet every man can still get up and sing.

CHORUS

So line up boys and sing this chorus, shout this chorus all you can.
We want the people there, to hear in Leicester Square,
That we're the boys that never get downhearted.
Back, back, back again in England, then we'll fill the flowing cup,
And tell them clear and loud, of that Ruhleben crowd,
That always kept their pecker up.

SECOND VERSE

Oh, we send our love and kisses, to our sweetheart or our missus,
And we say the life we lead is grand.
And we stroll around the tea-'us, where the girls can sometimes see us,
And we say it's just as good as down the Strand.
Yet there sometimes comes a minute, when we see there's nothing to it,
And the tale that we've been telling isn't true,
Down our spine there comes a-stealing, just a little homesick feeling,
Then I'll tell you boys the best thing you can do...

CHORUS

The song was written by C.H. Brooks with music by Ernest MacMillan and was first sung on 8 May 1915. It soon became the prisoners' 'National Anthem' and was sung at the many reunions after the war. The verses were even published in a Government White Paper, as well as in *The Times*.

CHAPTER 4

Home Front

❧❧

Well, as we have seen, war broke out irrespective of what action the British were going to take. Germany would probably have been victorious if Britain had not intervened; but intervene we did!

On 6 August 1914 we dispatched the British Expeditionary Force (BEF). It was small by Continental standards, only 120,000 men of whom 75,000 were regulars, the others being reservists. In addition we requisitioned 240 ships, 165,000 horses, London buses, delivery vans and 1,800 special trains which were all in place within sixteen days of war breaking out. They were up against 1.7 million German troops, although the French had 2.4 million men in the field.

After the initial euphoria and celebrations following the declaration of war, reality slowly began to sink in. Men were required at the Front in their thousands which meant that, by 1916, conscription was introduced. Fear of invasion began to occupy people's minds, and defence was therefore a priority. Rationing became a problem, and women had to replace men in industries but they were also required at home and at the front to look after the sick and injured. The civilian population had not previously experienced such problems or fears. It was a logistic nightmare but somehow the British spirit prevailed and somehow life at home struggled on.

As indicated, fear of invasion was high on the agenda, particularly in the coastal areas around Clacton. Each district or parish had to have in place a Local Emergency Committee whose responsibility it was to ensure that the local inhabitants were aware of what they had to do in case of invasion. For example local farmers, smallholders and estate owners had to provide a survey of their number of animals, equipment, employees etc. Although invasion was considered

Troops on the march. (Author's collection)

unlikely, in the event of a landing the civil population were instructed to destroy everything that might be of use to the enemy, farmers to destroy all livestock humanely by shooting them, not by letting them bleed to death or disembowelling them, and evacuate the district by an agreed route.

The Tendering District, which Clacton and surrounding areas were part of, sent out instructions to all the parishes of the district of what to do in case of invasion.

The opening paragraphs of the notice read as follows:

> An invasion is improbable but an invasion is not impossible and hence the civil population must be prepared and organized for it.
>
> In case of an invasion in the Tendering District the business of the civil population will be:-
>
> 1.   To destroy everything that might be of service to the enemy.
> 2.   To evacuate the District entirely.
>
> If an invasion occurs, the civil population will know for the first time that what war really means. All conditions will be altered; things which previously had great importance will suddenly cease to have any importance and martial law will be in force. The supreme duty of every citizen will be calmly, promptly, obediently and with the utmost goodwill, to do his share in the general scheme of operations. Citizens who lose their heads or refuse to obey instructions, even though such instructions may seem harsh, will be helping the enemy and endangering not only the lives of their fellow citizens but the safety of the Empire.
>
> In each parish the carrying out of the scheme is in the hands of the Parish Emergency Committee and the Chairman of the Committee is the chief authority for such purpose. The Parish Committee, therefore, must engage sufficient number of helpers (who may or may not be special constables) and also secure the co-operation of the regular police. All helpers will be authorized to wear white armlets with the letter **T** thereon in red. The armlets must be not less than 5 inches wide. It is suggested that local ladies be asked to make them.

A scheme of Emergency Orders was also set in place which consisted of either 'A warning order' whereby helpers who had previously been selected would be quietly summoned, tools likely to be of use to the army collected, labourers made available to help the military authorities and the inhabitants be informed, but not alarmed. Nothing else was to be done unless the order to evacuate was given.

If given by church bells being rung violently or by other agreed means, the inhabitants were to take nothing more than clothes, blankets, jewellery and food and drink for forty-eight hours with them. They would make their way via the previously-agreed evacuation route.

Agreed routes for our parishes were as follows:

> From Clacton – Coppen's Green, Cross House, along main road for 1¾ miles to St Osyth, Chisbon Heath. St Osyth Wick, Ainger's Green, Great Bentley, Point 94 on ½ in. map north of Thorington Station, along the main road through Frating for one mile. Frating Green, Ball's Green, Great Bromley, Bromley Cross, Ardleigh Station, Ardleigh Wick, Rankin's Corner. Long Road, Great Horkesley, Little Horkesley, Wood Hall, along main road for three miles to Mount Bures and into the Petty Sessional Division of Halstead.
>
> From Brightlingsea – Cross G.E.R. at Thorington Station, Frating Green, Great Bromley, Bromley Cross, turn right and in northerly direction to Badley Hall, Hungerdowns, across railway, Dedham, Stratford St Mary, Higham, Stoke-by-Nayland, Nayland, Bures and into the Petty Sessional Division of Halstead.
>
> St Osyth – Chisbon Heath, Rough Heath, Ainger's Green, cross G.E.R. North of point 73 0n ½ in. map, through Great Bromley, cross main road at point 96, Raven's Green, Hare Green, Cowey Green, Great Bromley, Bromley Cross, Burnt Heath, Ardleigh Wick, Langham Moor, Boxted Heath, Great Horkesley, Little Horkesley, Wood Hall, along the main road to Rectory, Mount Bures and into Petty Sessional Division Halstead.
>
> From Holland – Thorpe Cross, New Hall, Beaumont, The Oak, Stone's Green, Little Bromley, Bradley Hall, Ardleigh Station, Ardleigh Wick, Langham Moor, Boxted Heath, Great Horkesley, Little Horkesley, Wood Hall, along main road three miles to Mount Bures and into the Petty Sessional Division of Halstead.

From Frinton – Kirby Cross, Kirby-le-Soken, New Hall, Beaumont, The Oak, Stone's Greed, Wix, Bradfield, Dickey Hall, Lawford, Stour House, Jupeshill Farm, Dedham, Straford St. Mary, Higham, Stoke-by-Nayland, Nayland, Bures and into the Petty Sessional Division Of Halstead.

From Walton – Kirby-le-Soken, Beaumont, Stone's Green, Tendring Workhouse, Tendering Heath, Mill Green, Workhouse Green, Little Bromley, Badley Hall, Hungerdowns, across Railway, Dedham, Straford St Mary, Higham, Stoke-by-Nayland, Nayland, Bures, cross river Stour and into Petty Sessional Division of Halstead.

Their ultimate destination was Oxfordshire.

On the basis that many families did not travel very far in those days, we assume maps were handed out and people were instructed to familiarize themselves with the scheme. Where possible there would be guides helping them on their way. It is surprising that many of the routes included main roads. In general, main roads had to be left clear for the military, so if they were included the evacuees had to keep to the left so as to leave at least half the road clear for troops.

There was a motto and it was not 'Each for himself' but 'Each for all'. All this sounds very dramatic but the government just wanted the population to understand that the measures were precautionary and that there was no need for alarm.

Another restriction put in place was the feeding of wild animals, the concern here being that it was a waste of food, especially after rationing came into force in January 1918. The cause of food shortages was twofold, firstly many men from the farming industry joined the armed services, which left the country short of agricultural workers, the second cause which helped to make the situation worse was when on 9 January 1917 Germany declared unrestricted submarine warfare. This meant that our merchant fleet was at risk of being sunk. The Battle of Jutland in June 1916 was not a victory but it at least kept the Germany fleet in port and maintained the British blockade, creating a serious food shortages for the Germans but also the escalation of submarine warfare.

The government therefore encouraged people to grow as much food as possible themselves, and also established the Women's Land Army in 1917, to replace those who had left their farms to fight. So

Recruitment poster.

wherever you looked, women came to the country's aid; you found them in the fields, in the factories, included dangerous munition factories, you found them in the hospitals at home and overseas, and they were looking after their families as well. There is no doubt they helped Britain win the war.

Though there is no doubt there were shortages of food in the large towns and cities, did it really affect places like Clacton and the surrounding coastal villages? They did not have backyards like city dwellers but they had gardens were they could grow their own food, or there were areas where allotments could be established so rationing in the countryside was probably not so severe.

Voluntary Aid Detachments

On the outbreak of war, various organizations sprang into action, the Red Cross for one which in 1909 had formed a Joint War Committee with the Order of St John, working together under the protective emblem of the Red Cross.

The committee organized not only fundraising but recruited volunteers to work alongside its professional staff. Their primary role was to help the naval and military medical services in treating sick and wounded sailors and soldiers. This included men as well as women and they were all trained in first aid, and some also received training in nursing, cookery, hygiene and sanitation. They were given the title of Voluntary Aid Detachments (VADs). As you would expect, the majority of the women were trained as nurses, while the men took

Ricketts Convalescent Home, Clacton-on-Sea. (Author's collection)

on roles such as ambulance drivers, transporting sick and wounded soldiers from trains or ships to local hospitals. They frequently found themselves at the Front ferrying men back to the nearest medical centres, a role that was just as dangerous as if they were actually fighting as they would often come under heavy fire or in contact with some of the dreadful diseases that struck the troops such as cholera, typhoid and Spanish 'flu. By the summer of 1914 there were over 2,500 VAD establishments in Britain, with volunteers totalling 74,000 of which two-thirds were women and girls. The Clacton area was not short of volunteers coming forward and although Clacton had the Middlesex War Hospital (MWH) and the Essex & Reckitt's Convalescent Home (ERCH) which were in need of VADs, many went further afield. You could say that both the hospital and convalescent homes were Clacton's closest link with the fighting at the Front because of the thousands of troops that came to convalesce there.

Mrs Matilda Adams of Marine Parade, Clacton-on-Sea, signed on as a nursing member and her role was to assist the ambulance teams serving refreshments to the wounded at Clacton-on-Sea railway

Essex Convalescent Home, Clacton-on-Sea. (Author's collection)

station when they arrived during the night. She had previously worked for the British Red Cross.

Miss Beatrice Beaumont, who was a Hotel Assistant at Beaumont Hall Hotel on Marine Parade, not only organized all the work to look after wounded soldiers at Reckitt's but helped out on the ambulance trains with refreshments similar to Matilda. She worked for the Joint War Committee for seven years before resigning in October 1919. She had reached the rank of Commandant.

Miss Ida Christine Beard of Wellesley Road, Clacton-on-Sea, signed on in October 1915 and worked for the next three years as a cook and nurse at Gostwycke VAD Hospital in Colchester. Gostwycke House had been taken over by the VADs as a temporary hospital.

The following were also involved with nursing and general duties at the Essex & Reckitt's Convalescent Home:

- Miss Maud Bryan, Marine Parade, Clacton – Assisted at the ERCH and assisting the ambulance train at Clacton Railway Station serving refreshments to the wounded.

- Mrs Maud Carter, Vista Road, Clacton – Nursing duties at the ERCH.
- Mrs Ella Chapman, Victory Road, Clacton – Nursing duties including general work and needlework at the ERCH.
- Miss Rebe Chisnall, Dunedin Connaught Gdns., Clacton – Household duties at the ERCH.
- Miss Dorothy Clack, Connaught Gdns., Clacton – Nursing assistance at the ERCH.
- Miss Dora Clark, Pier Avenue, Clacton, – Nursing assistance at the ERCH.
- Miss Lillian Clark, sister of Dora, Pier Avenue, Clacton – Nursing assistance at the ERCH.
- Miss Alice Cox, Holland Road, Clacton – Nursing assistance at the ERCH.
- Mrs Ada Curtis, Electric Parade, Clacton – Needlework at the ERCH.
- Mrs Minnie Drake, Old Road, Clacton – Nursing duties including needlework for the wounded at ERCH.
- Mrs Florence Friend, Avondale Road, Clacton   Nursing and needlework duties at the ERCH.
- Miss Mildred Lampard, Edith Road, Clacton   Nursing duties at the ERCH and also for the last two years of the war serving refreshments on the ambulance trains at Clacton Station.
- Miss Susie Johnson, Wellesley Road, Clacton – Teacher by profession but carried out nursing duties during the school holidays at the ERCH.
- Miss Grace Mann, Agate Road, Clacton – Needlework at the ERCH.
- Miss Gladys Page, Bocking Elm, Clacton – Nursing duties at the ERCH, commencing in January 1912 and still working there after the war.
- Miss Mildred Page, sister of Gladys, Bocking Elm, Clacton – Nursing duties at the ERCH, commencing January 1912 and still working there after the war.
- Miss Ada Osborne, Alton Road, Clacton – Needlework and nursing duties at the ERCH.
- Miss Lily Quilter, Jackson Rad, Clacton – Nursing duties at ERCH.

- Mrs Jane Salter, Hayes Road, Clacton – Engaged in January 1912 as Quartermaster, assisting the British Red Cross Society (BRCS) Essex/86 at the ERCH, ambulance trains, War Work Depot etc. was still serving after the war.
- Miss Freda Shadbolt, Avondale Road, Clacton – General assistance at the ERCH, joining at the outbreak of war.
- Mrs Elsi Shillingsley, Holland Road, Clacton – General assistance at the ERCH.
- Miss Sarah Ann Stringer, Colne Road, Clacton – Nursing duties and spent three years living in the ERCH until it closed but continued working for the VAD.
- Miss Daisy Stroud, Holland Road, Clacton – Nursing duties at the ERCH.
- Miss Edith Thomas, Chapman Road, Clacton – Nursing duties at ERCH during holiday periods.
- Mrs Emma Treby, Ellis Road, Clacton – General nursing duties such as canteen work and needlework for the patients at the ERCH.
- Miss Winifred Warner, Wellesley Road, Clacton – Teacher by profession, carrying out general nursing duties during school holidays at the ERCH.

The following is a further list of VADS who lived in Clacton but carried out their duties elsewhere:

- Miss Elsie Appleby, Mrs Dorothy Adair, Mrs Mabel Joyce Bacon and Miss Grace Bayley, Miss Vera Church, Miss Stella Mayhew, Miss Marie Gladys Page, Miss Kathleen Tweedie and Miss M.L. Webb were all involved with nursing duties.
- Miss Ethel Lamb (née Barker), Page Road, Clacton – Worked as a sister in Etaples, Northern France for the St John Ambulance Brigade.
- Miss Enid Dorothy Bocking. Carnarvon Road, Clacton – Worked as a clerk at Ampton Hall Hospital, Bury St Edmunds.
- Mrs Mary Harcourt Goldsmith, Winterbourne, Clacton – Was a paid Matron (£125 p.a. plus board, lodging and laundry) overseeing three houses, 140 beds at the St John Hospital, Regents Park, Southampton from May 1916 to the end of September 1916.

- Miss May Hempson, Great Clacton Hall, Clacton – Worked as a cook at nearby Thorpe Le Soken Auxiliary Hospital.
- Miss Jennie Martin, Oceana, Clacton – Paid head cook at British Red Cross Hospital, Netley, Hampshire.
- Miss Katherine Maude Ridley, Arthurholme, Clacton – Taken on as a Quartermaster, keeping stores, ordering goods, and kitchen superintendent at the Red Cross hospital, Ardleigh. For a short time at Singholme, Walton-on-the-Naze.
- Mr William Simpson, 7 Page Road, Clacton – Enlisted as an orderly working in France from 22 May 1917 to 8 February 1919. He was initially paid 28 shillings a week, rising to 35 shillings a week.
- Miss Florence Smith, Clay Hall, Clacton – Worked as a paid laboratory assistant at Colchester Military Hospital from January 1916 to January 1918.

Unfortunately we have little information on a Mrs Sykes of Wykeham, Clacton whose rank on engagement was that of a searcher. The only other information on her record states   Wounded or missing. Was she sent overseas and went out looking for the wounded: I cannot imagine that or was it a matter of recording those poor soldiers who were missing, presumably wounded?

Miss Maud Fletcher's engagement with the Red Cross began in 1912 and she resided at Reckitt's Convalescent Home throughout the war as matron and lady superintendent. She was awarded the Royal Red Cross Medal second class, being decorated by the King at Buckingham Palace on 12 December 1917. The decoration was awarded to army nurses for exceptional services, devotion to duty and professional competence in British hospitals. The first recipient of the Royal Red Cross Medal was Florence Nightingale for her work in the Crimean War at Scutari Hospital.

Mr George William Humphrey joined the Red Cross Motor Launch Department on 1 August 1916 as an engineer. He was posted to Mesopotamia until the end of the war. He was mentioned in despatches (*The Times*, 22 February 1919) and was awarded the Victory and British War Medals.

In most major towns Red Cross Work Depots were set up to collect and despatch clothing from working parties. Items were sent to the

Red Cross headquarters or directly to soldiers in auxiliary hospitals at home or abroad. St Osyth had Works Depot No. 4524. Mrs Emily Jane Tydeman, Clacton Road, St Osyth, worked there part-time doing needlework, and was awarded the Red Cross Badge. Mrs Mary Smith also of Clacton Road, St Osyth, worked at the depot continuously from November 1917 until the end of the war. The following are women from St Osyth who did approximately three hours needlework per week at the depot or at home: Miss Gertrude Archer in addition to doing needlework also help organizing the depot. Mrs Helen Ivy Jacques (née Archer), Mrs Kate Balham, Mrs Annie Bareham and Miss Lilla Beales.

Mrs Margaret Tate, who lived at Holland House, Great Holland, worked for the War Hospital Supplies Depot at Southend-on-Sea and was awarded the War Office Volunteer War Badge. Miss Ethel Marion Low of Great Holland Hall was a quartermaster and nurse from 1915 to 1919, but the location of her employment is unknown.

From Frinton-on-Sea, Miss Amelia Armitage from Connaught Avenue carried out part-time nursing and general service work at 'Singholm' Military Hospital, Walton-on-the-Naze (a VAD temporary hospital and now a care home) and Turret Lodge Casualty Hospital, Frinton-on-Sea, from July 1916 to April 1918.

Edward Baker from Frinton-on-Sea volunteered in April 1916 as a driver with the Motor Ambulance Section and part of his service was at Le Havre in France. During his time with the Red Cross he was promoted to the rank of sergeant. He terminated his involvement in April 1919.

Miss Margaret Amy Knight was living at the Rectory, Frinton, when she signed up as a nurse in March 1915. She worked at a number of places including the Middlesex War Hospital, Clacton. Her father, Reverend Knight, was the Rector of Frinton from 1911 to 1919.

The only person we have been able to find from Walton-on-the-Naze is Miss Florence Mary Austin who joined late in the war (1 August 1918) and appeared to be paid at the rate of £36 a year as a cook to a Miss Cooper.

Brightlingsea, on the other hand, had quite a few including four men. George Frederick Bush signed up in September 1915 as a chief mate on hospital ships at a rate of £18 per month. He soon found himself in Mudros and Alexandria and his area of engagement is recorded as 'Egyphan' (Egyptian). Unfortunately he suffered from gallstones and died on the hospital ship *Dover Castle* on

30 January 1916. HMHS *Dover Castle* was a steam ship initially built as a passenger/cargo ship for the Union-Castle Line in 1904. Soon after the outbreak of war she was requisitioned as a hospital ship. On 26 May 1917 while en route from Malta to Gibraltar she was torpedoed twice by the German U-boat *UC-67*, killing seven stokers but the remaining crew, including the wounded, were evacuated to HMS *Cameleon*. After the war the commander of the U-boat, Karl Neumann, was tried for sinking of the hospital ship at the Leipzig War Crimes Trials. Although he admitted sinking the ship his defence was that he was only obeying German Admiralty orders. The German believed that the Allies were using hospital ships for military purposes and therefore on 19 March 1917 informed German submarine commanders that they could attack hospital ships if they did not appear to be complying with German conditions. As he believed the orders to be lawful he was found not guilty – a lucky man.

The Rector of All Saints', Brightlingsea, the Reverend Robert Rendell also signed up in 1915 but because of his responsibilities his service was only part-time but he was on call twenty-four hours a day. He worked as a military hospital orderly and carried out first aid duties during air raids. The arrangement terminated after two years, he having reached the rank of quartermaster.

Miss Gladys Munson, although from Colchester, signed up on 19 June 1916 and worked for two years as a paid telephonist at the Brightingsea telephone exchange. The following women from Brightlingsea all worked as nurses: Miss Grace Emily Jane Bye, Miss Hattie Fieldgate, Miss Kitty Fieldgate, Mrs Kitty Henderson, Ms Mabel May Lewis, Miss Mary Louise Stammers, Mrs Annie M Hartland-Mahon and Mrs Ethel Maria Dickin who worked as a sister at the Auxiliary War Hospital, Foremarke Hall, Derbyshire.

Ethel (née Adhams) married Edward Percival Dickin in 1900. He went to Northampton Grammar School and then on to the University of Edinburgh, graduating with a Doctorate in Medicine (MD). The 1901 and 1911 censuses have them living at 51 High Street, Brightlingsea. The Red Cross VAD record has him signing on 25 June 1915 with the temporary rank of captain in the Royal Army Medical Corps (RAMC) and his first appointment was Officer in Charge of Medical Division, General Hospital, Tigne, Malta. Tigne Barracks in Malta was taken over in May 1915. Then on 13 June an officers' hospital opened in the officers' mess with forty beds. In September the following year the number of beds was expanded by the erection of marquees in the hospital grounds but by this time Edward had returned home and was working at the military hospital in Colchester. After the war he was awarded both the British and the Victory Medal. Edward was interested in history and was obviously fascinated by the history of Brightlingsea as in 1913 he had published *A History of the Town of Brightlingsea, A Member of the Cinque Ports*. He passed away in 1945.

Finally there was Frederick Charles Bill who lived at Upper Peak Place, Brightlingsea, who served as a private with the Field Ambulance, East Anglian Unit and was awarded the 1914-15 Star.

There were thirteen VADs from other parts of the county and country that worked in the Clacton area the majority at the Middlesex War Hospital, including Miss Evelyn Violet Allott from Herongate who was employed as a quartermaster and staff nurse from 8 August 1914. She worked at the Grammar School Temporary Hospital, Brentwood, Coombe Lodge Primary Military Auxiliary Hospital and Middlesex War Hospital, Clacton. She was honoured by the King at Buckingham Palace with the Royal Red Cross Medal second class on 12 December 1917. These are just a few of Britain's 125,000 VAD volunteers who by the end of the war had worked at home and abroad, 90,000 of them being women.

Recruitment poster.

Instead of joining the Red Cross, **Clara Gosling** enlisted into the Queen Mary's Army Auxiliary Corps, service number 2108 on the 7 September 1917 and she soon found herself in France. The Women's Army Auxiliary Corps was formed in 1917 as a result of Lieutenant General H.M. Lawson's report which recommended that the army recruit women for non-combatant duties in France and at home to free up more men to fight. The Corps was renamed Queen Mary's Army Auxiliary Corps in April 1918. From March 1917 to the end of the war over 57,000 women served in France, Belgium, Greece and Italy. They were divided into five sections: cookery, mechanical, clerical, medical and miscellaneous.

Clara was registered as a worker but we believe she was actually a nurse and she was killed on 7 November 1918 just four days before the end of the war. She was born in Brightlingsea to Henry and Clara in 1886. Surprisingly her father was a mariner. She is buried in a Commonwealth military cemetery in Rouen, France: it is not known how she died. Clara was awarded the Victory and the British War Medals. Her Victory Medal came up for auction in May 2015 and with various donations from local businesses, organizations and individuals the Brightlingsea Museum was able to purchase it. Clara is the only woman commemorated on the Brightlingsea War Memorial so, as the curator of the museum says, it is important that the medal stays in Brightlingsea. In an interview the curator went on to say that 'it is a real tribute not only to the women who went into the services but also to those who worked in the factories. There were a lot of soldiers and naval personnel in Brightlingsea during the war who often commented on what good billets they had and that was because of the women who were left behind.'

Christmas 1916: Thoughts in a VAD Hospital Kitchen

There's no Xmas leave for us scullions,
We've got to keep on with the grind;
Just cooking for Britain's heroes,
But, bless you! We don't really mind

We've scores and scores of potatoes,
And cabbages also to do,
And onions and turnips and what not.
That go in the Irish Stew.

We're baking and frying and boiling,
From morning until night;
But we've got to keep on a bit longer,

Till Victory comes in sight.

Then there's cutting the thin bread and butter,
For the men who are very ill;
But we feel we're well rewarded;
For they've fought old Kaiser Bill.

Yes! We've got to hold on a while longer,
Till we've beaten the Hun to his knees;
And then 'Goodbye' to the Kitchen;
The treacle, the jam and the cheese.

By M. Winifred Wedgewood

Mabel Edith Grigson was born in Clacton to George and Esther Grigson in 1882. The 1911 census has her living at Harold House, Jackson Road, Clacton-on-Sea, single and her occupation being that of a Sick Nurse Probationer. Presumably at some stage after the outbreak of war she enlisted into the Queen Alexandra's Royal Naval Nursing Service. Initially a reservist but it was not long before she found herself posted to Royal Naval Hospital Bighi on the island of Malta in the small town of Kalkara, where she was promoted to sister.

There were a number of military hospitals on the island, their first casualties of the Great War coming from the Gallipoli landings, 600 arriving on 4 May 1915. Later patients came from Salonkia following British and French forces landing there to assist Serbia in its war against Bulgaria. Then in 1918 the influenza epidemic saw another surge in patients and it was on 3 October, just a month before the end of the war, that Mabel died of dysentery and heart failure. She not only appears on the Clacton Roll of Honour but also on the 'Women of the Empire' memorial panel in York Minister. She is buried in the Malta (Capuccini) Naval Cemetery, Malta.

Mabel was the sister of George Jarat Grigson who became the coxswain of the Clacton Lifeboat *Albert Edward III* in 1907, after seventeen years as a member of the crew. Like Mabel he was born in Clacton-on-Sea. He took after his father who was originally from Brightlingsea and was also a member of the Clacton crew from 1883 to 1899. In the crew were other family members, Walter Norman Wilson and Edward Ernest Wilson.

On 11 December 1914 the *Western Mail* reported the following awards:

The Royal National Lifeboat Institution has awarded the silver medal to John Swan, coxswain of the Lowestoft lifeboat, in recognition of the crew's gallant services in rescuing nine men from the minesweeper *Condor* in very rough weather on November 22 and also to George Grigson, coxswain of the Clacton-on-Sea lifeboat, for the exceptional fine services of lifeboat, which lasted from the 2nd to the 5th inst. And eventually resulted in fifteen persons being saved from steamship *Harlington*. In both instances additional remuneration was granted to the crew of the Lifeboat.

Nine months later, on 28 September 1915 George and his 2nd Coxswain Jesse Salmon were awarded Silver Medals, Second Service Class for the rescue of the barque *Leading Chief*. The lifeboat had to make nine separate attempts to approach the vessel and finally they had to take the lifeboat over the submerged deck of the vessel in a most hazardous operation at night in heavy seas.

The *Essex Newsman* reported the rescue on 2 October 1915:

GALLANT RESCUE OF WRECKED CREW

Exciting scenes and gallant rescues characterised the wreck of the barque *Leading Chief*, which grounded on the West Sunk Sands on Tuesday afternoon. The Clacton Lifeboat got away in answer to the call for help just after 4.30 on Tuesday afternoon and she encountered a rough passage in high sea and strong but fair wind. Meantime the crew of the barque jettisoned some 30 or 40 tons of cargo, with the object of easing the strain and possibly floating the vessel off but the barque was obviously sinking and when the lifeboat reached her the crew were gathered on the poop with the water almost up to their necks. As the *Albert Edward* was approaching the barque's mainmast crashed down, missing the lifeboat by a few yards. In an attempt to board the barque George Stebbing, a lifeboat man, was swept overboard and was in the icy cold water a quarter of an hour before being hauled aboard again. To get the poop of the barque, where the crew were, the lifeboat had to approach the partly-submerged vessel 'bow on,' crossing her sunken deck and by means the wrecked seamen were got safely on board, leaving a vessel which was quickly breaking up and which soon became a total wreck. On starting for home it was found that the motor was out of running and so sails had to be depended upon for the homeward journey, which took the best part of the night owing to a strong head wind. Clacton being reached at 10 o'clock on Wednesday morning.

The crew of the barque and of the lifeboat were in a terribly exhausted condition. They were taken into the charge of Mr. C.J. Beaumont, the local representative of Shipwrecked Mariners' Society and conveyed to Southcliff Hall, where they soon recovered from the privations they had undergone, thanks to dry cloths and generous meals.

The *Leading Chief* was under the flag of Guernsey and in addition to the awards of the Silver Medals all the lifeboat crew received additional remuneration.

Then in January 1918 George was decorated again for the rescue of twenty-three men from the SS *Iris*. The weather was bitterly cold with snow showers and strong easterly gale. The master refused to leave the ship so the lifeboat stood by for several hours. As the weather got worse and with the sea washing over the vessel, the captain decided to leave. The crew were rescued with great difficulty and danger. Both rescuers and the rescued were numb and well-nigh frozen from their exposure of twenty-four hours in icy-cold weather. Again, as you would expect, it was reported in the local *Chelmsford Chronicle* on Friday, 4 January 1918. 'The Clacton R.N.L.I. lifeboat *Albert Edward* rescued 23 lives from a large Swedish steamer, which was totally wrecked on a sandbank about 16 miles off Clacton . . .' Then a few weeks later in the same paper it reported that George had been awarded the Third Service Clasp and Jesse Salmon his second in command the Bronze Medal and as usual the crew were awarded an extra monetary award of 20s.

In addition to these three instances George was involved in several other shipwrecks caused by ships running aground on the sandbanks around the Clacton coast line. Just proving that though it appears to be an ideal location for an invasion the sandbanks helped to form some form of defence. It also showed that everyday life was still going on while the devastating war in Europe was in progress. George retired as coxswain in 1919. A younger brother of George, Harold was also a member of the lifeboat crew and was no doubt involved in some of these rescues. Of his two other brothers, one was in the navy and the other in the army.

In October 2010 six of Clacton's volunteer lifesavers were recognized by having roads named after on a new housing estate, off St John's Road:

George Grigson
Jesse Salmon
Samuel Legerton
William Weekes
Albert Potter
William Schofield

There is no doubt that the British women helped to win the war. Their roles changed dramatically once the men disappeared off to the Front. One area where they made a tremendous impact was in the factories that had been converted to producing munitions. Nearly 900,000 women – teenagers, wives, mothers and even grandmothers – joined the ranks of those working in these dangerous factories. Many of the functions involved were once believed to be too strenuous for women. They worked long hours and though the work was fairly repetitive there is no doubt that many enjoyed contributing to the war effort and the camaraderie of working in a team. A number of women rose up through the ranks and became inspectors, managing not only women but also men, a situation many men were not too pleased about. There was also concern that wages would be slowly reduced as the women were getting paid considerably less than the men.

They became known as 'canary girls' because the exposure to TNT, which is toxic, slowly turned the skin an orange-yellow colour, similar to the plumage of a canary. The canary itself was often used by miners to detect toxic carbon monoxide in coal mines. The girls were also referred to as 'munitionettes'. Warners Iron factory in Walton-on-the-Naze was converted into a munitions factory.

War Girls

There's the girl who clips your ticket for the train,
And the girl who speeds the lift from floor to floor,
There's the girl who does a milk-round in the rain,
And the girl who calls for orders at your door.
Strong, sensible and fit
They're out to show their grit,
And tackle jobs with energy and knack.
No longer caged and penned up,
They're going to keep their end up
Till the khaki soldier boys come marching back.

There's the motor girl who drives a heavy van,
There's the butcher girl who brings your joint of meat,
There's the girl who cries 'All fares, please!' like a man,
And the girl who whistles taxies up the street.
Beneath each uniform
Beats a heart that's soft and warm,
Though of canny mother-wit they show no lack;
But a solemn statement this is,
They've no time for love and kisses
Till the Khaki soldier-boys come marching back.

By Jessie Pope.

A few days before the outbreak of war 3,000 men from four battalions of the Essex Territorials (the 4th, 5th, 6th and 7th) arrived at Clacton for their annual camp in a field near Great Clacton. They were part of the Essex Infantry Brigade under the command of Colonel Lawford, Brigadier-General. A detachment of approximately sixty men from the Essex Army Service Corps were there in charge of transport and supplying whatever was required in the camp. Stationed in a joining field was a strong corps of the RAMC. The local YMCA established a marquee for them with facilities for writing letters, recreation etc. The *Essex Newsman* then reported on 1 August that all leave in the Territorial camp had been cancelled and those officers who had not joined the camp were to report immediately. Within days of war being declared, Field Marshal Sir Evelyn Wood V.C visited and inspected the 5th Battalion, of which he was Honorary Colonel.

Middlesex War Hospital

On Thursday, 2 July 1896 *The Times* reported that the Duke and Duchess of York visited the Middlesex Hospital at Clacton to open a fete in celebration of the opening of the new convalescent home connected with the hospital. The home cost nearly £30,000 and was intended for the reception of patients from the hospital. The maintenance of the home was to be provided by the income from a legacy left by Mr Henry Spicer.

On the outbreak of war the Board of Governors of the Hospital and Convalescent Home offered the hospital entirely for the treatment of wounded and sick soldiers. There were initially many difficulties to

Middlesex Hospital, Clacton-on-Sea. (Author's collection)

be overcome, in particular the provision of an adequate surgical and medical staff. The problem was that although the War Office was very enthusiastic about the offer, the fact was that most surgeons had already been mobilized for home duty and those that had not were eager to get to the Front. Also the hospital could not afford to pay any surgeons to do the work. The Board decided that the only option they had was to ask the hospital gynaecological surgeons, Messrs Comyns Berkeley and Victor Bonney, who were too old for military service, if they would volunteer to act as honorary surgeons in charge of the hospital. This they readily agreed to and they were to stay in post from August 1914 to February 1919. Over the next four and a half years the hospital received 9,242 patients, all direct from France, none from the other theatres of war or on home service. They were delivered in 129 convoys.

Miss. G. Morgan was the matron and in addition to her organizational skills she had gained experience of military nursing and hospital administration during the Boer War. This was of great benefit as the men who were sent to military hospital would still be under the control of commissioned officers, this obviously was not the case at the Middlesex. There is no doubt that she deserved the Royal Red Cross Medal 1st Class, which she received from the King. Next in line would be the sisters, nurses and VADs.

There is no doubt we are indebted to our medical practitioners, especially in times of crisis and we probably do not appreciate that at times they may suffer. For example, take Mr. R. F. Mann who was the first X-ray operator at the Middlesex Hospital. The following is a report from the *Dundee People's Journal* of 2 December 1916:

ANOTHER X-RAY OPERATOR GIVES HIS LIFE

After manfully bearing the pain of the X-ray dermatitis for many months, Mr R.F. Mann, of Harrow, has fallen a victim to his sense of duty. He was the first X-ray operator at the Middlesex Hospital and as such was in constant practice for the last 17 years, commencing before the present safety practices were in use. Four years ago he was medically advised to give up his work but refused to do so and since the outbreak of the war the demand on his services was so great that it must have hastened his end. In addition to his work at the Middlesex Hospital he undertook the work of radiographing wounded soldiers at the Clacton branch and for the Duchess of Bedford's Military Hospital at Woburn. Notwithstanding the fact that within twelve years he had undergone four serious operations, he remained at his post until last July, when another operation ended his activities – unbelievable dedication.

The notification of the first group of patients was received by telegram from the Port of London stating that a convoy had been despatched consisting of 'cot cases' and 'walking cases'. The main problem was that it was not possible to keep a store of food sufficient for an influx of a hundred or more men so that whenever a telegram was received informing the hospital of a new convoy of men, the housekeeper was kept extremely busy collecting supplies. The greatest difficult always appeared to be obtaining sufficient bread and on many occasions a donkey-cart had to be taken out to collect bread from near and far.

The transference of patients from train to the hospital was often a lengthy and fatiguing process and sometimes made more difficult if Zeppelins were on the prowl and the lights had to be turned out. However, admission at the hospital was well organized. The matron would stand by the front door with her nurses in attendance and as each patient was brought in she would note his complaint and get a nurse to take him to his allotted ward. The nurse would then return for the next patient. Those patients who were able to walk were sent to the hall for their supper, normally a bowl of hot soup, and then detailed to have baths. Others would have their supper in bed and be washed.

The *Essex Newsman* reported on 19 September 1914 that the first convoy had arrived on a Great Eastern Railway hospital train containing over 100 wounded soldiers, at Clacton at 6.30 pm on

British wounded waiting to be transferred back to 'Blighty'. (Author's collection)

Sunday. They were conveyed to the Middlesex Convalescent Home which was in the process of being converted into a war hospital for the duration. Space had been provided for 150 beds.

A large crowd had gathered outside the station for several hours before to greet with cheers the gallant heroes. Most of them, though a little bedraggled, were able to walk unaided to the waiting transport, just a few had to be helped and there were only five stretcher cases. They were all in excellent spirits considering the ordeal they had been through. The majority had been wounded at the Battle of Mons; others had been wounded in later engagements. Refreshments were served to the men on the platform by the Red Cross nurses and a detachment of the RAMC from Colchester assisted in the removal of the more seriously injured cases.

One of the wounded proudly showed off a German pistol which had belonged to an officer, another had a German helmet and one was wearing a German coat, which he stated he had got from the German who had wounded him. Several of the public received mementoes from the soldiers, bullets etc that they had picked up from the battlefield.

One of the earliest casualties received by the hospital was Private William Balmer of the 2nd Battalion Royal Inniskilling Fusiliers, quite possible one of the first 100 wounded soldiers to arrive. He had written to his family in his home town of Coleraine, Northern Ireland, informing them that he had been injured a fortnight earlier in both thighs while on active service with his regiment at the Front and that he was making rapid progress at the Middlesex Hospital, Clacton. He had been in the army for fifteen years. Balmer had landed with his regiment at Le Havre on 22 August 1914 and within days was involved in the Battle of Le Cateau and by 5 September was in the Battle of the Marne, sometimes referred to as the 'Miracle of the Marne' which went on for seven days and it is possible it was in this engagement that he was wounded.

Another casualty was Private Charles Frederick Clarke, aged 19 years, of Grantham. He had joined the Grantham Territorials in August 1914, underwent training in Luton and proceeded to France in February 1915. In August 1915 he was wounded in the face, for which he underwent treatment at a convalescent camp at Etaples. He made a speedy recovery and rejoined his regiment at the end of the month. Then on 13 October, while taking part in an attack, he was gassed. He was initially conveyed to the Middlesex Hospital (Clacton-on-Sea) and later to a convalescent home in Ongar, Essex.

As one would expect, soldiers from the Australian contingent were often patients at the Middlesex. Two wounded Australians, Private Walter Ernest Herriott and Private Albert Jas. Thomson, died of their wounds while being cared for at the Middlesex. They were buried with full military honours, the Durham Light Infantry providing the escort, band and firing party. There was a large attendance at the funeral that was conducted by Rev. J. Silvester, vicar of Great Clacton and Rev. J. Elvy, Wesleyan minister at Clacton. A floral display, included tokens from the wounded soldiers' fund and the Red Cross, was laid.

The following is a classified list of the injuries and diseases of the soldiers treated at the hospital:

- Gunshot Wounds 4,622
- Shell Shock 110
- Gassing 304
- Burns 26
- Trench Foot 415
- Accidental Wounds 178
- Accidental Fractures 140

- Local Inflammatory Disorders 268
- Acute Specific Fevers 282
- Trench Fever and Fever of Uncertain Origin 715
- Diseases of Nutrition and Metabolism 104
- Diseases of the Nervous System 80
- Diseases of the Eye, Ear and Nose 138
- Diseases of the Mouth, Throat and Larynx 40
- Diseases of the Lung and Pleura 346
- Diseases of the Heart 127
- Diseases of the Blood Vessels 34
- Diseases of the Abdomen 383
- Diseases of the Urinary System 220
- Diseases of the Genital System 104
- Disease of the Joints 317
- Diseases of the Muscles 189
- Diseases of Lymphatic Glands 12
- Deformities 87
- Lightning Stroke 1

Total 9,242

Middlesex Hospital staff during the First World War. (Author's collection)

The Middlesex Hospital appeared to be the senior hospital in the area to deal with war casualties but Ricketts Convalescent Home also took its fair share of injured while the Clacton Cottage Hospital looked after the local population.

From as early as 1914 the following soldiers had been buried in Clacton Cemetery, in addition to Walter Herriott, who were believed to have died in the local military hospital of illnesses or of their wounds:

- Robert Stranaghan – 20 November 1914.
- Sydney Munton – 4 November 1914.
- Robert Muirhead -16 November 1914.
- Albert Edward Brawn – 4 November 1914.
- Arthur Kelly – 25 March 1915.

In February 1916 the *Chelmsford Chronicle* reported that a local soldier, Private Charles Page of the Duke of Cornwall's Light Infantry, aged 19, was hit by a train while on leave when endeavouring to cross the line, thinking he had time to do it safely. He was found by PC Havers lying on the grass near a footpath from Old Road to Vista Road which crossed the line at Clacton. His right hand was reduced to a pulp and practically severed just below the wrist. He was taken to the Cottage Hospital where the hand was amputated just above the wrist. His parents, Mr and Mrs William Page, lived in Dudley Road, Clacton-on-Sea.

The *Chelmsford Chronicle* also reported in September 1916 that a concert was given at the Operetta House in aid of the Cottage Hospital and many of the soldiers at local convalescent homes were present.

Herbert F. Reynolds was from Suffolk but was lodging with a lady in Kirby Cross, a village very close to Frinton-on-Sea. He had enlisted at Colchester on 20 November 1915 into the Queen's Own (Royal West Kent) Regiment, service number 11330, as a private. He was obviously eager to join up but his employer for various reasons did not want to release him until they had no option, a little surprising as his papers have his occupation as a gardener. On 15 November 1916 he qualified as a Signaller 1st Class just a couple of days before he went off to France for a year. He recorded his memories for Age UK:

> My employer would not release me until November 1916; which
> kept me on edge all the time as I was eager to get to grips with

the enemy to at least help bring about the ending of the war for all time (a phrase current at the time).

However when I reached the barracks at Maidstone it seemed like entering a prison complete with Sergeant Majors as prison officers. No Home from Home here I thought. The rifles that were handed to us seemed to weigh ½ ton. But the surprise was that within a few weeks I enjoyed it all and was feeling fitter than ever before in my life.

One could relate many experiences of battles of the Somme and Ypres, bridges and railways captured which may be too ghastly to describe but one experience during the fighting in France stands out in my memory. About six of us were detailed to capture a stronghold of machine guns and snipers about 100 yards away. Just before dawn we crept cautiously towards the enemy. When we reached them, they were having an early breakfast, plenty of coffee and black bread etc.

We sprang on them so suddenly they dropped their mugs of coffee and every one of them, twenty in number held their hands up in surrender. Not a shot was fired or a bayonet used. We came back to our lines with our bag of prisoners all safe and sound.

He was wounded in August 1918 and was home by 1 September and the following is what he had to say about his recovery:

I cannot but recall, after being wounded, the wonderful way in which we were treated by the Red Cross. All the way from the battlefield to hospitals, the journey from Rouen to Southampton across submarine infested seas. Then to various hospitals and finally convalescent in England. The Red Cross treated us as VIPs indeed. Nothing was too much trouble for the Doctors and Nurses.

There is no doubt whatever that we who have survived so long owe a deep debt of gratitude to the Red Cross of Britain and overseas – long live the Red Cross.

Herbert was finally demobbed on 8 January 1919.

Home Guard

Initially it was planned that the Territorial Force would be responsible for home defence but as we know the BEF though putting on a good show

Captain Joseph Parish.
(Phyllis M. Hendy)

took a real hammering in the first few months of the war which meant that the Territorial Force had to abandon their home defence role and go instead to support the regular army in France.

The fear of a German invasion in the first couple of years of the war was ever-present so some form of home defence had to be established. Several schemes were put in place, one being the setting up of a Volunteer Training Corps (VTC), or what we would today call a 'Home Guard'. These groups were normally made up of men either too young or too old to enlist. Unfortunately, it did give those who did not want to join up an excuse not to volunteer. However, as the need for men increased the VTC became the subject of constant scrutiny.

One such platoon was set up at St Osyth and Joseph Parish of Brazier Farm became its captain. It was estimated that the St Osyth Platoon, which was part of the 5th Essex Volunteers, at times numbered ninety men. It was after a day's work and at weekends they came into their own. Their role would be to guard key installations such as factories and railway lines, also keeping an eye open for saboteurs and spies signalling to enemy planes and vessels and finally give an early warning of invasion.

In its early days the War Office did not take the VTC very seriously and would not supply its members with weapons or military uniforms, although many of them, being farmers, would have been very good shots. They were given red armbands with the letters 'GR' in gold giving the organization its nickname 'Gorgeous Wrecks'. Later in the war the War Office took over responsibility for the VTC and basic training, uniforms, ranks and weaponry were supplied.

When the threat of invasion disappeared the VTC was stood down and its duties were taken over by a new regiment, the Royal

St Osyth home guard. (Phyllis M. Hendy)

Defence Corps. Lessons were obviously learnt because within eight months of the outbreak of the Second World War, the government called for volunteers to form the Home Guard.

Women's Royal Naval Service (Wrens)

The WRENs, the women's branch of the Royal Navy, was formed in 1917. It was disbanded in 1919 but revived at the outbreak of the Second World War in 1939. They took on over a hundred different jobs to help relieve the men such as cooks, stewards, despatch riders, intelligence duties, administration, wireless telegraphist, radar plotters, weapons analysts, air mechanics etc.

Mrs Beatrice May Browne from Frinton joined the Wrens when she was only 17 and was demobbed in 1919 when they were disbanded. She re-enlisted in 1939 and served another eight years, which included a spell aboard HMS *Victory* at Portsmouth, attaining the rank of Chief Officer and in 1945 was awarded the British Empire Medal (BEM). She became a founder member and President of the Walton-on-the-Naze branch of the Royal Naval Association and Vice-President of the National Association of Wrens. On their disbandment in 1919 there were 7,000 Wrens

Mrs Beatrice May Browne.
(Brightlingsea Museum)

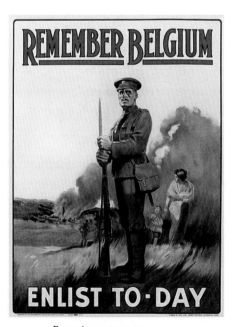

Recruitment poster.

Belgian Refugees

It was not only the soldiers we had to look after but also the Belgian refugees. When Belgium refused to give free passage to the Germans for them to attack France, they invaded in force in what became known as 'The rape of Belgium' and naturally this provoked the sympathy of the world.

Hundreds of thousands of Belgians fled the slaughter, but where to? As we know, Britain has a long history as a safe haven for refugees. We gave homes to French Protestant Huguenots in the seventeenth century and to Russian Jews in the nineteenth century. Belgium was admired in Britain for its resistance which gave the French and British time to mobilize. As one of the guarantors of Belgium's independence, Britain was willing to take in refugees and within a short period of time around 250,000 arrived in the country. A War Refugees Committee (WRC) was sent up and within weeks of publishing an appeal for accommodation, it received 100,000 offers. One such was reported by the *Chelmsford Chronicle* as early as 25 September 1914: 'Several offers have been made by Clacton residents to take in Belgium refugees and a fund is being started to which everyone in the town is asked to guarantee from 1d to 1s a week towards boarding the refugees.' Unlike previous refugees, at the end of the war both the British and Belgian governments appealed for them to return home and by 1921 more than 90 per cent had done so.

The Zeppelin Threat

As I have previously stated, before the war the towns in the Clacton area had become established holiday resorts. The war and the initial fear of invasion greatly affected their trade and hotel managers, bed and breakfast owners and shopkeepers experienced a drop in visitors and a serious fall in their income. Due to the drop in visitors the various councils started to cut back on bus and train services which exacerbated the situation. The local authorities and various associations such as the Clacton Advancement and Advertising Association worked frantically to persuade people that there was nothing to fear. They placed advertisements in several London daily newspapers explaining that their resorts were safe and in full swing. One journalist wrote that the holiday season at Walton was being enjoyed by many:

> Bathing was in full swing. Hundreds of children were paddling and disporting themselves on the sands, the sunlit waters were dotted with rowing boats, the 'Walton Belle' came in and went out on its usual trip, the Band Pavilion esplanade was filled with visitors enjoying the delightful music of the 'White Band', anglers were pursuing their peaceful pastimes on the pier – in fact there was not a disturbing note anywhere.

A somewhat exaggerated statement as the number of holidaymakers to Frinton fell by 10 per cent and Walton and Brightlingsea saw a drop of 25 per cent. Many others defaulted on their bookings, resulting in some being taken to court. The lack of bookings during August and September caused Clacton, Frinton and Walton to lose two-fifths of their normal lucrative holiday business. Also the Belle Steamers which bought daytrippers to these seaside resorts from London were faced with drastically reduced numbers, resulting in the sailing season being brought to an abrupt end on 30 August 1914.

However, you can understand their fear, especially the fear of Zeppelins. As early as the night of 15/16 April 1915 a Zeppelin crossed the North Sea and hugged the Walton and Clacton coast, eventually dropping two bombs on Maldon. Fortunately they did very little damage and nobody was hurt. In addition twenty incendiaries landed in fields around the Maldon area but the only casualties were three hens.

Then on 10 May Zeppelin *LZ 38* commanded by Hauptmann Erich Linnarz dropped its bombs in the Southend area. A dozen houses were destroyed and Agnes Whitwell, aged 66, was killed when an incendiary bomb crashed through the roof of the house, setting fire to the bed she was sleeping in with her husband, who was unable to save her. While escaping Linnarz dropped a card. 'You English, we have come and we will come again, Kill or Cure, German.' He did return as promised on 26 May, again crossing the coast near Clacton and dropping seventy incendiary bombs on the Southend area before returning home.

However, life went on and at nearby Walton-on-the-Naze 'B' and 'C' Companies of the 2/8th (Cyclist) Essex Regiment stationed there held a sports day at Ashes Farm on Whit Monday May 1915. There was a very large attendance of spectators and the six hours of sport was followed by an al fresco dance.

Another regiment that descended on the Clacton area for training during the war years was the Yorkshire Regiment in November 1916. Charlie Payne from London, a clerk in a music publishing company, was called up at the age of 33 in November 1916 and enlisted in 'D' Company, 24th Provisional Battalion, 5th Yorkshire Regiment, and he was immediately sent with a group of seventy men for training at Clacton. He wrote a long letter back to his wife on 6 December 1916 and at the end of the letter he added a P.S: We are known as 'Clacton's Town Guard'.

Prisoners of War

Over ten million service men and civilians were captured during the war and sent to detention camps, resulting in various prisoner of war funds being set up. One was set up at St Osyth in the autumn of 1917 as it was known that at least six men from the area were held in POW camps:

- Sergeant Arthur Amos – East Surreys – Gandeligon, Germany.
- Lance Corporal William Cook – Rifle Brigade – Munster, Germany.
- Corporal John Kemp – Rifle Brigade – Stanmuble, Germany
- Private Charles Last – 2nd Norfolk – Angora, Turkey.
- Private Arthur Moss – Kings Royal Rifles – Bavaria.
- Private James Simmons – East Surreys – Ingoldstadt, Germany.

Unfortunately William Cook was to die on 22 October 1918 from wounds received, just twenty days before the Armistice was signed.

The *Chelmsford Chronicle* on Friday, 17 August 1917 gave the following report on Essex Regiment prisoners of war:

> The Essex Regiments' Prisoners of War Fund has now over 300 men to provide food parcels for, each man coasting the fund £2.2s a month. The 'adoption' systems is the best. The adopter guarantees the cost of each man's parcel and keeps in touch with him by writing. The parcels are sent through Mrs Stephenson, of 75 Carlisle Mansions, S.W.1, hon. Sec. to the fund. It would undertake to adopt its own prisoners. Braintree already does this very thoroughly; also Grays.
>
> There are prisoners in Germany needing adoption from Colchester, Brentwood, Southend, Laindon, Hutton, Newport, Romford, Stansted, Woodford, South Ockendon, Hadleigh, Dunmow and Saffron Walden.
>
> Mrs Stephenson will be very pleased to furnish men's names and addresses to anyone who will undertake to 'adopt' a prisoner; or to any committee who will be responsible for prisoners from its own town or district. There are Essex prisoners of war in hospital at Jerusalem and Damascus, to whom at present only money can be sent to buy food. £1 a month is sent to these men. They come from Colchester, Stansted, Clacton, High Easter, Brightlingsea etc.

We also had German prisoners in camps in England. One such, at Water Lane, Stratford experienced a daring escape on 10 June 1918 when five German prisoners escaped through a 30-foot tunnel. The following is an extract from the report from the *Essex Newsman*:

HUN OFFICERS' ESCAPE

Four German officers and a man acting as servant made their way out during the dark hours of the morning. One officer and the servant were arrested by the police at Ilford an hour or two later and the others were captured on the Essex coast at Walton-on-the-Naze on Wednesday.

The method of escape was discovered by a small hole in the garden of an adjoining house, on top of some rockery work. This was discovered to be the mouth of a shaft ten feet deep and about eighteen inches in diameter. This shaft led to a horizontal passage, which had been tunnelled under a barbed-wire fence and through a two-foot brick wall into a basement kitchen of one of two old houses used for the camp. The opening in the basement had been cleverly hidden with paper matching that already on the walls. Towels were hung over this and a table loaded with crockery was placed against the entrance to the tunnel. As far as is known, the men had no tools except table knives. The excavated soil was found hidden beneath the floor boards. Considerable difficulty was encountered while excavating the last bit of the upright shaft, which gave access to the garden, for roots of a tree had to be cut through. How two of the officers, both big men, managed to crawl through such a small tunnel is a mystery to those in charge of the camp.

The remaining three German officers, Johann Brane, Hugo Thielman and Edmund Klaiss, a U-Boat commander were recaptured at Walton-on-the-Naze. They were noticed by PC Bird and Special Constable Greenwood. Although they left the camp in uniform the officers were wearing civilian clothes when caught. They had with them tinned food and dried bread and their dirty appearance gave the impression that they had been sleeping out.

Conkers

In 1918 rationing was introduced in Britain due to the German U-Boats sinking ships carrying food. A government committee was set up to look at ways of using any available resources. One of the schemes they came up with was to get children from the rural schools to gather seasonal fruits such blackberries, crab apples and

Rationing poster.

sloes during school hours for jam-making. School logbooks inform us that many schools took up the challenge. The fruit was packed into specially-provided baskets of a regulation size and sent immediately by train to special factories where it was made into jam mainly for the soldiers. The schools received payment which on many occasions was distributed to the children.

In the autumn of 1917 one of the most surprising notices of the war started to appear on the walls of classrooms and Scout hut across Britain: 'Groups of scholars and boy scouts are being organized to collect conkers . . .This collection is invaluable war work and is very urgent. Please encourage it.' It was never explained to schoolchildren exactly how conkers could help the war effort. Nor did they seem particularly to care. They were more interested in the War Office's bounty of 7s 6d (37.5p) for every hundredweight they handed in and for weeks they scoured woods and lanes for the shiny brown objects they usually destroyed 'playing conkers' in the playground.

Even members of the House of Commons and the public were kept in the dark about the reason for collecting conkers. The only official statement was printed in *The Times* on 26 July 1917: 'Chestnut seeds, not the green husks, are required by the Government for Ministry of Munitions. The nuts will replace cereals which have been necessary for the production of an article of great importance in the prosecution of the War.' So why were they so vital? Well it had been discovered that they could be used to make acetone, a component of the smokeless propellant for shells and bullets known as cordite.

Cordite had been used by the British military since 1889, when it first replaced black powder. It consisted chiefly of the high-explosives nitroglycerine and nitrocellulose (gun-cotton), with acetone playing the key role of solvent in the manufacturing process. Prior to the First World War, the acetone used in British munitions was made almost entirely from the dry distillation (pyrolysis) of wood. As it required almost a hundred tonnes of birch, beech or maple to produce a tonne of acetone, the great timber-growing countries were the biggest producers of this vital commodity, and Britain was forced to import the vast majority of its acetone from the United States. An attempt to produce our own acetone was made in 1913 when a modern factory was built in the Forest of Dean. But by the outbreak of war in 1914, the stocks for military use were just 3,200 tonnes, and it was soon obvious that an alternative domestic supply would be needed. This became even more pressing during the spring of 1915 when an acute shortage of shells – the so-called 'Shells Crisis' – reduced some British guns to firing just four times a day.

The British government's response was to create a dedicated Ministry of Munitions, run by the future Prime Minister David Lloyd George. One of Lloyd George's first initiatives was to ask the brilliant chemist Chaim Weizmann of Manchester University if there was an alternative way of making acetone in large quantities. Weizmann said yes. Developing the work of Louis Pasteur and others, Weizmann had perfected an anaerobic fermentation process that used a highly vigorous bacterium known as Clostridium acetobutylicum (also known as the Weizmann organism) to produce large quantities of acetone from a variety of starchy foodstuffs such as grain, maize and rice. He at once agreed to place his process at the disposal of the government.

In May 1915, after Weizmann had demonstrated to the Admiralty that he could convert 100 tonnes of grain to 12 tonnes of acetone, the government commandeered brewing and distillery equipment, and built factories to employ the new process at Holton Heath in Dorset and King's Lynn in Norfolk. Together they produced more than 90,000 gallons of acetone a year, enough to feed the war's seemingly insatiable demand for cordite (the British Army and Royal Navy alone fired 248 million shells from 1914 to 1918.)

However, by 1917 as grain and potatoes were needed to feed the British population, Weizmann was tasked to find another supply of starch for his process that would not impact on the already limited food supplies. He immediately began experimenting with conkers, aware that they grew in abundance across the country, and found that the yield of acetone was sufficiently high to begin production. This in turn prompted the nationwide appeal for schoolchildren to collect conkers. So in October 1917 country wide call went out for school children to gather up Horse Chestnuts. St Osyth children collected several hundredweight and were rewarded by the school with a 'CONQUER [sic] PARTY'. Unfortunately teething problems meant the manufacturing process did not start until April 1918 and it was soon discovered that the chestnuts did not provide the yields expected and production ended after three months.

Accidental Deaths

Tragedy hit Walton-on-the-Naze in November 1917 when Lance Corporal Frank William Pidgeon of the North Somerset Yeomanry who were stationed in the area was accidentally shot and killed during routine musketry training.

It would appear that he was holding the sighting disc while Private Swift was going through his rapid firing test. They were both lying on the ground when the accident happened. Dummy cartridges were being used but a live one somehow got mixed in and was placed in the clip with the dummy ones and it exploded on the second pull with the cartridge penetrating Pidgeon's right eye and passing through his head, killing him instantly. At the coroner's inquest the jury returned a verdict of accidental death and exonerated everyone involved. A few days earlier Pidgeon had heard that his brother had been killed at the Front. They were the only support for their widowed mother Priscilla.

Six months earlier, on 9 June, Private Frederick James Harris, a rifleman with the 32nd (County of London) Battalion, which was also in the Walton area, was found drowned on the shore. At the inquest it was stated that he was last seen alive walking towards the sea. The tide was low at the time and his body was recovered from 9 inches of water.

Reading through the local and national newspaper archives other than reports of what was going on at the front you could get the impression that life was going on normally. Children went to school, adults went about their daily tasks, holidays were taken, individuals got married – in fact Frinton-on-Sea became a favourite honeymoon destination – and sports and entertainment continued, albeit on a limited basis. Courts tried criminal offences, workers went on strike, people went to church and Parliament sat.

CHAPTER 5

Conscription

❧✤

Conscription refers to the process of compulsorily calling up men and women for military service. During the First World War men (and only men) who were conscripted into the armed forces had no choice but to go and fight.

In Britain conscription has only been deemed necessary on two occasions, during the First and Second World Wars. First World War conscription ended in 1919 but the compulsory military service that began in 1939 for the Second World War didn't come to an end until 1960, with the last National Servicemen leaving three years later.

Within a year of Great Britain declaring war on Germany it had become obvious that it was not possible to continue fighting by relying on voluntary recruits. In 1914 the British Army had approximately 710,000 men at its disposal. For more than 100 years both the government and the British public had been against conscription. The Secretary of State for War, Lord Kitchener, recognized that the British Army was far too small in comparison to the French and German ones and wanted to build an army of seventy divisions.

Lord Kitchener. (Author's collection)

Lord Kitchener's campaign – promoted by his famous 'Your Country Needs You' poster – had encouraged over one million men to enlist by January 1915. But this was not enough to keep pace with mounting casualties. The government saw no alternative but to increase numbers by conscription – compulsory service. Parliament was deeply divided but recognized that because of the imminent collapse of the morale of the French army, action was essential. In March 1916 the Military Service Act was passed. This imposed conscription on all single men aged between 18 and 41, but exempted the medically unfit, clergymen, teachers and certain classes of industrial worker.

Men who were called up could appeal to a local Military Service Tribunal. Reasons given for being exempt included health, already doing important war work, or moral or religious reasons. The last two groups became known as conscientious objectors. A total of 750,000 men appealed against their conscription in the first six months. Most were granted an exemption of some sort, even if it was only temporary. Conscientious objectors were often exempted but in most cases were given civilian jobs or non-combat roles at the front. Only 2 per cent of those who appealed were conscientious objectors, of whom about 6,000 were sent to prison. Thirty-five received a death sentence but were reprieved immediately and given a ten-year prison term instead.

A second Act passed in May 1916 extended conscription to married men. However, conscription did not apply to Ireland at this time because of the 1916 Easter Rising, although in fact many Irishmen volunteered to fight. Conscription was not popular and in April 1916 over 200,000 demonstrated against it in Trafalgar Square. Although many men failed to respond to the call-up, in the first year 1.1 million did enlist.

One of the public protests was when the Brightlingsea Tribunal granted only three months exemption to a young man whose parents were both dead and was the only carer for his blind and crippled brother and two younger siblings. The local newspaper commented that 'The confidence of the public appears to have been rudely shaken'. A month later a protest meeting was held in the town and one speaker commented: 'On some of these tribunals there were gentlemen who decided that other people's sons should go to war while their own skulked at home behind a coward's conscience.' Unfortunately I have not been able to establish what happen to this young man: one would hope that at appeal he was totally exempted. During the last months of the war, the Military Service (No. 2) Act raised the age limit to 51. The total number of men conscripted into the British Armed Forces was 2,277,623, 46 per cent of all British Army recruits.

The *Chelmsford Chronicle* reported on 14 July 1916 that Albert H. French, a dairyman, 29 and married from Brightlingsea, was refused exemption and leave to appeal to the Central Tribunal was also refused, as he had already had time to make arrangements since 4 February. Assuming he did enlist, it would appear that he survived the war. At the same tribunal a Hackney pawnbroker named Gerbold, single, who also owned a farm at St Osyth, claimed that the latter was his principal occupation and he therefore sought exemption on that ground. The chairman of the tribunal, Captain Howard, said the applicant would do the farm good by going away. There was laughter and the appeal was dismissed, but leave was given to appeal to the Central Tribunal.

In August 1916, Sidney John Sharman, single, 24, bootmaker, Walton-on-the-Naze, was appealed for by his father Mr J. Sharman and the case was adjourned for medical examination. Lance Corporal H.E. Edgar of a Provisional Battalion, Frinton, the only son of a widow, appealed for exemption from foreign service; Appeal dismissed.

At the same tribunal as the previous two a Mr N.R. Page of Clacton appealed for Mr Jeffery, a single man of 30 and a foreman vegetable and fruit grower: The Chairman: 'Can't you get one of the conscientious objectors who are working so hard in this neighbourhood?' (Laughter)

Applicant: 'No sir, I cannot.' The appeal was dismissed but a month was allowed before the man was called up.

It was not unusual for companies to appeal on behalf of their employees, In October 1916 Cramphorn Ltd appealed on behalf of C.E. Stock, a married man aged 35 living in Clacton. The case was dismissed but he was given a month's grace. In November 1916 the Essex Convalescent Home in Clacton appealed on behalf of its gardener W. Hutson who was married and 40 years of age, again it was disallowed but he was given a temporary exemption until 16 December. He does not appear on the list of Clacton men who served so it is possible he managed at a later date to dodge the call-up.

In October 1916, Essex County Council appealed for G.H.B. Gould, 37, married, living at Clacton, architectural assistant.

Mr G. Topham Forrest, the County Architect, told the tribunal that Mr Gould was doing important survey work. He had been passed for labour work at home only and he had been temporarily exempted by the Clacton Tribunal on domestic grounds. That exemption had now run out but he had been a special constable since October 1914. He was granted an exemption under the Army Council instructions of 9 August, whereby married men of 35 and upwards who were doing satisfactory service as special constables were exempted.

Appeals could go either way: for example in August 1916 the Military appealed against the certificate of conditional exemption granted to H.E. Hammond, single, 19, and F.L. Frost, single, 20, employees of Messrs. H. Browne and Sons Ltd., nautical instrument makers, Brightlingsea. Captain Howard admitted that the lads were doing good work and six months' exemption was granted in each case. Again at the same tribunal, William Charles Taylor, married, fishmonger, of Clacton appealed on business grounds and said he attested as a conscientious objector. The Chairman said 'I am glad you have dropped that', but the applicant replied that he had not: 'I attested before I knew married men were to be called up.' The appeal was dismissed and leave to appeal further was refused. On the Clacton Roll of Honour there is a Charles William Taylor of the Royal Fusiliers but he was wounded on 27 July 1916 in the attack on Delville Wood and later died on 21 September 1916, so he cannot be our man. The only possibility found is a C. Taylor from Clacton who appears on a list of men from Clacton who survived the war, but unfortunately no further records could be found to establish whether this is the same Taylor. In March 1916 a married Frinton man, Rowland Stanley Jull, applied for total exemption on the grounds that he was a resident engineer at the Frinton Electric Light and Power Works. He was given temporary exemption for three months.

An attested man was a volunteer who did not wish to serve immediately, but who instead took an oath promising to serve at a later date when summoned. This scheme left the army with a pool of committed men to call on, if and when they were needed. The individual was given an armband to wear to signify that they were prepared to serve and do their duty. This helped to relieve much of the pressure which young men at the time must have felt, enabling them to live within their communities without the shame of the 'white feathers' which were distributed to those alleged to be cowards.

The Order of the White Feather was founded in August 1914 by Admiral Charles Fitzgerald. The idea was to shame men into enlisting in the British Army and who better was it to hand them out than our women. Many prominent feminists and suffragettes joined the campaign. It did, however, create a few problems and the authorities issued employees with badges reading 'King and Country' to indicate that they were serving the war effort and those men that had been discharged due to injury or sickness were given a Silver War Badge.

In March 1916 there was a rather unusual case when fifteen applicants, all from the 108th Provisional Battalion of the Queen's (London) Regiment, came before the Walton-on-the-Naze Tribunal. Three applications were refused altogether, one was allowed two months, five were allowed three months, four were allowed six months and one was allowed three months with the recommendation to the military authorities to allow him to be reinstated in his trade as a core-maker. In the remaining case, that of a corporal who was one of eight sons, all of whom were serving with the Colours, the Tribunal gave a total exemption.

A similar case was held at about the same time at the Clacton Tribunal with thirty-two applications from Home Service Territorials who did not want to go abroad to fight. All of them were asked the same question 'Will the separation allowance made to your relatives be the same if you go abroad as it will be if you continue to remain in England' and in every case the answer was 'Yes' 'Well, then why do you object to going abroad?' enquired the Tribunal; the general reply was 'I might get killed.' The Tribunal seemed to find this response rather extraordinary, stating that it seems to take eighteen months of war for some men to discover this and then, when their country needs them, they jib. Conscience certainly turns some men into curious creatures. Their vision gets blinded and tribunals are needed to show them the way. Twenty-five of the applications were refused.

It appeared that individuals from all walks of life tried it on: at the same Clacton Tribunal, a director of the Clacton Cinema applied for total exemption for the manager and operator, on the grounds that he was indispensable. A temporary exemption was granted, to enable the applicant to find a suitable substitute. Tribunals were still being held just months before the end of the war.

CHAPTER 6

Welcome the 'Diggers'

❧⚜❧

The 'Diggers' – who? Well, they were our Australian cousins from the other side of the world. Out of a population of four million, 313,781 Australians came to our aid, along with  3,011 members of the Australian Army nursing service. There were never fewer than 50,000 Australian troops in Britain. For many of them it was an adventure and a trip of a lifetime, but 60,000 would not return to their loved ones.

Aussie hat.

The Digger

The Digger's a fellow that's fond of fun,
But likes a game that's fair;
If he back's a horse he wants a run,
And a jock that's riding square;
He isn't out looking for trouble or strife,
But he'll go for all he's worth
In defence of his cobber, his girl, or his wife,
And the land that gave him birth.

The British troops where affectionately known as 'Tommies', the French as 'Poilus' but where did the name 'Digger' come from? Well, it came from the Gold Rush days when the goldminers were known as 'Diggers'.

It was on Brightlingsea that from August 1916 until the end of the war that over 5,000 Australians engineers descended, with each spending several months in training, in fact many came back several times. By the time the Aussies arrived Brightlingsea had got used to

AIF engineer officers at Brightlingsea.

the military being there. HM Forces had invaded the village in the autumn of 1914, attracted by the suitability of the local area for engineer training. As well as four field companies of Kitchener's Army it was also being used by Territorial field companies from all parts of the country. In 1915 a School of Military Engineering (SME) was set up and thousands of officers and NCOs passed through the course.

Although the town was used to the military being there they had become quite excited about the prospect of their first overseas soldiers, especially as they were Australians who had made a name for themselves at Gallipoli fighting the Turks. The first arrivals were new recruits direct from Australia, part of 11th Field Company that had been formed in Adelaide four months earlier. They had sailed over in a converted ocean liner, the *Suevic*. They landed at Plymouth, barracked at Lark Hill on Salisbury Plain and a few weeks later arrived at Brightlingsea for training in bridge and pontoon building on the

Colneside creeks. The 11th was part of the 3rd Australian Division which was commanded by one of Australia's most famous soldiers, Major General John Monash. He was the only one in this division at this time who had seen action, having commanded a brigade at Gallipoli. When he landed in England with the 3rd, two first-rate British regular officers were detailed to watch over him, Lieutenant Colonels G.H.N. Jackson and H.M. Farmar, but they soon both became his admiring devotees.

Monash was born on 27 June 1865 in Melbourne, Victoria to a German-Jewish family and became a civil engineer. He received numerous decorations, not only from the British but also the French and Belgians. He was often referred to as the 'best man in France' but, although he might have been offered command of an army if the war had continued into 1919, it is unlikely a Jewish colonial militiaman of German origin could ever have become a British Commander-in-Chief. As his biography indicates, however, he felt more English than German. When he died in 1931 he was granted a state funeral to which approximately 300,000 people turned up.

The 11th and their commanding officer for the first month, Major Robert Donaldson, were warmly welcomed at Brightlingsea and the following evening many attended a concert or took to the local pubs. This was followed by taking part in a naval and military sports day in a meadow near the railway station, the competitors including a company of Highland engineers and crews of the Royal Navy boom trawlers. Their stay was extended by a month to train in trench-building, mining and other work, including helping to build defences along the Clacton coast.

Then in early September another group, the 10th, joined the 11th and it was not long before these two Australian companies and the locals heard the distant sound of war as in the early hours of 24 September they could see and hear the dreaded Zeppelins as they passed overhead on their way to London. There were twelve Zeppelins on the raid, eight of an older type heading for the Midlands and four new super-Zeppelins including *L 33* heading for London. On its return journey, *L 33* was hit by an anti-aircraft shell and damaged by Royal Flying Corps aircraft. It was forced to land near the village of Little Wigborough opposite Brightlingsea and Mersea Island on the other side of the river Colne.

Remains of L 33 *at Wigborough. (Author's collection)*

There were no serious casualties and what followed was a typical German and English scene. The Zeppelin's commander, Captain Alois Böcker, and twenty-one other Germans marched in formation along a lane near the village, aiming to find a boat to commandeer somewhere in the estuary to take them home. Unfortunately for them, they came across Special Constable Edgar Nicholas who insisted they came with him. Eventually they were handed over to a military escort who took them to an army camp on Mersea Island. This is believed to be the only time a parade by a hostile force took place in Britain in the two world wars. The next day several of the Aussies and no doubt a number of locals crossed over the water to the village to look at the wreck and pick up bits of the Zeppelin as souvenirs.

The Federation of Essex Women's Institutes occasionally produce publications of their member's memories. In one such, *Within Living Memory*, published in 1995 we find two members' recollections of the Zeppelin coming down:

> My earliest memory is of the Zeppelin coming down at Wigborough in 1916, which my brother Eric, two years older than me, was taken to see. I was very angry because I was considered too young to go. However, he brought me back a small bunch of ripe blackberries picked from the hedge of the field where the Zeppelin came down. The German crew gave themselves up to the local police and were taken into custody as prisoners of war and the Zeppelin caught fire and burned itself out. The skeleton

framework remained in the field for some time and many photos were taken of it.

A Zeppelin came down at Peldon and father took me out to see it, we brought home a small piece of fuselage. The Strood was zigzagged with sandbags and there were soldiers on duty there. This is the Wigborough Zeppelin.

On 26 October a New Zealand Field Training Company arrived, replacing the 10th and 11th. The commanding office was Major St John Keenan who had also seen action in Gallipoli, so at the time he had had more combat experience than anybody else at Brightlingsea. Over the next two years this was the way of life in Brightlingsea, with various Australian companies and the occasional New Zealanders coming and going, normally only spending a few months at a time there for training or retraining. Other than the first recruits, many were coming from the front and they probably saw it as a well-earned rest. although each morning they were awakened by the bugler sounding the reveille, followed by a parade and gathering of tools before marching off to the various training grounds. They had a significant

The bugle. (Author's collection)

impact on the town's population of 4,500. It was in their leisure time that they were to become a vibrant part of life in the village.

When the Australians left in 1919 a bugle was given to a seven-year-old boy, Harold Crosby. It was to be heard again after the Second World War when the local Air Training Corps (ATC) band borrowed it. When the band disbanded it was handed back to Harold for safekeeping, and when he passed away it was left to his son. It is now on display at the Brightlingsea Museum.

Brightlingsea was the only training camp on the east coast and had been chosen as an engineer training area because of its geography. The River Colne with its tidal creeks offered excellent practice for bridge building along with the soft sandy soils for trench and mining practice. In charge of the training camp for the duration of the war was the British Colonel Norton.

Army engineers, as the name suggests, were not combat troops but their skills were vital to the outcome of the war. They may not have gone 'over the top' but they were often found in No Man's Land setting up barbed wire with or without the infantry in support. Even when they were several miles behind the front line building a railway, roads, bridges or a hutted camp they frequently came under fire. Basically they were jacks-of all-trades.

They were normally given the rank of Sapper and they were essential to the running of the war. Without them, other branches of Allied forces would have found it difficult to cross the muddy and shell-ravaged ground of the Western Front. Their responsibilities included constructing the lines of defence, temporary bridges, tunnels and trenches, observation posts, roads, railways, communication lines, buildings of all kinds, showers and bathing facilities and other material and mechanical solutions to the problems associated with fighting in all theatres of the war.

The training ground was about a mile from the village just before you reached the Colchester to Clacton Road in the vicinity of All Saints' Church, Alresford Creek, between Moverons Farm and Hall Farm. The camp was established on the recreation ground in Regent Road and it was here during the warm summer months the troops and junior officers were billeted in canvas bell-tents but in the winter they were billeted with families in the village. Within the camp was a separate section for the British. There were one or two brick buildings put up as stores and toilets, otherwise everything else – canteens, messes, medical centres etc – was under canvas. Part of the reason for using the recreation ground was to acclimatise the men to living in tents but those that had seen action in France did not require to be acclimatised in this way as they would have lived in dugouts and huts, not tents. During the winter the recreation ground was used as an additional training ground and the men would have their meals in the various church halls.

With Britain imposing conscription in 1916, the Australian Prime Minister Hughes tried on two occasions to impose a similar law on his citizens but it was rejected. This meant that every Australian soldier was a volunteer. The question is why did such brave men travel half-round the world to fight in such a terrible war, was it for adventure or the fact that the majority were of British ancestry or had themselves ventured to this far-off land to make their fortunes and felt the need to come back and help defend the 'Mother Country'. Saying that, there were many with German, Swiss, Dutch, French, Italian etc ancestry who made up the 'New Australians' who also came.

They arrived with the following popular song ringing in their ears:

Australia Will be There

We are not out for conquest,
For we have heaps of room,
Where stately gums are growing,
And the golden wattles bloom;
We're leaving dear Australia
Because the cannon's roar
Of overbearing foemen
Calls us to England's shore.

Chorus

We Australian lads will very gladly share
Any dangers loved Old England has to bear,
Long before the rattle of her drums sound anywhere,
We're on the move for the country we love,
We Australians will be there.

We soldiers of Australia
Rejoice in being free

And not to fetter others
Do we go o'er the sea,
Old England gave us freedom,
And when she makes a start
To see that others get it,
We're there to take our part.

We are not out for plunder,
We covet no man's gold;
We fight not for a fortune,
Like buccaneers of old,
Our wheat fields and our pastures
Are ample for us all;
We're going to stand by those who have
Theirs backs against the wall.

By John Beukers

The words that really hit home were: 'Old England gave us freedom, and when she makes a start, to see that others get it, we're there to take our part'. I know Britain has been criticised for its colonization of various lands but as our minds have developed over the centuries we have endeavoured to make all people of the world free. This may be another reason why we ended up in getting involved in this devastating war.

With this song in their hearts you can imagine the change they brought to the sleepy village of Brightlingsea. It was not long before the social life of the depot was well under way, which naturally affected the whole village. The various churches embraced them. A 'khaki choir' sang at the Wesleyan chapel and they provided a harpist, Driver Francesco Pisania, to play at the church. The soldiers and the locals invited each other to various plays and concerts, including a circus, and a gymkhana. The New Zealanders had their own band and orchestra and the Australians tended to bring theirs up from Christchurch and for the next two years they were seen around the village whenever there was the opportunity. Think about it: the only music the locals at this time would have heard was possibly the church organ or the Salvation Army band: very few could have afforded the primitive gramophones. In November 1917 a literary and debating society was formed, meeting weekly. So Brightlingsea was experiencing what many other towns and villages throughout the kingdom would not experience for many years, an active social life with music. We must not forget the sports events they also organized, be it cricket, football, rugby, athletics, boxing and even the odd card game. So it was not all drinking down the local! You could be forgiven for forgetting a war was raging just across the North Sea.

It was not only Australian and New Zealand engineers that trained at Brightlingsea but also regiments from all over Britain. The *Dundee, Perth, Forfar and Fife's People's Journal* reported on Saturday, 2 September 1916 that the Dundee Royal Engineers displayed their prowess on the sporting field at Brightlingsea. They competed in a sports day against the Australians and the Royal Navy, some 250 personnel taking part. A feature of the meeting was the fine running of Sapper J. Porter of the Dundee Engineers, who finished first in the 440 yards, half-mile and one mile.

Two weeks later we have the *Chelmsford Chronicle* reporting on another sports meeting at Brightlingsea, this time between the Royal Navy and the Australian engineers. One of the events was the tug of war in which the ship-riggers met bluejackets and teams from the Engineers. Neither the seaman nor the riggers could hold their own against the burly Anzacs.

With this vast number of soldiers descending on the village, be they Australians, New Zealanders or British, they often outnumbered the local population so it's not surprising that a number of relationships were formed. There were also a number of families who had established Australian connections, where a generation or so back members of their families had emigrated to find a better way of life. Then there were others that had not long been in Australia but joined up. Arthur Lewes was one who had seen action with the 1st Australian Battalion on the Somme, and took the opportunity to revisit his home.

Arthur was an example of the New Australians: he was 26 when he arrived in Australia from Brightlingsea in 1907. His occupation at the time was that of a ship rigger. Sailors could put their rope skills to work in lifting and hauling, in an era before mechanical haulage, cranes etc. He enlisted on 19 April 1915 as a Private (2168) into the 1st Battalion, 18th Reinforcement. The unit embarked from Sydney, New South Wales, on board HMAT *Kyarra* (A55) on 3 June 1916.

HMAT Kyarra. *(Author's collection)*

At the time he was living at 3 Crown Street, East Sydney, New South Wales. His parents were Mr G. and Mrs E. Lewis of Hurst Green, Brightlingsea. He was killed in action at the Second Battle of Bullecourt on 6 May 1917.

The First and Second Battles of Bullecourt were part of the Arras offensive. The British plan was to support the French offensive on the Western Front on the Aisne River and it was agreed that they would launch an attack at Arras a week earlier to draw in German reserves which would then not be available when the French attacked. Part of the British plan was to take the town of Bullecourt and this was going to be the job of the Australians. The attack was unsuccessful with the Australians losing over 3,000 men, but then three weeks later the Australian 2nd Division with the help of the British 62nd Division attacked again and this time were successful. However, 18,000 British and Australians and 11,000 Germans were killed or wounded in the battle, of which Arthur was one. He was awarded the British War Medal and the Victory Medal and is commemorated on the Australian National Memorial at Villers-Bretonneux, France.

In late May 1918 HMAT *Kyarra* left Tilbury for Sydney, carrying 2,600 tons of Australian mail, hospital supplies and medical staff, when she was struck by a torpedo from the submarine *UB-57* in calm waters around Anvil Point just off Swanage, Dorset, killing six of her 126 crew.

Martin James French was living in Sydney when he enlisted in January 1916 into the reinforcements of Field Company Engineers, 2nd Military District of the Australian Imperial Force (AIF). His initial training took place at the Engineers Depot, Moore Park, Sydney. Then on 10 May 1917 he boarded the *Clare McGillivray* at Melbourne arriving at Plymouth on 25 July 1917. He did, however, receive seventy-two days detention for 'breaking ship' while in Fremantle. From August 1917 to February 1918 he undertook further training at Brightlingsea. By early March he was in Rouelles, France at the Australian Infantry Base depot with the rank of Sapper. On 10 March he transferred to the 12th Field Company with whom he served for over a year in places such as La Novella, Amiens, Villers-Brettoneux and Gentelles. In April 1919 he returned to England before sailing for Sydney aboard the *City of Exeter* on 12 July.

Martin was born in Orange on 17 December 1877. In 1899 he was working in his father's (Nicholas) hotel, the Federal, as a barman. Between 1903 to 1908 he lived in Kalgoorlie, Western Australia. working as a tram conductor. When he signed up he was back in Sydney working as a salesman. After the war he worked for a time with his brother Tom, as a store manager then as a traveller in Westbury, Tasmania. Then in 1928 he moved to Wagga Wagga, New South Wales, where his three sisters lived. He married Elizabeth Scott in 1933. He went on to serve in the Second World War and died in Wagga Wagga in January 1954. His obituary stated that he was a keen sportsman and a member of the town's 1st AIF cricket team.

Patrick Maher had a couple of spells at Brightlingsea but does not appear to have had a typical war. Patrick was born in Ballarat, Victoria, in 1880, and he saw active service in the Boer War with the 10th New Zealand Contingent. He was discharged on 1 September 1902, returned to New Zealand and in 1904 married Elizabeth Copper, moving back to Australia in 1912 with his family of six. He was 35 when he enlisted on 17 February 1916 into the Light Horse but on 23 March 1916 he transferred to the 10th Field Company Engineers with the rank of Sapper, service number 10301. Why did he sign up at this age? Was it because he missed the excitement of active service or he needed the extra money to help support his expanding family? His occupation at the time was that of a labourer. His medical record shows that he was fit for active service.

After initial training he left Melbourne aboard HMAT *Runic* (A54) on 20 June 1916, reaching Plymouth, England on 10 August 1916, moving on to France on 23 November 1916. There followed periods of illness at various field hospitals: 3 December 1916 to 9 December 1916, 19 May 1917 to 26 May 1917 (bronchitis) and 30 August 1917. On 30 July though he boarded the hospital ship *Jan Beydel* for England. Admitted to Woking Hospital on 31 July 1917 before being transferred to 1st Australian Auxiliary Hospital, Harefield on 27 August 1917.

He was discharged on 30 August 1917, and then spent the next four and half months at various depots in the Dorset and Wiltshire area before finally arriving at Brightlingsea on 18 January 1918 but by 14 March he was back in hospital, this time with mumps. He returned to Brightlingsea on 4 April 1918 for a three-month stay before being sent to France to rejoin his unit on 4 July 1918. Two months later, on 9 September, he was back in hospital again with 'Gastritis', transferred back to England on the Hospital Ship *Formosa* and eventually discharged from Southern General Hospital, Stourbridge on 24 October. After a couple of moves he ended up in Brightlingsea again on 29 November 1918 for a couple of months before being transferred to the Australian Reserve Brigade at Heytesbury, Wiltshire.

However, it was not long before he was once more back in hospital, this time for a two-week stay with influenza. The on 14 March 1919 he wrote to his wife:

> Dear Wife and Children
>
> I think it is about time I started writing to you again. I thought I would be home or nearly home by now but I am still in this God forsaken place. It is now nearly 3 months since I last wrote to you. I was expecting to get away any time after the middle

of February but my bad luck was in the way. I was not keeping very well during my last weeks at Brightlingsea. I left there as I thought for home on 29/1/1919 and ended here in camp on Salisbury Plain. I was only here a few days when I got on a boat roll and was ever so pleased with myself, but while waiting for the boat to go I got influenza and was sent to hospital and was there 3 weeks. I asked the doctor every day to let me out as I was on a boat roll and at last he let me go. When I got back to camp the boat had sailed that very morning and I was too late for the next boat as the roll had gone in. I paraded before the C.O. but he told me he could do nothing and now I am here waiting for the next boat but there is no sign of any as yet. The last boat that took the boys from here left on Saturday and all my mates are gone on it and I am here now and I do not know a solitary soul . . . If Daisy is going to school you must be very lonely – well you won't be lonely any more when I come home. Forgive me for not writing but I really expected to be on my way by this time. So nothing more this time and I hope you hear I am on my way before you receive this. So au revoir, big kisses and best of love to the little kiddies and your dear self.

I remain your fond husband Pat.

Unfortunately, he never made it because on 2 March he was back in hospital, this time with appendicitis, dying on 25 March. Well, what a battle he had, not on the Western Front against the enemy but against his own failing health. Of the two years and nine months he was with the 10th Field Company Engineers he appears to have spent only nine months at the Front. A battle I am sure he would have preferred to have fought at home, in fact if he had he probably would have lived a full life instead of leaving behind a wife and five children.

Sapper Patrick Maher was buried on 28 March 1919 in Tidworth Military Cemetery, Wiltshire, Plot number A. 82 and has a Commonwealth War Graves Commission headstone. From the burial report of Sapper Maher:

Coffin was Elm with Brass Mounts – Deceased was buried with full Military Honours. The coffin draped with the Australian flag being borne to the graveside on a Gun-carriage, preceded by a Firing Party from Headquarters A.I.F. Depots in United Kingdom. Six Australians supported the Pall. The 'Last Post' was sounded and volleys fired over the grave. Headquarters A.I.F. Depots in United Kingdom were represented at the funeral.

Maher is commemorated on:

- Australian War Memorial, Canberra – panel 24.
- Mollingghip State School Honour Board.
- Mollingghip Roll of Honour – Mollingghip Hall.
- WW1 Avenue of Honour Arch in Ballarat, Victoria.
- Also tree number 3796 – Avenue of Trees, Ballarat.

On the CWGC headstone is the inscription:

He Died an Australian Hero
The Grandest Death of all

John Cade was another Australian who spent time at Brightlingsea who never knew when to give up. However, on this occasion, unlike the Patrick Maher scenario, the authorities step in.

John was born at Michelayo on 24 October 1890. He moved with his family to Canberra in 1909, attending Monaro Grammar School and Gatton College. When war broke out John was in Queensland, Jackarooing. He enlisted at Townsville, Queensland, on 8 February 1915 but in April 1915 was discharged for being medically unfit. He had suffered from a bout of malaria in 1914.

Unperturbed, he re-enlisted and was appointed Second Lieutenant. By October he was with his battalion, the 25th, in the area around Armentières when he fell ill and was hospitalised with a liver infection and influenza. He finally returned to his regiment in May 1916 and took part in the Battle of Pozières (23 July). The battle was part of the Somme Offensive, initially a two-week struggle for the village of Pozières and the ridge on which it stands. Though the British were involved it was primarily an Australian battle. The Allied forces eventually captured the plateau north and east of the village, putting them in a strong position to threaten the German stronghold of Thiepval.

John had led two charges and after being buried by exploding shells three times he was finally shot in the ankle and rendered unconscious by gas. He was sent to hospital in England to recover not only from the injuries received but also from shell shock. In February 1917 he was back in Australia, but six months later he embarked from Sydney with the 47th Battalion and immediately attended the engineers' school at Brightlingsea. However, it was soon realized he had not fully recovered from his experiences at the front and was now suffering from memory loss and depression. He was returned to Australia and discharged on 28 June 1918. He married Alice Dawson in October 1919 but, still not satisfied, enlisted for service in the Second World War on 30 May 1942 aged 52, and discharged just over a year later on 24 November 1943. He died on 28 September 1958.

He is commemorated on the:

- Queanbeyan RSL Wall of Remembrance, Crawford St, Queanbeyan NSW.
- Michelago Public School Roll of Honour.
- Michelago District Roll of Honour World War 1, Ryrie Street, Michelago.

On 13 November 1916 a contingent of 340 men arrived at Brightlingsea which included a number of trainee junior officers. The eldest of them was Second Lieutenant Cyril Lawrence. He was born in New Zealand in 1889, emigrating to Australia with his family in 1909. Prior to enlisting in 1914 he worked as an engineer. His initial rank was that of a Sapper with the 5th Field Company of Engineers. He became a prolific diary writer, which has been published by Ronald East – *The Gallipoli Diary of Sergeant Lawrence of the Australian Engineers 1st A.I.F 1915.*

His first taste of action was with the 2nd Field Company at Gallipoli. The Gallipoli campaign against the Turks was Winston Churchill's idea which unfortunately went terribly wrong. The first landing took place at 6.30 am on 25 April 1915. The Expeditionary Force consisted of 70,000 British, French Australian and New Zealand soldiers, of which the Australians and New Zealanders accounted for 15,000. The peninsula was heavily defended by well-armed Turkish troops.

Lawrence's unit arrived on Gallipoli as reinforcements in early June and he recorded in his diary his first impression of the area: 'Above all the thing that meets, or rather hits, the eye is the number of "dugouts" . . .The whole landscape is covered with them. It looks for all the world like a mining camp.'

As we know from other diaries the fighting was not continuous and the soldiers often had several days of rest:

> We had a glorious swim after dusk. The Turk guns seldom fire after dark . . . the beach is just crowded – all men though.
>
> Each man has to cook his own rations, gets his own firewood and everything . . . Our rations are as follows: breakfast – tea and sugar, no milk, six biscuits per day (hard as Hell too), a small piece of cheese, a quarter pound of jam and one rasher of bacon. Lunch – tea only. Tea – stew or bully beef and tea, no milk.

By the end of June he was not feeling very well: 'I feel pretty sick and weak today – have had dysentery and neuralgia since I landed here.'

The plan was to knock the Ottoman Empire out of the war by opening up the Dardanelles Straits, capturing Constantinople and link up with Russia. The initial bombardments by the Navy started in mid-February 1915 were ineffective but they were followed up by the landings in April at Cape Helles and by the Australians and New Zealanders on the western Aegean coast. The expedition was met by fierce Turkish opposition and by August there was stalemate. The Allied forces only ever advanced a few hundred metres from the shore, enduring suffocating heat and being surrounded by rotting corpses that drew thick swarms of flies. They lacked water and thousands died from dysentery. Although the campaign diverted substantial Turkish forces away from Russian front, it did not produce the desired results. Finally it was decided to withdraw and this took place between December 1915 and January 1916.

During the campaign Cyril Lawrence was promoted to sergeant and this is what he had to say in his diary when he became aware of the evacuation plan:

> How can they leave this Place? Ours, because it is our and ours alone: we fought for it and won it, even leaving that out of the account, just think of all it means, the leaving of this place. It has grown upon one: we took it and tamed it and somehow its very wildness and ruggedness grips you. You can't leave it.

But leave they did and Company Quartermaster Sergeant A. L. Guppy had this to say in verse:

War graves, Gallipoli. (Author's collection)

Not only muffled is our tread
To cheat the foe'
We fear to rouse our honoured dead
To hear us go.
Sleep sound, old friends – the keenest smart
Which, more than failure, wounds the heart
Is thus to leave you-thus to part,
Comrades, farewell!

The Allies' casualties amount to approximately 280,000, with the Turkish forces losing approximately 250,000. The evacuation, however, went very smoothly and the majority of the units ended up in Egypt.

The Gallipoli campaign was a defining moment in Australian history. Taking place only thirteen years after the federation of Australia, it was the first major international conflict in which this young nation had been involved. The Australian and their New Zealand colleagues became known as the Anzacs (Australian and New Zealand Army Corps). April 25th is Anzac day and is commemorated every year.

By November Lawrence had come via Bournemouth to Brightlingsea and he was not very complimentary: 'This must be the most deadly place in England.' Within a month, however, Lawrence was on the move again, this time he was posted to the Western Front and by Christmas he was building a narrow-gauge supply railway across the muddy devastation of the recent Somme battlefield. While in France he made a brass trench-art bracelet from a German shell for his sister Clarice. After he returned to Australia he had the following engraving on the reverse: 'France 1916 SGT. C Lawrence 1/A.I.F. Brass from German Shell.'

The Battle of Menin Road in September 1917 was part of the Third Battle of Ypres, commonly known as Passchendaele. This was where Lieutenant Lawrence rebuilt a captured enemy strongpoint under fire for which he was subsequently awarded the Military Cross. Two weeks later he was struggling with his unit along the Helles Track, Jabber Track and Anzac Ridge, past Zonnebeke when they were scattered by enemy fire and shells which killed five. Lawrence called on two NCOs and got them to rally the men, taking them forward to Broodseinde, the village just beyond Zonnebeke, to rebuild another German position. It was for this action he was possibly recommended for a bar to his Military Cross.

The Battle of Menin Road was an offensive operation undertaken by the British Second Army in an attempt to take sections of the curving ridge east of Ypres, which the Menin Road crossed. This action saw the first involvement of Australian units (1st and 2nd Divisions AIF) in the Third Battle of Ypres. The attack was successful along its entire front, though the advancing troops had to overcome formidable German entrenched positions, which included mutually-supporting concrete pillboxes, and also resist fierce German counter-attacks. A feature of this battle was the intensity of the opening British artillery support. The two AIF Divisions sustained 5,013 casualties in the battle. Another quote from Lieutenant Lawrence: 'The concussion is simply awful. No one could image it unless they had actually experienced it. Nothing but great spurts of flame, screaming and sizzling of shell and banging and crashing of big guns. At times it becomes so terrific . . . it is simply one great throbbing, pulsating jolting roaring inferno.'

By September 1918 Lawrence was back at Brightlingsea, where he took over the investigation of possible spies. This was an obsession of the Senior Naval Officer, Lieutenant Commander Mahon. who from the early days of the war believed that there were enemy agents based around the town who were signalling to enemy aircraft or U-boats. It might seem laughable today, but a hundred years ago it was a scary thought. For some three hours around midnight each nights any lights seen were reported. There were at least four lookout posts around the

Ypres after two years of war. (Author's collection)

town watching the Colne and observers were watching the Blackwater and the open sea from Mersea. No spies were ever found.

Cyril Lawrence was promoted to lieutenant colonel in March 1917, returning to Australia on 24 January 1919. He continued to serve with the Australian army, returning to full-time duty in 1941, being appointed chief engineer then temporary colonel in April 1942. Volunteering for the AIF in July 1942, he was promoted to temporary brigadier. He retired in June 1944, finally moving to South Africa to be with his family in the 1970s. He died in 1981.

The first of the Brightlingsea trainees to be killed was Sapper John Dahl, service number 9445. John was actually born in Zurich, Switzerland, in 1871 to Bertel Christian and Caroline Dahl (née Burkli). The family moved to Queensland, Australia in 1873 and Bertel and Caroline were married there in 1874. Three sisters were to follow, Anna and Caroline in 1877 and Sophie in 1881. John's father died young in 1887, which saw his mother become stationmistress at Darra station on the Ipswich line. John joined the Queensland Railway as a lengthsman and labourer until 1901. By then he and his mother were living in Buderim Mountain, his occupation being that of a fruit grower. Although he had been born in Switzerland he decided in 1898 to become an Australian citizen and on 12 March 1898, at the age of

Lieutenant Colonel Cyril Lawrence at Brightlingsea. (Australian War Memorial)

27, took the Oath of Allegiance at Darra. On 7 August 1912 at the age of 41 he married Grace Addison in Brisbane, and a son was born on 19 May and was named John Addison Dahl, but unfortunately Grace died in childbirth. John then moved back to the Buderim area and worked as a carpenter.

On 10 December 1915, at the age of 44, John enlisted in Brisbane. Age limits and physical standards had been relaxed by this time, allowing men of his age to enlist. He was assigned to the 11th Field Company Engineers, Section 3 of the AIF. It was a newly-formed unit and on its first deployment. Basic training was carried out at Enoggera in Brisbane. From here the company was posted overseas, embarking on 31 May 1916 aboard the *Suevic*, arriving in Devonport, England on 21 July 1916. At some point the unit arrived at Brightlingsea for more training. They left Southampton for France on 24 November aboard the *Nirvana*.

After less than a month in France and having endured the cold, wet and muddy conditions, John became the first of the company and the first Brightlingsea Australian trainee to be killed. It was a high explosive shell that took his life while he was in the support line at Armentières on Christmas Eve, December 1916. He is buried at Cite Bonjean Military Cemetery, Armentières, Plot 111, Row C, Grave 21. He was survived by his mother and sisters, Caroline, Sophie and Anna, who became guardians to his son John.

There is no doubt there were a number of colourful Australians who spent time at Brightlingsea. Take Herbert Lockington Freshwater, for example. He was in fact born in Bedford in 1890. He arrived in Sydney from London on board the *Orsova* on 1 February 1912. Shortly afterwards he sailed to the British Solomon Islands and at the age of 26 was a plantation manager at Waimari, San Cristobal. He returned to Australia on 3 October 1916 on board the *Matunga* and a month later enlisted on 6 November 1916 at the Sydney Showground Camp with the Field Company Engineers (1st Army Troop Company). He gave his father as next of kin – Thomas Freshwater, 97 Castle Road, Bedford, England. Although passed fit for service it was found that he had suffered from malaria. He had twelve months' previous military service with the Frontiersmen in England. The Legion of Frontiersmen was a paramilitary group formed in Britain in 1905 by Roger Pocock, a former constable with the Canadian North-West Mounted Police and a Boer War veteran. It was prompted by fears of impending invasion of Britain and its Empire. Its headquarters was in London but branches were formed throughout the Empire.

Freshwater was obviously a bit of a cad, often finding himself being punished for minor offenses. For example, while at the training camp he was fined £1 for refusing to obey an NCO's order. His unit finally left Melbourne on board the *Clan McGillivray* (A46) on 10 May 1917 arriving at Fremantle. He failed to re-embark on the 22 May going absent without leave. Eventually he re-embarked on 29 June, disembarking at Plymouth, England on 25 August. His first camp was Parkhouse, near the village of Shipton Bellinger. Then he moved on to the Australian Engineers Training Depot (AETD) at Brightlingsea for further training.

He left Brightlingsea at the end of January 1918 for Rouelles in France with the rank of Sapper. We are not sure how much action he saw but he was back in London on 5 December 1918 and finally discharged from the AIF on 20 September 1919. He was awarded the

British War Medal and Victory Medal. Ten days later, on 1 October, he was on his way back to the Solomon Islands and there he married Lillian Osmond in the Hallows Chapel, Pawa, in November 1927. It was the first European marriage to be held on the island. Lillian died in a private hospital at Hawthorn, Victoria on 16 May 1937.

His adventures did not end there. He remained on Guadalcanal during the Japanese occupation in the Second World War along with a group of tough Australian miners working the alluvial gold leases 3,000 feet up in the mountains. The war correspondent Winton Turner reported:

BRAVE MINERS OF GUADALCANAL

GUADALCANAL, Fri – A plucky group of tough Australian miners remained on Guadalcanal during Japanese occupation, working their alluvial gold leases 3000 feet up in the mountains.

They were Messrs. F M Campbell, A Andresen, H L Freshwater and A Wilmot.

I have examined some of this Guadalcanal gold, 80 per cent, pure metal. Gold has rarely been won at greater risk of life. Hostile natives and Jap patrols were a constant hazard for the miners.

Wilmot was murdered by natives and his body was found in a mutilated condition. Natives had come on him while he was reading. But before he died he left a clue by placing his spectacles in the book describing how natives had crept up on a white man and killed him.

A native suspect was arrested, held for some time but is now serving in native prison. Truly strange things can happen in the tropics . . .

Herbert died on 8 October 1944 at Double Bay, Sydney. He is commemorated on the Buderim Mountain Roll of Honour.

The Australian Young Men's Christian Association (YMCA) arrived at Brightlingsea in November 1917. It took over the High Street Recreation Rooms, set up a library with over 500 books, arranged weekly sing-songs and liaised with the Red Cross at Colchester who were helping to look after many wounded in its hospitals. The YMCA was to stay to the end of the war.

Like any other, the depot had its problems, especially with those going absent without leave, though most of these were because after a day or two days' leave in London or Colchester around the pubs and girls, they missed their last train home. Their punishment for these offences would probably been a reduction in pay, being confined to barracks or stand to attention for a time after training. If the absence was for a longer period then the individual would face a court martial with proceedings being held at Brightlingsea. The panel was made up of three judges who included two officers from the barracks and an independent major from another base. Unlike the British, the Australians, no matter how serious the offence, never imposed the death penalty.

The numbers at the depot varied considerably from a couple of hundred men to over 1,200 troops, peaking at 1,275 men in June 1918, and this did not include a small detachment of 200 British personnel. By August and September things were beginning to move in the right direction for the Allies and victory was beginning to look possible. It was around this time that a Brightlingsea SME student, Lieutenant Hunt from Victoria, on his first day at the front performed one of the bravest deeds of any field engineer at Cerizy, on the banks of the Somme. He saw one of his sappers wounded by the Germans on the opposite bank. He crawled through a hail of bullets and somehow managed to carry the man back to safety. His company commander, Major Riddell, put him forward for the Victoria Cross, but instead he was given the DSO which normally only went to company commanders. His story is told in C.E.W. Bean's history of the First World War. Bean was a war correspondent and historian, born in New South Wales but educated in England. He actually taught for a short time at Brentwood School in Essex.

As one would expect many relationships were formed, resulting in over thirty marriages at Brightlingsea alone. The majority of Australians took the English wives back home but three remained behind plus two New Zealanders. Very little has been written about the Australians at Brightlingsea other than one book which is a 'must read' entitled *Australians at Brightlingsea: The Anzacs Stay in the Town: 1916-1919 & Afterwards* by Julian P. Foynes. The main reason for his interest is that his grandfather, George Rickwood, was one of the Australians who stayed behind.

George was the son of a Kentish immigrant and was born in Glebe, Sydney. He became Sydney harbourmaster, having also been a lifeguard at Bondi Beach and a boilermaker at the shipyard on Cockatoo Island just across the water. He was working on the cruiser *Brisbane*, the first major warship built by the Australians, when war broke out. He enlisted in 1915, trained as a sapper, he came over to England with the 39th Infantry Battalion and received further training on Salisbury Plain and then in France.

George was wounded when the 3rd Division was halted around Tyne Cot on 12 October 1917. The AIF was involved in two attempts to take Passchendaele, the first on 9 October 1917 known as the Battle of Poelcappelle, and the second on 12 October, the Battle of Passchendaele. It was these actions, fought in the wind and rain and what was left, after the constant shelling, of the mud-covered, cratered landscape of Belgium, that provided the popular name for the whole Flanders offensive, 'Passchendaele'. These battles were a failure, the units employed in them being decimated and demoralized. All too many AIF graves in Tyne Cot carry the ominous dates, 9 and 12 October 1917.

Half of George's battalion were casualties during this week's offensive. He remustered as an engineer and arrived at Brightlingsea in July 1918. He played rugby for the depot team and married a local girl, Lilian Uncles, with who he had four children. He spent the next three decades living the life of a typical Brightlingsea seafarer. He had a narrow escape in the Second World War in 1941 when a German aircraft bombed a minesweeper being repaired at the jetty: a mate of his was killed. He died in 1951.

At 10.45 am on Monday, 11 November 1918 the telephone rang in Lieutenant Colonel Nicholson's office with the news that a ceasefire will come into operation in quarter of an hour's time. At that time, 11 am, all the ships in the Estuary could be heard sounding their sirens and hooters and the depot was given a half-day off.

The depot finally closed its doors on 30 May 1919 and of the 5,000-odd 'Diggers' who passed through Brightlingsea around 300 were killed. I have only mentioned a few of the men that set foot in Brightlingsea to read the full story I again suggest you read Julian Foyne's book.

On a Good Front

A 'buckshee' ride with changes three,
'Wake up, dig! Here's Brightlingsea.'
On right, a river meets the ocean brown
Whilst the marshland rises up the town—
Slumbering and dreaming of its ancient glory,
When Celt and Saxon waged their battles gory.

No hearty hand at station meets you,
Until the provost picquet greets you.
With 'Gotcher pass, not late, damn glad!'
I'm hookem, give us a smoke, me lad'.
Up winding streets with swag you trek
And reach the camp right on the Rec.

On parade the 'fall-in' sounds,
Then a 'Precious' voice rebounds—
'As you were—smarter on the left!' and why?
For there some dinkum detail Diggers sigh
Whose deeds have made the cliffs of Anzac ring
To whose boots the muds of Flanders cling,
Now, sluggard, to attention spring.

'Officers, take post', delivered now,
With chaste salute and courtly bow;
The band strikes up some martial air,
For a march to the Ford or the mine-fields fair,
Perhaps it's the 'Hard' where the pontoons are weighty,
But you may get a nod and a wink from your katie.
A bonny girl with a tam o'shanter,
Who'll giggle at your harmless banter,
'Where you be going, boy?' in her minor key,
Which starts down at A and becomes a big C.
And at night you find that all the good 'possies'
Are strongly held by tarts and Aussies.

> Soon we shall leave this village behind,
> For the land where the sunshine and wattle's entwined;
> Good-bye then the sprats, the rice pudding and stew,
> Alas! Good Essex Friends, we'll bid you Adieu.'

By Sapper Fred Johnston.

The stalwart sons of Australia who came to help the Mother Country in her hour of need will always be remembered by the folk of Brightlingsea. The town's Recreation Ground, that had been taken over by the military and closed to the public in 1915, was eventually reopened in early 1921.

CHAPTER 7

The War at Sea

❧❦

The Essex

From North to South, from East to West
The Essex give their very best
Leaving their homes, forsaking all,
Responding nobly to the call
Of King and Country, round the flag.
They rally grandly; do they lag?
No! The trumpet calls and off they go
To help their brothers; downhearted? No!

Author unknown

Being an island, the one fear Britain had, as already mentioned, was of an invasion, especially if the conflict was a European one. The last major invasion as we all know was the Normans in 1066, though there had been a number of major attempts since, such as the Spanish Armada in 1588 and during the Napoleonic Wars 1799–1815 which was why the Martello Towers were built along the South Coast and this part of the Essex coast. Also with our huge empire to police, it had been British policy to have the world's largest navy to defend our shores and our empire. We must also not forget that being an island nation, Britain was heavily reliant on imports from overseas. So to maintain its dominance, at the beginning of the twentieth century the British Admiralty believed that the navy would need to be larger than the next two largest navies put together. However, it soon became obvious that this might not be possible, so they decided to settle for a 60 per cent margin.

Prince Wilhelm, the future Kaiser Wilhelm II, on his many visits to Britain to see his grandmother Queen Victoria and his cousins, was very impressed by the Royal Navy. In fact Queen Victoria made him an honorary admiral in the Royal Navy. Wilhelm was particularly grateful and promised he would always take an interest in Britain's fleet as if it was his own. With both his fascination with and concern about the strength of the Royal Navy he decided that Germany must have a navy to challenge Britain's dominance. He had previously told the Prince of Wales, the future Edward VII, that one day he would have a fleet of his own.

In the decade before the Great War, Europe was going through turbulent times and Germany expanding her navy did not help the situation. The First Sea Lord, Admiral Sir John Fisher, became concerned about Germany's intention as early as 1906 and therefore started to draw up plans for a naval war against Germany and within a couple of years it was obvious the German Navy was catching up, so with Admiralty pressure the Government decided to build eight new battleships of the Dreadnought type, the first of which had entered service in 1906. These were much more powerful than any previously-existing battleships.

By August 1914 Britain and Germany's respective naval strengths were:

	Britain	Germany
Dreadnoughts available	22	15
Dreadnoughts building	13	5
Battlecruisers	9	4
Battlecruisers building	1	3
Pre-dreadnoughts	40	22
Coast defence ships	–	8
Armoured cruisers	34	8
Protected cruisers	52	17
Scout cruisers	15	–
Light cruisers	20	16
Destroyers	221	90
Torpedo boats	109	115
Submarines	73	31
Total	**609**	**334**

Poster. (Author's collection)

In addition to Britain's superior numerical strength, its biggest advantage was that its sailors were long-service professionals and thus better trained and more experienced than the three-year conscripts who made up a large proportion of German naval personnel. Also the large British merchant navy provided a further source of trained seamen. Tirpitz (Germany's Grand Admiral) had thought that conscription would be an advantage for Germany because it would be able to recruit more sailors than Britain, but he was wrong.

The obvious route for the invasion of Britain if it ever came about was the short trip across the Channel but France would have to be subdued first so the flat lands of the east coast of Essex would have made a good alternative landing place, despite there being 70-odd miles of the North Sea to cross. The authorities therefore considered that the Clacton coast was one of the country's danger zones, so it was soon apparent from the amount of naval personnel around that Brightlingsea should be developed into a significant naval base, to control the Thames estuary and surrounding waters.

By April 1915 the shore base at Brightlingsea was fully established and had been named HMS *Wallaroo*, presumably after the *Pearl*-class cruiser launched in February 1890 and handed over to the Australian Navy in September 1891. In November 1914 she became a guardship at Chatham before being transferred to Brightlingsea were she was anchored just below the Martello tower. It is understood that she became the flagship of the base commander, Rear Admiral Napier, who stayed there for the first two years of the war. She was a light cruiser of 2,575 tons and the largest warship assigned to Brightlingsea, armed with eight 4.7in guns. The ship was sold for scrap in 1920. At its peak there were about 520 personnel at the base including 30 officers. Fortunately the base was never attacked and the patrols never spotted any Germans. However, it did provide some support for the secret HMS *Osea* and in April 1918 Rear Admiral Keyes' flagship and four other destroyers anchored nearby before their famous raid on Zeebrugge.

HMS *Osea* was a shore base for coastal motor boats (CMBs – torpedo-carrying speedboats) on Osea Island, tucked in the mouth of the River Blackwater. During the First World War it was a remote, secluded and secretive base. The CMBs were initially stationed in Kent but were too exposed, so the decision was taken to move them to Osea

Island. Its location proved to be a great success as it was protected on three sides but the CMBs were still able to reach the open sea in a matter of minutes.

The Zeebrugge raid in April 1918 was an attempt by the Royal Navy and 200 Royal Marines to block the Belgian port of Bruges-Zeebrugge in an attempt to deny its use to German submarines. The operation was led by the cruiser *Vindictive* with two Mersey ferries, *Daffodil* and *Iris II*, plus two old submarines. The Marines' job was to land and destroy German gun positions. Unfortunately the wind changed and the smokescreen to cover the ships was blown offshore, so the Marines came under heavy fire and suffered many casualties. It also forced the blockships to be sunk in the wrong place and the submarines collided with the viaduct. It was not the success hoped for and within a few days the canal was reopened to submarines at high tide. The British suffered 583 casualties and one destroyer sunk, while the Germans suffered only 24 casualties. However, the heroic action did result in the award of eight Victoria Crosses.

Zeebrugge
A Vision on the Way
'What craft be ye that sail the midnight seas
And what may be your burden, or your task?'
'We have no speech for watches such as these,
And who art thou who dost make bold to ask?'

'I ask as one who has e'er now made bold,
And fain would know the matter of your quest –'
'Hast thou then ever been a boy, of old
Creeping by night to rob a hornet's nest?'

'Ay, have I and I found it perilous sweet,
Without the compass of a single star;
I know not even that my pulses beat
More joyful fast the eve of Trafalgar!'

Author unknown

Serving on board HMS *Wallaroo* while it was at Brightlingsea was Stoker 1st Class **William Richard Mercer**, service number 120715.

William was born in Kent in 1861, and died of illness on 28 February 1916 and is buried in All Saints' Churchyard, Brightlingsea.

Brightlingsea's seafaring tradition meant that many local men served on cargo ships and ocean-going yachts. Merchant shipping was often easy prey for the German U-boats. One such ship was the SS *Seven Seas*, a British cargo steamer which was torpedoed and sunk by *U-37* on 1 April 1915 just off Beachy Head en route to Liverpool. Lifeboats were lowered but were dragged down by the sinking ship. Nine of her seventeen-man crew were drowned including the master. A boat containing the survivors was picked up by a destroyer and the occupants were taken to Newhaven. Amongst them was a local man, William Eady of New Street, Brightlingsea.

The day before *U-37* had sunk the French ship *Emma*, twelve miles off Beachy Head. The ship was nearly blown in half and only two of her crew of twenty-one survived after swimming for over an hour before being picked up. As usual the Germans made no attempt to rescue them. On 25 March, en route to Boulogne, the *Delmira* was also attacked by *U-37* but this time the ship managed to beach herself and there were no casualties. Not a bad week's work, but on 30 April on her homeward journey *U-37* hit a mine near Sandettie in the Straits of Dover. All thirty two of the crew were killed.

Eady was born in Brightlingsea in 1876 and lived with his parents Henry and Amelia in Lower Green Street. We find in the 1901 census at the age of 25 he had moved and was now living in Mile End Road, London and his occupation was that of a Fireman. He married in 1908 and at some point joined in the Merchant Navy, service number 349461. He was awarded the Mercantile Marine Ribbon and British Medal Ribbon on 31 January 1920 but his Mercantile Marine Medal (MMM) and British Medal do not appear to have been issued until the following year, with the MMM being sent to the Queen Victoria Seaman's Rest. William died in 1954 aged 79.

Benjamin (Ben) Chaplin was born in Brightlingsea in 1872 into a seafaring family, his father also being named Benjamin. He married Rosabelle Caroline Savory at All Saints' Church on 1 December 1906. He had followed in his father's footsteps as a mariner. The 1911 census has Ben, his wife, three sons and a daughter living in Itchen, Hampshire, and he is registered as a master mariner.

Local sources tell us that he was the famous captain of the ship *Bloodhound*: the problem is, which *Bloodhound*?

- HMS *Bloodhound*, a gunboat launched in 1871. Guns 2 x 6pdr; commissioned in 1914 for service off the Belgian coast, reverting to harbour service in 1916.
- HMS *Bloodhound*, a hired trawler, built it 1890. Guns 1 x 3pdr; saw service as a boom defence vessel from June 1915 to 1919.

It is more likely that it was the latter because his next posting was as acting Lieutenant of HM Yacht *Seadawn*. She was patrolling the Thames estuary when she hit a mine. Ben was seriously injured and died in Chatham Hospital on 6 July 1918. He had previously been awarded the Distinguished Service Cross (DSC.) which is given in recognition of gallantry during active service against the enemy at sea. He was also award the French Croix de Guerre and would automatically receive posthumously the Victoria/British Medal and possibly the 1914/15 Star.

Walter B. Dines was another mariner born into a seafaring family but was to die due to an unfortunate accident on 25 August 1915. He was born at Brightlingsea in 1885. At the time the family were living in Sidney Street, and his father Benjamin was a mariner. The 1901 census shows Walter as a mariner's apprentice, and they had moved to Spring Road probably because the size of the family. In addition to Walter there were three other sons and three daughters. He married Ellen Charlotte Verrall on 27 December 1909 at All Saints' Church. Ellen was born in Hailsham, Sussex so presumably he met her on one of his voyages. At his inquest he was described as an Able Seaman and Rigger and he was carrying out salvage work on HMS *Clementina*, a 625-ton armed Admiralty yacht that had been serving as an auxiliary during the war. The *Clementina* had been involved in a collision with the SS *Adam Smith* on 5 August 1915 near Tor Cor Point, Northern Ireland, a notorious area for shipwrecks. She was re-floated but beached nearby in Cushenden Bay.

It was here where it is believed Walter fell from a mast either on *Clementina* or the *Linnet* which was helping with the salvage work, he fractured his skull, dying in Cushendall Cottage Hospital. He is commemorated on the Roll of Honour in All Saints' Church and on one of the memorial tiles around the inside of the church in memory of local men lost at sea.

It is not known how far the seafaring family of Dines went back but the Nurse family from Brightlingsea went back at least to the early 1800s. Silas Nurse was born about 1811 and the 1841 census registers him as a mariner. His son, David Rochford Nurse, was born on 23 September 1856 and was baptised on 7 December 1856 at the Wesleyan Methodist Church, Brightlingsea. He followed his father into the Merchant Navy and one of the ships he served on as an able seaman around 1893 was the *Anemone*. He had married his wife Rachel in 1876 and they had five daughters and five sons, Silas, Ernest, **Rochford**, Frederick and Jack.

Frederick unfortunately died in 1891 at the age of five, while the other four followed their father into either the Merchant Navy or Royal Navy. Silas's occupation is recorded in the 1901 census as a mariner but in 1903 he married Elizabeth and at around the same time he became a police constable in the Billericay district. By 1939 they were back living in Brightlingsea and Silas was a retired police pensioner. Elizabeth passed away in 1944 and he married Grace Saville in 1947 at the ripe old age of 70 but died two years later.

Rochford was the next to go to sea, the 1901 census has him listed as a mariner and at some later date he enlisted in the Royal Naval Reserve (RNR), rank deck hand, service number 9741.DA, and at the time he was living in Hull with wife Hannah. He served aboard HM Trawler *Robert Smith* along with other shipmates from the Hull area. On 21 July 1917 she was attacked by the German submarine *U-44* (Kapitänleutnant Paul Wagenführ) north-west of Lewis in Scotland. All hands, twenty-five in total, were killed. Under Wagenführ *U-44* had a very successful career from March 1916 until August 1917 sinking twenty-two merchant ships, with two more damaged and three taken as prizes. The U-boat was finally sunk on 12 August 1917 when it was rammed by HMS *Oracle* off southern Norway. All forty-four crew lost their lives. Rochford is remembered on the Chatham Naval Memorial and has a memorial tile in All Saints' Church.

Next in line was Ernest Nurse. He was born on 16 October 1892 and was a local fisherman before enrolling in the RNR on 16 November 1914, rank: seaman, service number 6759 He served aboard HMS *Juno*, a second class cruiser with a crew of 450. Between January 1915 and February 1919 HMS *Juno* spent time in Irish waters, the Persian Gulf and the East Indies. The only notable action she appears to have

HMS Juno. *(Author's collection)*

been involved in was the British attack on Dilwar, 13–15 August 1915. Following German encouragement, the local Tangistani tribe attacked the British at the port of Bushire on the Persian Gulf. Britain complained to the Persian government and demanded reparations; until these were paid Britain determined to occupy Bushire and to attack Dilwar to punish the insurgents. Warships, one squadron from the 16th Cavalry and the entire 11th Rajput Regiment were sent to Bushire, along with two captured Turkish guns, only one of which was later found to be serviceable. Meanwhile the Germans in Bushire were believed to have slipped away to Shiraz; soon afterwards the Khans astride the Shiraz road blocked it and cut the telegraph wires running inland.

On 10 August 1915 a British expedition left Bushire to carry out punitive measures against Dilwar. The ships involved were:

- HMS *Juno* (Captain D. St A. Wake) – 11 x 6in, 8 x 12pdr and 1 x 3pdr guns.
- HMS *Pyramus* – 8 x 4in and 8 x 3pdr guns.
- HMIMS *Lawrence* – 4 x 4in and 4 x 6pdr guns.
- HMIMS *Dalhousie* – 6 x 6pdr guns.

The designated landing party, under Commander Viscount Kelburn, Royal Navy (HMS *Pyramus*), consisted of:

- Captain G. Carpenter, Royal Marine Light Infantry (RMLI), with fifty NCOs and Marines from HMS *Juno*.
- Nine Marines from HMS *Pyramus*.
- Eleven petty officers and seamen from HMS *Juno* manning machine guns.
- A demolition party of one warrant officer and twenty men from HMS *Juno*.
- Four signallers from HMS *Juno*.
- One medical officer and ten stretcher bearers from HMS *Juno*.
- Twenty-four Seedie Boys (locally-enlisted stokers) acting as ammunition and machine-gun carriers.
- Major C. E. H. Wintle with one officer and 280 sepoys of the 96th Berar Infantry.
- Five machine guns.

Because of unfavourable weather, the landings could not commence until 11 August and even then conditions were still difficult. An inshore current took the boats 1,600m away from the planned landing site. HMS *Juno* bombarded the foreshore at a range of about 7,250m with her 6in guns but the fire had little effect on the enemy and whilst the boats were being hauled ashore the Tangistanis opened fire with their rifles from trenches.

A base was eventually established but not before *Juno* had lost four men killed and seven wounded. Ernest was part of the *Juno* landing party. While the Marines continued to attack the tribesmen *Juno* helped out in shelling various targets, but due to an error shells landed amongst the Marines, wounding some and demoralizing others, this obviously delaying the success of the expedition. The landing party and the boat crews had taken a total of fifty-five casualties from the fighting, most of these due to the 'friendly fire' incident, and eleven casualties from heatstroke. The Tangistanis were believed to have lost a considerable number of men. Ernest survived the war, being demobbed in January 1919 but obviously remained in the RNR, finally being discharged on 19 January 1937. On his return to Brightlingsea he married Lilian Finch and returned to his pre-war job of fisherman. He died in 1950.

The last of the brothers, Jack, was born in September 1896, and he enlisted the Royal Navy on 6 January 1916, service number 8847A. He was assigned to HMS *Pembroke* which was the name given to the training barracks at Chatham. The barracks had a gunnery school, new-entry training centre, church, canteen, infirmary, gym, swimming pool and a large parade ground. A month later, on 10 February, he transferred to the fleet messenger ship HMS *Isonzo*, then at the end of the month to HMS *Prince of Wales*.

Prince of Wales was a pre-dreadnought battleship, the sixth of seven ships of the Royal Navy to bear that name. When war broke out the ship became the flagship of the 5th Battle Squadron. The squadron was assigned to the Channel Fleet and based at Portland. From here it patrolled the English Channel. Then on 14 November the squadron transferred to Sheerness to guard against a possible German invasion but was back in Portland by the end of December 1914. *Prince of Wales* was then sent to the Dardanelles to support the Anzac landings on 25 April 1915 but by May she was on her way to the Adriatic until January 1918 before returning to harbour service.

Although Jack's records show he was transferred to *Prince of Wales*, for how long is not known because we see that he was discharged from HMS *Isonzo* on 20 February 1919, returning to *Pembroke* the following day, eventually being demobbed on 16 May 1919. He returned to Brightlingsea, and stayed in the RNR until he was discharged in 1941, discharge number 727413. He died in 1961 aged 64.

One of Brightlingsea's most famous mariners was Edward Isaac Sycamore. He was born on 24 August 1855 in Chelmsford, and by the time he was 12 he had started work as a fisherman. In 1875 he started yachting with the Marquis of Ailsa, which was to launch him on career that was to make him one of the world's best-known racing yacht captains between 1890 and 1929. In fact, the 1881 census has him staying at the King's Head Inn, Harwich, occupation captain. By 1891 he was living with his wife Elizabeth, daughter Edith (aged 7) and son William (aged 1) at 51 New Street, Brightlingsea, occupation master mariner. His career included two America's Cup races being a crewmember aboard *Valkyrie III* in 1895, the captain on this occasion being William Cranfield. They lost to the yacht *Challenger*. Edward skippered his next attempt in September 1895 with *Shamrock II* from

Valkyrie 111. *(Mersea Museum)*

the Royal Ulster Yacht Club but was beaten by the yacht *Columbia* of the New York Yacht Club.

During the 1890s he worked for Rear Admiral the Hon. Victor Montague and on parting company to further his career, Montague presented him with a silver watch, and he was also presented with an engraved stopwatch from Admiral Lord Charles Beresford who at the time was Commander-in-Chief of the Channel Fleet. After 1903 the America's Cup competition was not held again until 1920, mainly due to the War.

In 1906, while sitting in the Swan Hotel having a drink with a farmer friend and discussing their respective skills, he challenged the farmer to a ploughing match, to prove that by using his compass he could plough a furrow as straight as the farmer could. The challenge was accepted. Edward won and when Sir Thomas Lipton of the *Shamrock* heard about the contest he presented a cup to be competed for annually. When years later horses were replaced by machinery, the matches were discontinued. The cup was initially placed in the local

Miss Sycamore taking part in the ploughing match, 1907. (Author's collection)

Crew of Valkyrie 111 *in 1895. Edward Sycamore is seated third from the left in the second row. (Mersea Museum)*

bank but later given to the Brightlingsea Sailing Club. It is one of the many cups raced for.

Edward's excitement was not going to end with the America's Cup or racing up and down a ploughed field. In 1914 he had command of the German-owned 15m yacht *Sophie Elizabeth* and along with the Kaiser's yacht *Meteor IV* they were being towed by a torpedo boat to England for Cowes Week when war broke out. They had passed through the Kiel Canal and were in the North Sea but suddenly the torpedo boat slowed and then turned and towed both boats at high speed towards the Elbe and finally berthed at the naval base at Cuxhaven. The *Sophie Elizabeth* was left for a time moored against a buoy. Captain Sycamore wired the owner but did not get a reply: not a happy crew.

A few hands went ashore with the captain to get water. Then in the early hours of the morning, with all hands fast asleep, a launch came alongside and an armed officer ordered them to leave the yacht with their personal belongings. They were taken ashore and marched to a prison under armed guard. The crew were all placed in separate cells and given a meal of bread and black coffee. After being searched they were released and sent back to the yacht without their belongings.

The owner of the yacht arranged to meet the crew at Hamburg where there was a Grimsby boat still lying there, crowded with British refugees caught in Germany. The crew tried to join them but the boat was prevented from sailing. Eventually, through the owner's influence, they were put on a train for Denmark, but at some point the train was stopped and the crew and other British refugee passengers were once again searched and jailed. Captain Sycamore was in fact placed under guard. Once again they were released and put on another train which eventually took them to Esbjerg where they managed to get passage back to Harwich and home. You can imagine their families were relieved at their safe return but as you would expect the crew, like many of their contemporaries, offered themselves for sea service as members of the RNR or as volunteers.

The *Chelmsford Chronicle* reported the story:

BRIGHTLINGSEA SKIPPERS SAFE

Capt. E Sycamore of Brightlingsea arrived home on Tuesday (11th August) from Denmark, where he had being staying with the British Consul, after being detained in Germany. He states that he had some rough experiences in Germany, being twice imprisoned. He left his crew in Denmark; they were expected to follow on. Captain Sycamore arrived with nothing other than what he was wearing, all his luggage having been taken from him while in Germany. Capt. Sycamore brought a reassuring message with regard to Captain James Taylor, of Brightlingsea who, with his wife, is imprisoned in Hamburg.

He also reported that when in Germany he and his crew saw several mine-layers being painted to resemble the boats running from Harwich to the Hook of Holland and from Queenborough to Flushing.

It is possible that the generosity shown him and his crew may have been due to him being well known to the Kaiser, whose yacht he regularly beat, if being jailed a couple of times counts as being generous! Sycamore would have been allowed home because of his age, but as previously mentioned his crew would normally have been interned. So I suppose the Kaiser was being generous.

Later in an interview with the Admiralty Board Sycamore was asked; 'What do you know about navigation?' He answered: 'I guarantee to take any vessel you like to give me from Dover to Rosyth in thick weather quicker than any of you gentlemen sitting round the table.' At this, they gave him a commission and he was enlisted into the Royal Naval Volunteer Reserve (RNVR) as a lieutenant. He took command of a motor launch *ML 350*, and he also commanded *ML 352* and *ML 5*. All three were based at Newlyn, near Penzance on the Cornish Coast. These

Edward Isaac Sycamore. (Mersea Museum)

small launches were designed for harbour defence and submarine chasing or air-sea rescue. On 1 April 1918 Sycamore was promoted to captain, eventually being demobbed on 13 September 1919 at the age of 64. He returned to his yachting career and was still captain of the *Shamrock* on his 74th birthday in 1929. He died on 9 April 1930.

Sycamore was not the only Brightlingsea mariner to be interned in Germany. Captain John Norton, age 66, from Brightlingsea and master of the barge *Tintara* was interned at Remagen. He had been arrested with his crew including his son **Fred**, Sid Gentry and Albert Garnham from Brightlingsea. Captain Norton told the *Chelmsford Chronicle*, reporting on his release in December 1914, that when he was arrested he had about £10 in his pocket, which the Germans took, but they overlooked a half-sovereign. He also said the black bread they gave him made him sick. He managed to get an interview with the American Consul who said: 'My dear man, you have no business here at your age. I can't give you any relief but I can give you your passage money to go to England.' The Captain was hesitant as he wanted to stay with his crew, but the consul advised him against this and gave him 45 marks and said he would give the crew 10 marks each. On leaving Germany he recorded that the towns were full of wounded men, bread was eight pence a loaf and meat eighteen pence a pound. His biggest surprise was when he returned to the Thames that everything was as he left it. The Germans had informed him that London was in ruins.

The rest of the crew including his son Fred were interned, apparently at Ruhleben. As the British blockade of Germany slowly took hold, prisoners became an economic burden on the German war effort. Fred unfortunately died of pneumonia while a prisoner in 1917: his father must have been greatly distressed considering he was released. Like many others who lost their lives due to the war his memory is remembered on a memorial inscription at All Saints' Church, Brightlingsea. The barge *Tintara* was interned in a small riverside port on the Rhine River called Oberwinter, Remagen. *Tintara*, along with another British barge called *Carisbrooke Castle*, was returned by the Germans in November 1918. More bad news was to fall on the Norton family later in the war.

Barge Tintara. *(Mersea Museum)*

Sidney Mildmay Gentry is recorded in the Ruhleben survival register as living in Barrack 5, having been born on 1 December 1895 in Brightlingsea, and described as being a seaman on the *Tintara*, with his Brightingsea address being given as 7 Francis Street. From the Ruhleben Football Association (RFA) Season 1915 handbook it is noted that he was working as a seaman in Remagen when he was arrested on 1 August 1914. He was initially interned in Remagen, Donaueschingen and Berlin before being sent to Ruhleben. The fact that he was mentioned in this handbook suggests he possibly played in the barrack's football team. The records also show that the inmates also played cricket in the Ruhleben Cricket League.

Another Brightlingsea man, Percy Edmund Gould, was the second officer on the *Campeador* and was arrested in Hamburg on 16 October 1914 and after a brief spell of imprisonment on the hulks there, was transferred to Barrack 8 at Ruhleben. He was obviously a keen footballer as the camp magazine informs us that he played for the Barrack 8 against Barrack 20 in the RFA Cup Final in April 1917. The first match ended in a draw 1-1, the replay was three days later and Barrack 8 lost 3-0. Percy was born in Clacton in 1893 but on the outbreak of war was residing in Brightlingsea. Also at Ruhleben, in Barrack 5 according to the survival list, was a Albert Edward Garnham, born 5 November 1872 from Chelmondiston, Suffolk, a seaman from the *Carisbrook Castle* or should this have read *Tintara*?

In war there are a considerable number of barbaric occurrences, and one such happened at Ruhleben. Captain Charles Fryatt with his crew of the merchant ship SS *Brussels* was captured by the Germans on 22 June 1916 off the coast of the Netherlands and interned at Ruhleben. Although he does not seem to have a connection to the Clacton area he had often sailed out of the port of Harwich just a few miles further along the Essex coast.

Captain Charles Fryatt.

In the previous eighteen months he had had several run-ins with German U-boats. In particular on 28 March 1915 he was ordered to stop by *U-33*. On seeing that the U-boat had surfaced to torpedo his ship, Fryatt ordered full steam ahead and proceeded to try to ram *U-33*, which forced it to crash dive. Following his capture he was court-martialled by the Germans, found guilty as a *franc-tireur* (an illegal combatant) and shot. Rather a strange decision considering the Germans were from February 1915 attacking merchant shipping in British waters without warning. In 1926, following a long investigation, it was concluded that the action of the German authorities amounted to murder.

Winston Churchill, who had become First Lord of the Admiralty in 1911, believed that whoever controlled the high seas would win the war but this also meant that the English Channel had to be kept free of the German Navy. This was done by stationing a large number of warships in the North Sea in an attempt to keep the German fleet in port. The fighting on land in the early months of the war was going badly but as usual British morale was boosted when the Royal Navy won the Battle of Heligoland Bight on 28 August 1914. Heligoland is a small archipelago located twenty-nine miles off the German coast. The islands became a naval base and the civilian population were evacuated to the mainland. The British attacked German patrols, in so doing destroyed three light cruisers, two torpedo boats and one destroyer plus damaging several other vessels. In the process 712 German sailors were killed, 149 wounded and 336 taken prisoner. The British casualties were very light. This defeat resulted in the Kaiser ordering his surface fleet to stay in port. Though this is what the British wanted, it did unleash the U-boats which created a big threat to British shipping.

Involved in the Heligoland Bight operation were the armoured cruisers HMS *Aboukir*, HMS *Cressy* and HMS *Hogue*, which a month later on the morning of 22 September 1914 were attacked by *U-9* commanded by Kapitänleutnant Otto Weddigen. The three ships were on patrol in the North Sea without escorting destroyers as they had been forced to seek shelter because of bad weather. Weddigen had been ordered to attack British transports at Ostend but had dived because of the bad weather. On resurfacing he spotted the three British cruisers. She fired her first torpedo at 6.20 am which struck *Aboukir* on her starboard side. She quickly began listing and capsized, having only managed to lower one lifeboat. *Hogue* approached her sinking sister-ship to help the survivors but in so doing she was struck by two torpedoes at about 6.55 am. She sank within 20 minutes. *Cressy* then attempted to ram the submarine without success before she was hit at 7.20 am, sinking 35 minutes later. Several Dutch ships and British fishing trawlers helped to pick up survivors. In total 62 officers and 1,397 men lost their lives, 837 being rescued.

The following three sailors who appear on the Clacton-on-Sea Roll of Honour lost their lives that day and were possible the first Clacton men to be killed in the Great War. **Frederick Hammond** was born on 5 October 1876 to Sarah and Charles at St Osyth. The 1891 census has him working as a general labourer but by September 1896 he had enlisted in the Royal Navy, service number 283493, engaged as a stoker. His first ship was *Pembroke II* (the shore base at the Royal Naval Air Station at Eastchurch) and he served on several others before joining HMS *Aboukir* on 2 August 1914. His naval record states that he was killed or died as a direct result of enemy action

U-boat sinking a merchant ship. (Author's collection)

and his body was not recovered for burial. In addition to appearing on the Clacton Roll of Honour he also recorded in the memorial register kept at the Chatham Naval Memorial and on *De Ruvigny's Roll of Honour*.

The Marquis De Ruvigny's *Roll of Honour* features biographies of over 26,000 men of the Army, Navy and Air Force (all ranks) killed in the Great War, 7,000 of which include photographs. The majority of the biographies relate to deaths in the early years of the war, although there is some coverage of deaths in 1917 and 1918. At the beginning of the war, the notion of an all-encompassing biographical listing of each serviceman killed in the Great War would have seemed perfectly feasible. In the early months a quick, easy victory was expected, but it quickly became clear that the war would be long-lasting and the disasters of 1916 and 1917 making those early months of patriotic optimism seem a distant memory. By then it was perfectly clear that the De Ruvigny's ambitions were entirely unachievable. Nonetheless, this roll offers a unique glimpse of over 26,000 men who gave their lives, and stands as a tribute both to the men themselves and the perseverance of its compilers.

William 'Willie' Page from Clacton was also killed when HMS *Aboukir* was sunk. He was born on 29 September 1889 at Clacton and had enlisted on 28 April 1908 for five to seven years. Service number SS2347. His first ship was *Pembroke I* and it would appear that he was one of the ship's cooks. Like Hammond above, he served on several other ships before spending time at Chatham. He joined HMS *Aboukir* on 2 August 1914. His body was never recovered. He left behind his wife Alice who was living at the time in Castle Road, Clacton-on-Sea. He is remembered on the Clacton Roll of Honour, *De Ruvigny's Roll of Honour* and the Chatham War memorial.

Not appearing on the Clacton Roll of Honour is William Thomas Page from Great Clacton. He does not appear to be related to Willie Page above. He was born on 7 November 1879 at Great Clacton to Robert and Caroline Page. He enlisted on 15 April 1899 for twelve years, service number 291867 and his first ship was *Pembroke II* but again served on many other ships before joining HMS *Aboukir* on 2 August 1914 as a leading stoker. In 1911 he married Florence Fisher in the Biggleswade District, Bedfordshire. In 1912 their son Jack was born, followed in 1913 by Clarence. He was now a Naval Reserve man and they were living in the High Street at Henlow when he was called up. On 2 October 1914 the *Biggleswade Chronicle* reported:

HENLOW NAVAL MAN LOST IN NORTH SEA DISASTER

Much anxiety has been felt in the village respecting the fate of William Thomas Page, husband of Mrs Page of High Street, Henlow. Mr Page was a leading stoker on HMS *Aboukir*, one of the victims of the North Sea disaster and as no tidings of him could be heard for some days, it is feared he had perished. These fears, unfortunately, were confirmed on Monday, September 28th when Mrs Page received a telegram from the Admiralty informing her that her husband was not among those saved. Mr Page was a naval reserve man 35 years of age and previously settled in Henlow some few years ago, he had served 12 years in the Navy on board HMS *Amazon* and other warships. On the outbreak of the present war he was called up and drafted to HMS *Aboukir*, which was engaged in patrolling the North Sea until the fateful morning. The *Aboukir* was one of the ships taking part in the Heligoland engagement. Mr Page married the daughter of Mr and Mrs Fisher of High Henlow, who with her two infant children mourn his loss. He will be remembered as a quiet, steady workman, a good husband and father and was respected in both Henlow and Arlesey, at which latter place he worked previous to being called up for service. Much sympathy is expected for his wife and children, the eldest of which is barely 2½ years old. At St Mary's Church on Sunday the Vicar made reference in the prayers to those who had fallen in the war from the parish.

Harry Osbourne from Arlesey was also on the *Aboukir* and was rescued. He said that the last he saw of William was on the Monday evening when they were on the deck together smoking their pipes. Another survivor told Osbourne he saw William just before the ship went down and he was in a very fearful way because he could not swim. He is commemorated in *De Ruvigny's Roll of Honour*, the Chatham Navy Memorial and Arlesey War Memorial. The Clacton Roll of Honour has in fact a William Page listed, regiment, Royal Fleet Reserve but no date of when he died. Could this be our William Thomas?

Appearing on the Clacton Roll of Honour is **George Ernest Hatcher** a Leading Stoker on HMS *Hogue*, service number 299240 who was killed on 22 September 1914 when the ship was sunk. He, like the others above, had already spent twelve years in the Navy and was in the RNR when he was called up. Although he appears on the Clacton Roll of Honour I have been unable to trace his connection to the town. Again like the others he appears in *De Ruvigny's Roll of Honour* and the Chatham Navy Memorial.

Walter William Ingate was a Brightlingsea man who also went down with HMS *Hogue*: his body was never recovered. Walter was born in Tollesbury, Essex, on 16 March 1886 but on the outbreak of war was living with his wife Kate when on leave at 149 Sydney Street, Brightlingsea. He had enlisted in the Royal Navy on 16 March 1906 and served on a number of ships before transferring to the RNR, returning to active duty on the outbreak of war. He is remembered on the Clacton Roll of Hour, the Chatham Naval Memorial and in *De Ruvigny's Roll of Honour*.

On 31 October 1914 the seaplane carrier HMS *Hermes* was torpedoed by *U-27* and sank off Ruylingen Bank in the Straits of

Dover. She had been used to ferry seaplanes and stores to France. The previous day she had arrived at Dunkirk, the next morning she set out for home but turned back because a German submarine was reported in the area. Despite zigzagging she was torpedoed and went down with the loss of forty-four men, one of whom was **Claude Herbert Jeffers,** from Little Clacton. Claude was born on 4 December 1882 and on 4 December 1900 at the age of 18 signed on for twelve years, his occupation at the time was being of a waiter. The first ship he served on was HMS *Northampton*. After twelve years and several ships he was demobbed and joined the RNR. Re-joining HMS *Pembroke 1* on 2 August 1914 as a Leading Seaman, and on 25 August 1914 he joined HMS *Hermes*. He left behind his wife Edith and young son Leslie.

Among those saved from the wreck were George Southerwood of Great Holland and James Parmenter of nearby Upper Kirby. The papers reported that when Southerwood – a chief stoker – was blown into the sea by the force of the explosion, he found Gunner Parmenter swimming quite close to him. The two seaman were half an hour in the water. Southerwood was nearly exhausted when he was helped aboard the rescue vessel by Parmenter. Both survived the war.

The next serious engagement was the Battle of Dogger Bank in the North Sea on 24 January 1915. The British had intercepted and decoded German wireless transmissions that a raiding squadron was heading towards Dogger Bank. This raid had come about because of a previous German raid in late 1914 when they bombarded Scarborough, Hartlepool and Whitby, killing 108 civilians and wounding 525. The British public were outraged, so the Admiralty was making sure this did not happen again. They sent five battlecruisers, seven light cruisers and thirty-five destroyers which must have been quite a surprise for the smaller, slower German squadron.

In the action that followed the Germans lost one armoured cruiser, the *Blücher*, and had one battlecruiser heavily damaged, killing 954, wounding 80 and 189 taken prisoner. The British had one battlecruiser and one destroyer damaged, with 15 killed and 32 wounded. The battlecruiser HMS *Lion* was out of action for four months.

Just prior to the Battle of Dogger Bank the battleship HMS *Formidable* was sunk after being hit by two torpedoes on 1 January

1915. She was the second British battleship to be sunk by enemy action during the First World War. At the time she was participating in gunnery exercises off the Isle of Portland supported by light cruisers. The fleet at night remained at sea on patrol and at 2.20 am *Formidable* was struck by a torpedo from *U-24* and a second at 3.05 am. The cruisers *Topaze* and *Diamond* came alongside to pick up eighty men. At around 5.00 am she rolled over onto many of the men in the water and sank quickly. A local Brixham trawler in two attempts was able to save 118 men. The loss of life of

Frederick G. Mayes. (Phyllis M Hendy)

Formidable was 35 officers and 512 men, of which one was **Frederick George Mayes**, Stoker 1st Class, who lived at St Osyth. He was born at St Osyth on 26 March 1892 and at the age of 19 enlisted in the Royal Navy. His first ship was HMS *Pembroke II*. He then served on HMS *Blenheim*, a first class protected cruiser, before transferring to HMS *Formidable* on 29 July 1914.

An interesting twist is that it is believed that the author Eric Knight's novel *Lassie Come Home* in 1938 was inspired by an event following the sinking of *Formidable*. A lifeboat containing dead bodies from the battleship was blown along the coast onto the beach at Lyme Regis. The local pub, called the Pilot Boat, offered its cellar as a temporary mortuary. When the bodies were laid out a half-collie dog named Lassie found her way amongst the bodies and began to lick the face of Able Seaman John Cowan. She stayed with him for a considerable time, apparently keeping him warm. He eventually stirred, was taken to hospital and made a full recovery. He returned to thank Lassie and all at the pub for saving his life.

While all this was going on there were a couple of smaller engagements going on down in the Pacific and South Atlantic. It started with the Battle of Coronel on t1 November 1914 just off the coast of Chile near the city of Coronel. This time it was an easy victory for the German Pacific Squadron led by Vice Admiral Maximilian Graf von Spee. The British squadron, commanded by Rear-Admiral Sir Christopher Craddock, was composed almost entirely of either obsolete or under-armed vessels resulting in the British losing two armoured cruisers and 1,570 men killed. The Germany casualties were only three wounded.

The shock of this defeat vibrated through the British Navy and they decided to send a large force to track down and destroy the victorious German squadron, which consisted of the two armoured cruisers SMS *Scharnhorst* and *Gneisenau*, three light cruisers, SMS *Nürnberg*, *Dresden* and *Leipzig*, and three transport ships. The British sent after them two battlecruisers, HMS *Invincible* and *Inflexible*, three armoured cruisers and two light cruisers. On 8 December 1914 at the Battle of the Falkland Islands the British battlecruisers sank all the German ships with the exception of *Dresden* and the transport ship *Seydlitz*, killing 1,871 and capturing 251 for the loss of 10 killed and 19 wounded. Admiral Graf von Spee was killed and went down with his flagship *Scharnhorst*. The light cruiser *Dresden* evaded destruction for three months before her captain scuttled her off Juan Fernandez Island on 14 March 1915, detonating her main magazine. This brought an end to German raiding on the high seas. As far as we have been able to establish there were no sailors from Clacton or surrounding areas involved in any these battles, other than possibly Herbert Bird who served on HMS *Indomitable* which was at Dogger Bank.

Britain continued to pursue a strategy to engage where possible and destroy Germany's High Seas Fleet, or keep the German force contained and away from Britain's shipping lanes. This was also beginning to strangle Germany's mercantile shipping. So in late May 1916 the High Seas Fleet planned to lure out, trap and destroy a portion of the Grand Fleet. However, the British intercepted signals that showed a major German operation was being planned. So Admiral Sir John Jellicoe sailed with the Grand Fleet as did Vice Admiral Sir David Beatty's Battlecruiser Fleet. On the afternoon of 31 May 1916 the Battle of Jutland began which was to turn out to be the largest naval battle of the war.

Beatty encountered Germany's Vice Admiral Franz Hipper's battlecruisers and in a running battle, Hipper initially got the upper hand before the British main fleet joined in and the High Seas Fleet turned for home and escaped. On the face of it, it would seem that Germany were the victors as Britain lost 14 ships out of 151 and Germany 11 out of 99, resulting in 6,094 British deaths, 674 wounded and 177 captured against Germany's 2,551 deaths and 507 wounded. However, Vice Admiral Reinhard Scheer's plan of destroying a substantial portion of the British fleet failed. The Royal Navy retained naval supremacy and the blockade was not broken. Germany therefore turned its efforts to unrestricted submarine warfare and the destruction of Allied and neutral shipping, which in the end brought America into the war.

HMS *Queen Mary* was the last battlecruiser to be built before the Great War. She had taken part in the Battle of Heligoland Bight, but missed Dogger Bank because she was in for a refit. At the Battle of Jutland she was fully involved in the action and scored three hits on the German battlecruiser *Seydlitz* but she became exposed due to damage to other ships resulting in hits from the battlecruiser *Derfflinger* and her magazines exploded. Her wreck was discovered in 1991 on the bottom of the North Sea. The site is designated as a protected place under the Protection of Military Remains Act 1986 as it is the grave of 1,266 officers and men. Two of the men were **Arthur Frederick Hobbs** from Clacton and **Frank Herbert Mills** who was born in Brightlingsea.

Arthur was born on 4 August 1883 and enlisted on 4 August 1901 at the age of 18 for twelve years. His first posting was HMS *Northampton*. Other ships included HMS *Victory*, *Vernon*, *Britannia*, and *Revenge,* eventually joining *Queen Mary* in September 1913. He was the son of Thomas Hobbs who was the landlord of The Ship inn, Great Holland, and husband of Blanche Ellen who was living at West Worthing, Sussex, when Arthur was killed.

The *Chelmsford Chronicle* reported his death on 23 June 1916:

> Able Seaman Arthur Hobbs, a torpedo man, a native of Clacton was lost with the *Queen Mary*. His father was at one time stationed at Clacton as a Coastguard and later took the Ship Inn, Great Holland which he held for 17 years. The deceased had been in the Navy nearly 15 years and was married only four months ago.

Frank H. Mills memorial tile, All Saints' Church, Brightlingsea.

Although Frank Mills was born at Hadleigh in Essex his record refers to him as being a native of Brightlingsea and he is commemorated with a monumental inscription in All Saints' Church, Brightlingsea, and on the Portsmouth Naval Memorial. He was the son of Thomas and Amanda Mills, and was born in Brightlingsea on 13 December 1893. The family later moved to Coventry. He enlisted in 1910 for twelve years and the 1911 census shows him as Boy First Class at a naval establishment at Portland, Dorset. It appears that he had joined the naval training establishment HMS *Impregnable* at Devonport in February 1910. On 13 December 1911 at the age of 18 he was allowed to join the Navy proper. He continued his training aboard the ships *Donegal*, *Albemarle*, *Cochrane* and *Excellent*, which was a gunnery training establishment. A year later he was promoted to Ordinary Seaman and then on 13 February 1913 to Able Seaman, service number J/7266. He transferred to HMS *Queen Mary* on 4 September 1913. He was awarded the 1914 Star and the British and Victory war medals.

Moving a little further round the coast to Walton-on-the-Naze, we find that **Henry Newcombe** is remembered on the their Church Memorial although we have not been able to find a connection other than he was either the nephew or brother of Harry Newcombe of 9 Broomfield Cottages, Walton-on-the-Naze. Henry was born on 2 January 1883 at St Pancras and joined the Navy in January 1901 for twelve years as an Able Seaman. His first ship was the *Northampton*, and he served on many ships with his last being *Victory II* at the end of his twelve years' service. He then joined the Royal Fleet Reserve (RFR) whereby those that joined did regular annual training and were liable to be recalled in times of emergency.

On his recall he found himself posted to HMS *Princess Irene*, an ocean liner that was requisitioned by the Royal Navy and converted to an auxiliary minelayer. In May 1915 she was moored in Saltpan Reach in the Medway Estuary in Kent. She was being loaded with mines on the 27th when she exploded and disintegrated. A total of 352 people were killed, Henry being one of them. Wreckage from the ship was flung up to twenty miles away, a girl of nine on the Isle of Grain was killed by flying debris and a farmhand died of shock. Other than three of her crew who were ashore at the time the only survivor was a stoker, who suffered severe burns. Henry is also remembered on the Portsmouth Naval Memorial: his body was never recovered.

Able-Seaman **Charles Baker**, 'Chuck' as he was affectionately known, of 11 Herbert Road, Clacton-on-Sea appears to have served the whole of war aboard HMS *Leda*. She was built as a torpedo gunboat in 1893 but converted into a minesweeper in 1909. From the outbreak of war she was one of a squadron of fleet sweepers attached to the Grand Fleet. They were kept busy sweeping the areas around the northern bases and chasing suspected U-boats. She had a top speed of about 17 knots but on one occasion exceeded 19 knots whilst chasing a U-boat.

He was obviously a man with a sense of humour and in early October 1914 he wrote the following letter home:

> We are still above water dodging about. Shall soon have the rough weather here. We've had a pleasant surprise. Some kind gent has given 600 gramophones to the navy. We had one come aboard to-day with 12 records. They have it playing to-night and it's great! Everybody is singing and it makes us all merry and bright, so to speak. Will give the Germans a little music as they go down to see how the mermaids are getting on. Nothing very exciting doing yet. I can hardly realize that we are in the middle of an awful war – least not yet; but we might when we get a few lumps of iron weighing about 1,252 lbs. flying round our heads like flies.

It would have been letters like this that would have helped keep up morale at home.

During the war it became the Merchant Navy's responsibility to not only service the home market but also supply the Royal Navy, and the transport of troops, armaments, raw materials and supplies for the army, in addition to providing both personnel and ships to supplement the existing resources of the Royal Navy. From the very start merchant ship losses were very high, with them peaking in 1917 when the German government adopted a policy of unrestricted submarine warfare. Although the adoption of the convoy system helped to reduce losses, by the end of the war, 3,305 merchant ships had been lost along with a total of 17,000 lives.

One such sailor who lost his life was **Joseph Benjamin Kittle**, a native of Clacton-on-Sea. He was aboard the SS *Joshua Nicholson* when she was torpedoed by *U-70* without warning at 6.30 am on 18 March 1917. The ship was defensively armed and en route from London for Alexandria when attacked off Wolf Rock, Land's End, Cornwall. The ship started to sink immediately and while the port lifeboat was being lowered she capsized and three men drowned. Another was blown into the water by an explosion. After the ship had gone down, six men came to the surface and clung to pieces of wreckage. Of these, three drowned over the next three hours, the remaining three being picked up at around 5 pm, exhausted but alive. In total twenty-six lives were lost including the ship's master. Joseph is commemorated on the Tower Hill Memorial along with 12,000 other men of the merchant service. He was 19 years old.

One of the major disasters that shocked Brightlingsea was the sinking of HM Yacht *Verona* on 24 February 1917. She was built in 1890 for the wealthy Australian J.R. Wood as a wedding present for his bride, the famous actress Elizabeth Jennings. The yacht was requisitioned by the Royal Navy and named HM Yacht *Verona* for anti-submarine patrol duties off the east coast from her base in the Moray Firth. She was equipped with small guns on her counter and two more at the bow. She was later modified to take a single depth charge. But before she could fire her guns or drop her depth charge she struck a mine laid by *UC-33* off Portimahomack. The yacht sank in less than a minute taking all her crew and her captain with her. Amongst those who lost their lives were four men from Brightlingsea: **Ridgeway Alfred Bragg**, steward, **Harry Thomas Doyle**, sub-lieutenant, **George Salmon**, cook, and **William John Steady**, able seaman. All are commemorated on the Brightlingsea Roll of Honour and the Merseyside Roll of Honour.

Unfortunately many sailors were killed in accidents rather than by enemy action. Able Seaman **Wilfred Leslie Eggleton** was aged only 19 when he was killed when HMS *Vanguard* was sunk by an internal explosion at Scapa Flow on 9 July 1917. *Vanguard* was a *St Vincent-*

class dreadnought battleship built in 1908. She saw action at the Battle of Jutland in May 1916 and at the inconclusive action of 19 August that year. Although the Battle of Jutland was seen as a success for the German Navy, they still took a battering and they had decided that another raid should be mounted as quickly as possible before the Grand Fleet took the initiative. They had decided on a dawn bombardment raid on Sunderland but due to mixed reconnaissance information and the fear of a major battle the German Fleet returned home. In the short skirmish that took place the British lost two light cruisers and the Germans had one battleship damaged. After this, *Vanguard* spent the rest of her time until that fatal night on routine patrols and training in the North Sea. The internal explosion appears to have been the result of faulty cordite. The ship sank almost immediately with the loss of all but two of the 845 men on board at the time. It is one of the most tragic accidents in the history of the Royal Navy. The wreck is now designated as a controlled site under the Protection of Military Remains Act.

Wilfred had enlisted in the Navy on his eighteenth birthday, 1 January 1916, for twelve years. He had previously been an errand boy, living with his parents in St Osyth. He saw service on a few ships before being transferred to HMS *Vanguard* on 5 June 1916, so he would have seen a little bit of action in August 1916, otherwise his career to date had been fairly uneventful. Bodies that were retrieved after the sinking now lie in Lyness Royal Cemetery, Wilfred's is not one of them. He is commemorated on the St Osyth War Memorial and the Chatham Naval Memorial.

Another was **Ernest George William Davidson,** husband of Winifred, of Red House, Third Avenue, Frinton-on-Sea. He was born on 8 June 1874 in Rangoon, British Burma. His father was a senior colonial police officer who had also served for a brief period in the Rifle Brigade. His uncle was Sir Arthur Davidson, a Royal Equerry from 1891 to 1922. It is understood that Ernest did not want to join the Royal Navy but it seemed he had no choice and joined in 1889 as a 14-year-old cadet. In April 1905 he was appointed captain of the destroyer HMS *Lightning*, in March 1906 captain of the gunboat HMS *Bramble*, in September 1908 captain of the torpedo gunboat HMS *Speedwell*, and then from 7 September 1912 to 20 April 1915 he was captain of the destroyer HMS *Lyra*. Finally on 3 September 1916 he was appointed to command HMS *Otranto*, an armed merchant cruiser.

The *Otranto* was built in 1909 to carry passengers and mail between England and Australia but within a week of the outbreak of war she was requisition by the Admiralty and converted into an auxiliary cruiser. She took part in the fateful Battle of Coronel on 1 November 1914, suffering five hits but survived the action. Following the battle she was sent to the Falkland Islands to act as a guardship, returning to England in March 1915 where her ex-Merchant Navy crew threatened to mutiny. Then in May 1915 she was sent to patrol the west coast of America returning to England in June 1918 to take up the role of ferrying American soldiers to the Western Front.

Just six weeks before the Armistice she was part of a convoy bring 20,000 US servicemen to Glasgow and Liverpool. On 1 October, *Otranto* collided with a French fishing schooner and sent her to the bottom, but luckily there was no loss of life. On 5 October the American escort ships handed over to two British warships off the west coast of Ireland for the final leg of the voyage. The weather by now had turned nasty, with the wind whipping up huge seas and making visibility very poor, and on next day *Otranto* and her fellow troopship HMS *Kashmir* found themselves too close to land and both needed to take action. The *Otranto* thought she had sighted Ireland and turned sharply to port, but *Kashmir* correctly thought the land was Islay and turned sharply to starboard, resulting in them colliding. *Kashmir* was undamaged and made it safely to port, but *Otranto* was badly holed forward on the port side. Davidson nursed the ship towards Islay and hoped for the best. The destroyer HMS *Mounsey* was able to rescue several hundred soldiers and crewman but 431 lives were lost including that of Captain Davidson. It was reported that he was last seen on deck, valiantly trying to organize some sort of evacuation for soldiers and crew left on board. His body, along with many others, were washed up all over Machir Bay. Ernest, you could say, has two graves, his actual one in Islay and one in with a memorial in Thurlestone Churchyard, Devon, where his wife Winifred is buried.

James Samuel Chatten was born in Cosford, Suffolk, on 11 May 1889 but at the time of his death on 27 March 1918 his mother was living at Clacton-on-Sea. He had joined the Royal Navy on 1 May 1907, just 18 years of age, as an able seaman for twelve years. At the time of enlisting his occupation was that of an agricultural labourer. His final ship was HMS *Kale*. She was a 'River' class destroyer named after the Rive Kale in Scotland. From August 1915 she was employed on the Humber in counter-mining operations and anti-submarine patrols. The ship was sunk when she struck a British mine in the North Sea, resulting in the loss of forty-one officers and men. It would appear that the commander had steered a course which was six miles east of the swept channel and straight into a prohibited area.

The death of **Ronald Joseph Robinson**, another Frinton man, was particularly unfortunate. He was born on 31 May 1897 and enlisted in the Royal Navy in July 1916. His last ship was HMS *Ebro*, an armed merchant cruiser on blockade duty, where he was an ordinary seaman. Along with three others he boarded the Norwegian ship *Najade* west of the Faeroes on 6 March 1917 to act as armed guards. *Najade* was ordered to head for Kirkwall in the Orkneys for inspection of her cargo. She was on her way there when she was sunk by *U-59* off Fair Isle. All four members of the armed guard which included Robinson lost their lives. He is commemorated on the Chatham Naval Memorial.

One of the roles played by small merchant ships were to act as decoys designed to lure submarines into making surface attacks, giving the ships the opportunity to open fire and sink them. They were known as 'Q-ships' and were heavily armed with concealed weaponry. One such was HMS *Prize*, or *Q21* as she was known. She was sunk by *UB-48* on 14 August 1917, but prior to that she had had a fascinating career.

She was a three-masted topsail schooner built at Westerbrock, Germany in 1901 and originally christened the *Else*. Within hours of the outbreak of war she became the first ship to be captured in the English Channel and was escorted back to Britain by a destroyer escort. With the Admiralty on the lookout for vessels suitable for decoy work, they requisitioned the ship and named her HMS *Prize*. She was armed with two Lewis machine guns and two large deck guns. One was concealed by a collapsible deckhouse while the second was on an ingenious retractable mount, under the hatchway covers of the after hold.

Prize left Milford Haven on 26 April 1917 under the command of Lieutenant William Sanders to patrol the west coast of Ireland. She was nearing the end of her patrol when her lookouts sighted *U-93*. Sanders called Action Stations as the U-boat moved to intercept, its commander Von Spiegel firing two warning shots. The crew of *Prize* executed a well-rehearsed plan, with six men running about the deck in mock panic, while the gun crews secretly took up their positions. The six-man panic crew then lowered the lifeboat and rowed clear of the ship as *U-93* continued to fire while approaching dead astern. Then only 75 yards away, *U-93* stopped dead in the water, this time firing its shells at the waterline. The time for subterfuge was over, Lieutenant Sanders stood up and yelled – 'Right boys now's your time, Raise the Ensign, Down Screens, Open Fire.' Both vessels opened fire simultaneously and both vessels were hit. A shell from *Prize* struck the U-boat's compressed air tank under the gun, destroying its sights.

The following is an extract from the British account of the engagement:

> The second round from *Prize* hit the base of the conning tower rendering diving impossible. The next round destroyed the gun and its crew. Remaining hits were on the aft part of the boat, her stern being turned towards *Prize*. Numerous casualties were caused amongst the German crew by *Prize*'s Lewis gun. Three survivors were blown overboard. The submarine proceeded for 3,000 yards before the engines stopped and it sank. An explosion with black smoke occurred as she slipped away beneath the swell, leaving behind just a few whiffs of smoke. In this short, savage engagement, the Q-Ship had fired thirty-six rounds in just four minutes.

The panic party then rowed around picking up the three survivors. Although Sanders believed *U-93* had sunk, it had in fact levelled off beneath the surface and, with Lieutenant S. Ziegner now in command, managed to limp home under cover of darkness.

All the crew received the DSM, Lieutenant Beaton was awarded the DSO and Lieutenant Sanders received the highest award, the Victoria Cross. He was also offered other assignments but decided to stay with HMS *Prize*. In June Sanders found himself in another scrap with a U-boat and he was wounded but by August, *Prize* was ready for action again and then came that fateful day 14 August 1917.

Prize with other ships was working off the north-west coast of Ireland when *UB-48*, on passage to the Mediterranean, came across her. The following is an extract from the U-boat's KTB (Kriegstagebuch – war diary):

> 16.30 3-mast schooner with Swedish flag observed. Forced the crew to leave the schooner after more hits with shells, thereafter we dived. 8 crew members observed leaving in a lifeboat and nobody left on the schooner. Could observe all of the schooners deck without seeing anything suspicious. Dived again at a range of 1000 m. Then the lifeboat was heading back towards the schooner and we signalled 'abandon ship'. With our deck gun manned we sailed nearer to schooner. Suddenly we observed people on the deck and the Swedish flag was changed with the British White Ensign. From the foredeck they opened fire with a small calibre gun and on the afterdeck they were turning a heavier cannon towards us. After I order Alarm and before we dived, my deck crew scored a hit close to the heavy gun on the afterdeck on the schooner. This hit maybe saved us, because there was no fire from this cannon, they only hit us with one shell from the small gun before we disappeared. Then we left but stayed in the area because we were determined to sink this ship.

The U-boat continued to stalk *Prize* then at 3.05 am on 14 August the U boat submerged and fired a torpedo but it missed. It fired a second at 3.25 am from 70m and this one hit the schooner amidships which resulted in a massive explosion. The schooner disappeared from the surface. The schooner and her crew of twenty-seven have never been found. One of them was Petty Office **George James Jarrett** from Brightlingsea where he had been living with his wife Annie at 37 Sydney Street. He had previously been awarded the DSM and Bar. George was born in Ballycastlea, Antrim, Northern Ireland on 18 January 1887 and on his eighteenth birthday enlisted in the Royal Navy, signing up for twelve years' service. By the time his time was up the war had been going on for over two years and he obviously stayed on with the RNR. He served on a number of other ships before joining the fateful HMS *Prize*. He is not only commemorated on the Brightlingsea War Memorial but also on the Plymouth Naval Memorial.

A year later, on 18 August 1918, **Robert Easey**, a Stoker 1st Class, service number SS/111863, was killed when the destroyer leader HMS *Scott* was sunk off the Dutch coast less than a year after she entered service. The cause of her sinking is somewhat unclear. It was first thought that she was torpedoed by *U-17* that had been patrolling and laying mines in the area, but it was later believed that she had in fact hit one of the mines that the U-boat had laid. HMS *Scott* was the first of a new destroyer leader class and was named after Sir Walter Scott. She was part of a group tasked to escort traffic from the Hook of Holland when HMS *Ulleswater* presumably hit a mine. HMS *Scott* went to her aid but also hit a mine and sank within fifteen minutes, with twenty-two men losing their lives. Robert's body was never found. Although from Great Holland, Robert had been born in Framingham, Suffolk and had enlisted on 27 March 1912 for twelve years, having previously been a draper's porter. He is commemorated on the Chatham Naval Memorial.

One of the most tragic accidents happened on the night of 28 March 1916. The light cruiser HMS *Conquest*, part of the 5th Light Cruiser Squadron of the Harwich Force, was in port at Harwich. She had seen some action in August 1915 when she took part in the hunt for the German minelayer *Meteor*. The ship's crew had gone ashore. Although it was an early spring evening the weather could only be describe as filthy, with a blizzard sweeping the coast: certainly not an evening to be in a small boat. However, thirty-nine men attempted to return in the ship's cutter. It foundered in the storm and all on board were drowned. The following eighteen of the men are buried in the cemetery of All Saints' Church, Walton-on-the-Naze. None of them are from the area:

- Barlow, William – Petty Officer.
- Brown, John – Engine Room Artificer 4c.
- Button, Frederick – Cook's Mate.
- Concannon, John – Petty Officer Stoker.
- Dillon, George F – Shipwright 2c.
- Gillingham, Sidney J – Stoker 1c.
- Grinton, William J – Ship's Steward.
- Howe, Frederick H – Petty Officer.
- Hunt, Walter J – Private, RMLI.
- Hughes, Edwin – Petty Officer.
- Maybank, John T – Ordinary Seaman.
- Mccloghrie, Thomas – Engine Room Artificer 5c.
- Mcgrath John R – Stoker 1c.
- Moody, Ernest C – Yeoman of Signals.

- Pearton, Charles – Stoker 1c.
- Phipps, Vivian G – Able Seaman.
- Simpson, Ernest K – Stoker 2c.
- Plant, Vivian G – Leading Signalman.
- Unknown Seaman.

It would appear that this is the worst single accident to involve the loss of life to members of one of the Royal Naval Ships, other than in action or on-board accidents of any description, since 1899.

To date there have been two Royal Navy ships named after the town of Clacton. The first was built in 1904 and was initially used as a passenger ferry but in October 1914 she was requisitioned and used as a patrol vessel (screw minesweeper). Pennant Number M30, she carried two 12pdr guns. She served in the Dardanelles, arriving at Lemnos on Saturday, 10 April 1915, fifteen days prior to the first engagements of the Gallipoli campaign. Lemnos was chosen as the gateway to the Dardanelles. Very little can be found of her involvement other than that on 27 July 1915 she arrived at Anzac Cove at 2.00 am to discharge troops and stores and take back on the wounded and left

The eighteen graves of those who lost their lives on HMS Conquest. *(Author's collection)*

HMS Clacton. *(Author's collection)*

at 12.30 pm for Mudros. Then on 3 August 1916 she was torpedoed and sunk by *U-73* at Chai Aghizi, Kavella Bay in the Aegean.

Though danger threatens
Britain's smiling shores,
The Glory of our past
Shall never fade
Our Mariners have
Justly held the seas
A Thousand years
Fearless and undismayed;
While absent you are
Ever in our thoughts,
Our prayers are with you
On the ocean wide,
We long to clasp your hand
When Strife is o'er
May heaven grant
No harm to you betide.

Unknown Author

The Brightlingsea naval base, which had served the country so well, was closed on 31 October 1921.

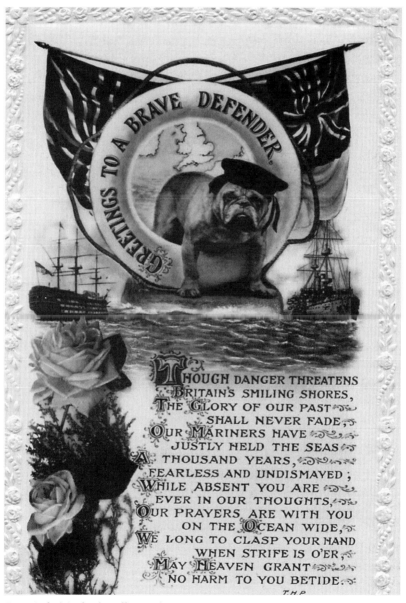

Postcard. (Author's collection)

CHAPTER 8

War in the Air

❧❦

Previous conflicts were fought either on land or at sea, but for the first time this war was also going to be waged in the skies, by means of balloons, airships and the new invention of aircraft. However, powered flight had only just emerged from its experimental stages, with the first flights being credited to two Americans, the brothers Orville and Wilber Wright, on 17 December 1903. Although previous individuals had built and flown experimental aircraft over very short distances, the Wright brothers were the first to invent the controls that made heavier-than-air powered flight possible. After several attempts, they finally covered a distance of 852 feet in 59 seconds.

As both sides experimented, it became clear that although initially air power would not win the war, it would provide considerable assistance to commanders

Recruitment poster. (Author's collection)

by improving reconnaissance and spotting. In fact from the very start of the war, huge observation balloons became a common sight above trenches as both sides tried to spy on each other. The Germans were a step ahead of the Allies in developing rigid airships, inflated with hydrogen and powered by gasoline engines placed in gondolas situated at either end of the long, cylindrical hull. They were patented in Germany as early as 1895 and became known as 'Zeppelins', named after their inventor Count Ferdinand von Zeppelin and by the time of the First World War the German Airline Deutsche Luftschiffahrts-ag (DELAG) had carried over 10,000 fare-paying passengers on over 1,500 flights. However, it soon became clear to the German military that they could be used for both reconnaissance and bombing.

It did not take long for the British authorities to recognize the threat of the Zeppelins and as early as September 1914 the Admiralty had given instructions for all lights on the seafront and public places at Clacton-on-Sea and Walton-on-the-Naze to be extinguished. However, the public would soon experience the devastation the Zeppelins could cause. The *Framlingham Weekly News* reported the following sighting on 24 April 1915:

HARWICH ESCAPES

> At Harwich, though an airship passed over the town about one o'clock, no bombs were dropped. The weather was very clear and bright and the craft could be seen distinctly. It passed towards Felixstowe coming from the direction of Clacton-on-Sea or Colchester. It showed no lights. It was flying at a good height and was going at the rate of forty miles an hour. At Maldon four bombs were dropped but though they fell within a few feet of houses, very little damage was done and nobody was injured.

Though Clacton and the surrounding area was to see a number of Zeppelins fly over, they did not record any bombs being dropped. There were in fact five large airship raids over Essex between March 1916 and September 1916. To the people of Essex they became known as the 'silent raiders'.

The airship raids in early 1916 caused the government major concern, and the result was the creation of a number of airfields in Essex and the Home Counties. By the end of 1916, fifteen airfields had been created in Essex, including one at Little Clacton and another at nearby Beaument in addition to the one already at Clacton. During the war there were over fifty Zeppelin raids, mainly aimed at London. The Germans' ultimate aim was to break British morale and even though some 700 people were killed and 2,000 seriously injured, all it achieved was the opposite, a strengthening of morale. The construction of rigid airships by the British lagged behind the Germans but by the beginning of the war the Air Battalion of the Royal Engineers had acquired a small fleet of non-rigid ships which was taken over by the Royal Naval Air Service (RNAS). The RNAS used airships principally to counter the U-boat threat.

With the continued advances in aircraft design it was not long before aircraft on both sides were being used, first for reconnaissance. It was estimated that an aircraft could gather more intelligence in four hours than a cavalry patrol could in twenty-four hours. However, it was not long before commanders realized that they had to stop the enemy flying over their territory, so pilots were armed with pistols and rifles and later bombs. It was not long before they were shooting at each other and 'dogfights', as they were known, became the norm. These dogfights actually began with pilots throwing grenades or grappling hooks at each other, before progressing to small arms and then later machine guns.

At the beginning of the First World War Britain had some 113 aircraft in military service, the French Aviation Service 160 and the German Air Service 246. By the end of the war each side was deploying thousands of aircraft. The Royal Flying Corps (RFC) was formed in April 1912 as the military began to recognize the potential for aircraft as reconnaissance and artillery observation platforms. It was in this role that the RFC went to war in 1914. The RFC also had a balloon section which deployed along the eventual front lines to provide static observation of enemy positions. Shortly before the war. a separate Royal Naval Air Service (RNAS) was established.

The RFC had experimented before the war with the arming of aircraft but the means of doing so remained awkward, because of the need to avoid the propeller arc and other obstructions such as wings and struts. In the early part of the war the risk of injury to aircrew was therefore largely through accidents. As air armament developed the dangers to aircrew increased markedly and by the end of the war the loss rate was 1 in 4 killed, a similar proportion to the infantry losses in the trenches.

For much of the war British pilots faced an enemy with superior aircraft, particularly in terms of speed and operating ceiling and a better flight-training system. Weather was also a significant factor on the Western Front with the prevailing westerly wind favouring the Germans. These disadvantages were made up for by determined and aggressive flying, albeit at the price of heavy losses, and the deployment of a larger proportion of high-performance aircraft. The statistics bear witness to this with the ratio of British losses to German standing at around 4 to 1.

When the RFC deployed to France in 1914 it sent four squadrons (Nos 2, 3 4 and 5) with twelve aircraft each which. together with aircraft in depots, gave a total strength of 63 aircraft supported by 900 men. By September 1915 and the Battle of Loos, the RFC's strength had increased to 12 squadrons and 161 aircraft. By the time of the first major air battles at the first Battle of the Somme in July 1916, there were 27 squadrons with 421 aircraft plus a further 216 in depots. The expansion of the RFC continued rapidly thereafter putting strain on the recruiting, training system and aircraft supply system.

At home, the RFC Home Establishment was responsible for training air and ground crews and preparing squadrons to deploy to France. Towards the end of the war they provided squadrons for home defence against German Zeppelin and later Gotha bomber raids. The RFC and the RNAS initially had limited success against the German raids, largely through problems of locating the Zeppelins and then reaching their operating altitude.

They were also deployed in the Middle East, the Balkans and later in Italy. Initially the Middle East detachments had to make do with older equipment but were eventually given more modern machines. The RFC (in small numbers) was able to give valuable assistance to the army in the eventual destruction of Turkish forces in Palestine, Transjordan and Mesopotamia.

In the final days of the RFC, over 1,200 aircraft were deployed in France and were available to meet the German offensive of 21 March 1918 with the support of RNAS squadrons. On 1 April 1918 the RNAS was merged with the RFC to form the Royal Air Force. At the time of the merger, the Navy's air service had 55,066 officers and

*Taunton E. Viney, DSO.
(Frinton War Memorial
Club)*

men, 2,949 aircraft, 103 airships and 126 coastal stations. The RNAS squadrons were absorbed into the new structure, individual squadrons receiving new squadron numbers by effectively adding 200 to the number so No. 1 Squadron RNAS (a famous fighter squadron) became No. 201 Squadron RAF.

One of our first air heroes was Flight Lieutenant **Taunton Elliott Viney**, born at Saffron Walden on 14 November 1891 to Arthur and Edith Viney. At the outbreak of war we believe they were living at 'Bratton', Second Avenue, Frinton-on-Sea. As a child he moved with the family to South Africa where he was educated at Grahamstown, returning to finish his education at Mill Hill independent boarding school in London. On the outbreak of war he returned to South Africa and enlisted as a private in Prince Alfred's Guards but after six months he returned to England and took up a commission in the Royal Naval Armoured Car Section before transferring to the RNAS on 20 May 1915, with whom he gained his pilots certificate on 1 July 1915 in a Cauldron biplane at the Royal Naval Air Station, Eastbourne.

On the 30 July 1915 he sent his mother the following letter:

> My dear mother, had a very nice crossing to Boulogne, where a Rolls Royce met us, or rather another man in a boat and brought here. Had a joy ride of 40 minutes this morning, shall be practising for some time. I xxxx hopefully nice lot of fellows out here, rather funny about my luggage at Frinton, wasn't I lucky, got it when I saw Mrs Dalgal yesterday morning – awfully nice of her. I like her very much. Dunkirk is very deserted the bombardment did a lot of damage. Xxxxxxxxxxx on second thoughts you might as well send all the soft white collars you can find and also white shirt. Remember me to all.
>
> Your dear and loving son Taunton E Viney

Then on 28 November 1915, accompanied by his observer Lieutenant Le Comte de Sincay, flying a Henri Farman 3620, they came across two German submarines six miles off the German coast. They destroyed the second by dropping two 65lbs bombs from 1,200 feet. They hit it amidships and as it broke up they could see both ends sticking up in the air. For this Viney was awarded the Distinguished Service Order (DSO) and promoted to Flight Lieutenant. The notice appeared in the *London Gazette* on 1 January 1916. The 3620 was a French-built plane and was named after its designer Henri Farman who was actually British (although his mother was French). He took out French nationality in 1937.

The airmen were credited with sinking the U-boat but the loss is not reflected in German records. However, *UB-6* and *UC-1* both suffered some damage from air attacks about the time in question.

The following article appeared in the *Gloucestershire Echo* on Monday. 6 December 1915:

A YOUNG AIRMAN HERO

The heroes of the aerial exploits of the war, it is interesting to notice, have been, practically without exception, young and 'raw' airmen fresh from the flying school.

Flight Su-Lieut. Taunton Elliott Viney, R.N.A.S., who bombed and sank the German submarine off the Belgian coast, is no exception to the general rule. He is only twenty-four and took his flying certificate only a few months ago.

The mother of Sub-Lieutenant Viney is living at Frinton-on-Sea with her daughter, Mrs Jamieson, the wife of a London stockbroker. To a representative Mrs Viney said:

'My son was born at Saffron Walden. He lived with us for seven years or eight in South Africa and was educated at Kingswood College, in Grahamstown; and when we came to England he went to Mill Hill School. At the outbreak of the war he returned to the Cape and joined Prince Alfred's Guards and served six months with the Union forces in South Africa. Then, in March of this year, he got a commission in the Armoured Car Squadron of the Royal Naval Volunteer Reserve. In June he obtained a transfer to the air service and on July 1st got his flying certificate and that is all there is to be told about him'. Mrs Viney concluded 'except that we are all very glad and proud.'

Viney was unfortunately killed on a bombing raid on Mariakerke Aerodrome on 21 May 1916. He was flying a newly-introduced Sopwith 1½ Strutter, serial number 9384, and was part of 5 Squadron, 5 Wing at Coudekerkue. His friend, Denis Felkin, claimed that he had crashed his stricken plane into the sea to prevent it falling into enemy hands. He is buried at Oostende New Communal Cemetery, Belgium. The Germans dropped a message that he had been picked up in deep water off Ostende and all efforts to revive him were unsuccessful. They afforded him a funeral with full military honours. His service record recorded that in addition to English he spoke French and that he was a good officer, hardworking and trustworthy.

A pilot of 3rd Squadron, Second Lieutenant **Reginald Davis** of Great Holland, aged 26, was killed during the Somme Offensive on the 20 October 1916. He is buried at Heilly Station Cemetery, Mericourt-Labbe, Somme, Plot V, Row A, Grave 8. The 3rd Squadron was sent to France on the outbreak of war and they initially operated in a reconnaissance role using a variety of aircraft types. They were heavily involved in the Somme offensive and a number of their pilots including Davis were flying French Moranes.

The *Chelmsford Chronicle* reported his death on 10 November 1916:

> Lieutenant R. Davies RFC, son of Mr and Mrs R. H. Davis of Lawn Cottage, Great Holland, was killed on October 20. Deceased was 26 years of age and had been in France about 16 months. He was in Canada at the outbreak of War, Joined the Alberta Dragoons and came over with the first Canadian Contingent. While in France he received his commission in the RFC.

By December 1916 and January 1917 the RFC on the Western Front were at a low ebb as more than half of its casualties had been brought down behind enemy lines and stocks of replacement aircraft were getting very low. General Hugh Trenchard (known as the father of the Royal Air Force), commander of the RFC, wrote to London complaining: 'You are asking me to fight the battle this year with the same machines as I fought it last year. We shall be hopelessly outclassed and something must be done.' As it turn out something was being done and updated versions of aircraft already in service were becoming available. No. 4 Squadron received deliveries of the BE.2g, a machine unfortunately almost identical to the current BE.2e which offered no performance improvements whatsoever.

It was possibly in one of these aircraft on 3 February 1917 that Captain **John Casely McMillan** was wounded by shrapnel from a close 'Archie' burst whilst on an artillery spotting mission. The term 'Archie' was RFC slang derived from an old music hall song called *Archibald, Certainly Not!* and it was used by the British military for German anti-aircraft fire. It came about by the fact that the future Air Vice Marshal Amyas Borton used to sing the song's defiant chorus – 'Archibald, certainly not! – Get back to work at once, sir, like a shot!' – as he flew his aircraft between exploding German shells. He died three days later 6 February 1917 at the age of 24.

John was born on 18 June 1892 in London only son to John and Helen and at the time of his death had been living at 'Duerdon' in Brightlingsea. He initially joined the Royal Scots Fusiliers, service number 204749, achieving the rank of second lieutenant. He obtained his 'flying ticket' (Pilot's Licence) number 2475 at the Military School, Farnborough on the 20 February 1916 in a Maurice Farman Biplane. He is buried at Contay British Cemetery, Contay, France and is commemorated on the Brightlingsea War Memorial and at All Saints' Church, Brightlingsea. He was entitled to the British War and Victory Medals.

Second Lieutenant **Douglas Woodman**, son of Mr George Alfred Woodman of 'Crumlin', Holland Road, Clacton-on-Sea, was killed in action on 11 March 1918 and is buried at the Vadencourt British Cemetery. He was 20 years of age and part of the famous 56th

John Casely McMillan.

Squadron RFC which flew the SE5a fighter/scout aircraft. In addition to successes in the sky, the squadron was also involved in various ground actions by conducting aerial attacks against troop movements and infrastructure such as railways yards and aerodromes. As there was no specific ground battle going on at the time he was killed, one can only assume he was lost in one of the many dogfights.

Not everybody who was killed in either of the air services was lost in action, Second Lieutenant **Alfred Wilfred Tolhurst** from Clacton was in training at Northfleet, Kent when he was killed on 6 October 1916, presumably in an accident. He is buried at Northfleet Cemetery.

Lieutenant **Dudley Howard Hazell**, son of Frederick and Winifred Hazell of Little Saling, Frinton-on-Sea, born in Epsom on 22 September 1895, appears to have initially enlisted in the King's Own Royal Lancaster Regiment following his training at the Royal Military College, Sandhurst (July 1914 to January 1915). In early November 1917 he was admitted to hospital and declared unfit for service for two months. It would appear that it was following this period of illness that he transferred to the newly-founded Royal Air Force. He flew a number of different aircraft and the total number of hours flown solo by the time he was transferred to France was twenty-four. Unfortunately he lost his life in unknown circumstances on 7 September 1918. He is buried at Cabaret-Rouge British Cemetery, Souchez.

Observer Lieutenant **Robert Edmund Horton** and pilot Lieutenant Charles Mossop were both killed in an accident while flying a converted Wight seaplane No 9859 on 12 August 1918 at Port-en-Bessin near Cherbourg, France. It is a little confusing what actually happened: one report states that they were killed while trying to land their damaged aircraft, while another that the tail-plane collapsed on take-off. Both were airman with 243 Squadron. Mossop had previously been awarded the DSO and Robert had been mentioned in dispatches. He was 21 years of age. Robert was born in Walton on 4 November 1897. The 1911 census has him living at Frinton with his grandparents, though at the time of the accident it appears his mother was living in the nearby village of Kirby Cross. He had attended Brighton College from 1906 to 1916 and is remembered on their Roll of Honour. He is buried at Tourlaville Communal Cemetery.

The fact that the war could also be fought in the air enabled the people at home to more fully understand the perils of war even though initially it might have caused little excitement. Sunday, 12 August 1917 was a glorious summer day and very few were giving a thought to the war and air raids, when at 5.40 pm a faint humming sound could be heard. The sound grew louder and people started to look skywards and excitement grew as they spotted nine aeroplanes approaching from the direction of Walton-on-the-Naze. No warning had been given although there was a warning system at Clacton. Initially there seemed some doubt as to whether they were British or not but when they got over the town the local anti-aircraft guns opened up. It took some ten minutes for the nine aeroplanes to clear Clacton's airspace but as soon as they had gunfire from warships opened up on another squadron of aircraft which appeared to be heading towards Margate in Kent.

By this time a great crowd had gathered to watch the spectacle of dogfights, flashes from the guns and shells bursting in the air. There was no panic and the excitement caused soon subsided. Evening church services continued as normal and there was scarcely a vacant seat at the Calonnade Band pavilion.

It transpired that these aeroplanes were part of a group of twenty German Gotha bombers which attacked Southend and Margate. Very little damage was done at Margate, where four bombs were dropped, demolishing a barn and one empty house, and there were no casualties. At Southend the situation was different: some forty bombs were dropped killing twenty-three civilians (eight men, nine women and six children) before our airmen managed to chase them back over the sea.

This incident was reported in the local papers all over Britain plus the national dailies, prompting W.J. Josling from Kingsway, Mildenhall, to pen the following poem:

The Southend Air Raid

While a brilliant sun was shining
O'ver Southend, fair and bright,
Some twenty German aeroplanes
Suddenly hove in sight.

With feverish, haste they dropped their bombs,
On murder they were bent,

And defenceless men and children
To a sudden death were sent.

Many of them were strangers,
Just come down for the day;
But, ah! The sad and aching hearts
Before they went away.

'Vengeance is mine; I will repay,'
Is what our Lord has said;
So we'll leave it there, with a silent prayer,
For the living and the dead.

Although we had taken a bit of a hammering at the Battle of Jutland
and had the U-boat menace to deal with we still managed to control
the seas and we were slowly winning the war in the air, but it was on
land that we had to win to put an end to this disastrous conflict.

CHAPTER 9

The Land War

❧

In all wars the final victory must be won on the land. However irresistible the armed forces of a country may show themselves by sea and air, the naval and aerial arms can never strike the decisive blow. They can guard and protect on the one hand, devastate, cow and paralyse on the other but they cannot break through the last lines of defence. That task must be left to the tanks and their supporting infantry.

This paragraph is from the opening of the foreword to the book *The Battle of Flanders* 1940 by Ian Hay. Although the book is on the opening battles of the Second World War it is also applicable to the First World War and the French Revolutionary and Napoleonic Wars of 1792–1815. Although the aircraft and tanks played a part in the First World War and our heroic navy as in previous conflicts continued to control the high seas, we had to defeat the enemy on land and this we did yet again but as we know it took four long years.

I say again, *if only* the British Army at the start of the war had been as strong in numbers as our allies and enemies the war might not have lasted so long, but we always seemed compelled to start a land war from small beginnings, unlike our navy which was the most powerful in the world, which meant our land forces had either to play for time or take desperate risks until they had been built up into an effective striking force. The entire history of the British Army is one of tales of early defeats, reverses or expensive resistances, only redeemed in the end, as resources and experience accumulated, by final victory.

Being an island with a large empire to defend, we had to put our navy first to ensure that our shores were safe from invasion and only then we could concentrate on building up our military strength and in this war it was going to take nearly two years. It was not going to be until 1 July 1916 when at last we had a highly-trained and fully-equipped army that went charging into the Battle of the Somme. Saying that we must not forget the courageous men of the original BEF who held the Germans for those two years enabling us to prepare for the Battle of the Somme and the final push in late 1918.

As already stated, the French, Russian and German armies were considerably larger than the British Army but it was a highly-trained professional force of approximately 700,000 officers and men. In 1914 the BEF numbered approximately 150,000 men, made up of six infantry divisions and one cavalry division. The infantry division consisted of infantry, artillery, engineers, Army Service Corps, and medical and veterinary services. By the end of the war the British Army consisted of approximately 4,000,000 men, including troops from the Dominions and the colonies.

The army had learnt many lessons from its various colonial wars, in particular the Boer War of 1899–1902. One result was a more practical uniform, one that was less visible, so from the beginning of the Great War the British solider wore a khaki uniform and cap, plus cotton webbing designed to carry all the equipment that an infantryman needed in the field. This comprised cartridge carriers capable of holding 150 rounds of ammunition, haversack, entrenching tool, bayonet, water bottle and pack. The webbing was surprisingly comfortable to wear and comparatively modern. As the war progressed there were a few changes to personal equipment, the first being the introduction of the steel helmet. Trench warfare resulted in a significant number of head wounds from shells bursting overhead. The French adopted a steel helmet in 1915, quickly followed by the British then the Germans in 1916.

The British helmet was designed by John Brodie and therefore became known by his name. A number of modifications were made to the helmet to make it more comfortable. What also became a necessity were gas masks. Initially several makeshift types of masks and goggles were used before the PH Gas Helmet was introduced in October 1915, PH being the chemical phenate hexamine which was impregnated into the cloth of the helmet to neutralize the gas. In the latter part of 1916 a more advanced mask was introduced – the Small Box Respirator consisting of a rubberized fabric mask attached via a tube to a metal canister carried on the chest containing absorbent filters.

The army's rifle was the Short Magazine Lee-Enfield, known as the SMLE for short. The Mk III version was introduced in 1907 with a longer sword bayonet than earlier models. Chambered for .303in ammunition, it had a fast bolt action combined with a ten-round magazine loaded from five-round chargers, which gave it a maximum rate of fire of fifteen rounds per minute. The rifle could also be equipped with a telescopic sniper scope, grenade launcher and wire cutters. Earlier versions of the Lee-Enfield and Lee-Metford were also used until the Mk III became available in sufficient numbers. Trench warfare on this scale was a new phenomenon, so as one would expect specific equipment was adopted such as various forms of periscopes, torches, lanterns, wire cutters and trench pumps.

The major battles in the early months of the war were the Battle of Mons where the BEF fought gallantly against overwhelming odds, followed by the Retreat from Mons and the Battle of the Marne where the BEF and the French eventually halted the German advance some twenty-five miles from Paris. It then became a question of who could get to the coast first and control the ports: the 'Race to the Sea' was on and the various battles that followed from it.

British troops resting behind the lines. (Author's collection)

Buses transferring troops to the Front. (Author's collection)

As the war progressed the maximum period of time the soldiers found themselves in the front-line trenches was normally only two weeks. They would be relieved to recuperate behind the lines. This would include not only a bath and de-lousing but sports, entertainment, extra training, letter-writing etc. This system went a long way to helping the men survive the trenches.

One of the events in the early days of the war that must have either amused or shocked the men was when they were waiting to be transported to the front. It was on 22 October 1914 when troops stared in disbelief at their transport; they expected vans or trucks but instead standing in front of them were thirty-six red London double-decker buses still with advertising painted on them. So as you can imagine there was much amusement among the British troops in particular the 1st Battalion, Connaught Rangers who were part of the Ferozepur Brigade (an Indian Army brigade) and were the first to board the buses at 8.30 am. More than a thousand London buses were sent to serve in France and Belgium during the war. The volunteer drivers found themselves in the army overnight and within a week were out in

France. Drivers would stay on the road for eighteen hours going back and forth collecting troops.

The following are a few stories of our brave men and the battles they fought in. They are not in a chronological order and the men do not all originate from our area but at some stage had a connection to it.

It is very difficult to imagine what it was really like on at the Western Front. Letters sent home by the troops in theory helped their loved ones get a rough idea of what they were going through. However, most of them are rather upbeat, in fact you get the feeling they were really enjoying themselves or maybe they did not want people back home to realize how grim it really was.

The following reports in the local paper in November 1914 give some idea of the bravery of the men. Corporal Raymond Webb, 1st Life Guards, in writing home to his mother of 2 Gordon Cottages, Clacton, informs her that he had been wounded in the leg and also in the ear by shrapnel. While recovering in the base hospital he was given the opportunity to go home but refused, saying he would rather have 'another smack at the enemy'. He then goes on to say that since the injury he has spent three or four days in the trenches, stating that 'it is a very rough job but we are getting round them and it won't be long now before we settle it'.

Then we have Private Frank Selby, 2nd Essex Regiment, Brightlingsea, who was wounded just after the Battle on Mons while taking a dispatch to an officer. He spent time in hospital, returned home and had a bullet removed from his shoulder. On his return he said that he took part in several ferocious bayonet charges and commented that the Germans, several as young as 16, fought shy of the cold steel. He also wrote that the Tommies were quite cheerful and usually entered into the charge singing 'Tipperary' or 'Get out and under'. Among the stories that he related was that a Scottish soldier, who after having his arm blown off by shrapnel, picked it up and took it with him to hospital. Private Selby spoke in praise of the way in which the English officers were treating their men.

The following letters also give us some insight of what it was like at the front.

The first letter dated 8 January 1915 is from James Kenneth Franks who was born in Clacton in 1893. We have been unable to locate his war records other than his medal card but it would appear that he enlisted at Colchester into the 1st Line (1st/1st) Regiment of the Essex Yeomanry.

The Essex Yeomanry was a cavalry regiment formed mainly by volunteers from the east of England. At the outbreak of war the regiment was mobilized along with the Eastern Mounted Brigade and by the end of August 1914 was in Woodbridge, Suffolk and had joined the 1st Mounted Division. At the end of November the 1st/1st Regiment left the Brigade and embarked for France arriving at Havre on 1 December 1915. It joined up with the Royal Horse Guards and 10th Royal Hussars as part of the 8th Cavalry Brigade, 3rd Cavalry Division near Hazebrouck.

> Last Monday our Brigade was called out as a Reserve. We went within a short distance of the firing line and could see the shells bursting quite close. We waited for some time but were not wanted, so we finally went to a farm where we rested for the night. The next day we still waited as reserve until evening when we were relieved by another Brigade. We have now retired to our winter quarters. This morning (Sunday) we saw a very exciting scene in the air. A German aeroplane ventured some distance over the firing line and dropped several bombs on a small town. It was fired upon at the same time and then pursued by two British aeroplanes but I'm afraid it managed to escape.

The next letter is from Trooper Don Wright, also from Clacton, to a friend:

> We get plenty of cigarettes and tobacco out here. One of the things I miss most is some good chocolate which is very dear here. We have to pay 1s 3d for chocolate which we could get in England for 7d.
>
> The weather at present is bitterly cold and always wet and makes me think of 'Sunny Clacton.' It turned out to be my luck on the first night in France to be on Guard which was a great moment. It is very amusing to hear the little French children ask us for an 'Anglaish Souveneer' such as one of our badges or a biscuit. Of course being Cavalry we get very little trench digging but we've had some of it. The entire Clacton Troop is facing the elements in a very good spirit, which is half the battle.

Soup on the way to the troops. (Author's collection)

> We have done a lot of moving since being here. On one
> occasion we travelled in horse trucks for about 18 hours – jolly
> good experience for us. You should see us sometimes; we have
> been three days at a time before being able to wash.

Like James Frank, I cannot locate any war records for Don Wright
other than his medal card and this tells us that he had initially enlisted
into the Essex Yeomanry, probably the 1st/1st Regiment as it states he
embarked to France on 30 November 1914. What is a little strange is
that it appears that at some point he transferred to the Royal Engineers
and then back again to the Essex Yeomanry. Like James he appears to
have survived the war and was awarded the 1914-15 Star along with
the Victory and British war medals.

The first major action the 1st/1st was involved in was the Battle
of Frezenberg Ridge (11–13 May 1915), part of the Second Battle of
Ypres. They made a gallant bayonet charge and succeeded in driving
the Germans from the trenches which threatened the flank of the 27th
Division. Five officers and sixty-five men were killed the attack.

This was followed by the Battle of Loos (26–28 September).
There was very little action for the regiment in 1916. It all changed

in 1917 when they took part in the first Battle of the Scarpe (9–12 April) which was part of the Arras offensive. The regiment's task was to secure the village of Monchy-le-Preux, a vital piece of high ground which at the time was held by German infantry. They had to ride across miles of exposed farmland covered with barbed wire and under constant fire from the enemy trenches but this is what they were trained for.

In letter home to his wife an artillery officer described what he had seen that morning:

> The most wonderful sight, It was a thing one could hardly believe to be real. It was a splendid clear open ground over a slight rise where I was standing at 9 a.m. I had passed them (Essex Yeomanry) on my way up and suddenly they passed me at the trot and as they got level they broke into the charge. They thundered past me with their swords and lances all in line. How they got through the fire I don't know, gaps appeared in their lines and riderless horses were everywhere, but on they went and crashed into the village which they took and held.

But by the time the Yeomanry were relieved two days later 135 of the 600 men who had taken part in the charge were dead, many more were wounded and almost all the regiment's horses, corralled in the town square, had been killed where they stood by a heavy artillery bombardment during which the officer was himself injured.

On 1 March 1918 the 1st/1st Regiment transferred to the 1st Cavalry Division and remained as one of the only six Yeomanry regiments to be posted to a regular cavalry division for the duration of the war. Due to the static nature of the Western Front the cavalry often fought dismounted as infantry. It would appear that Webb, Selby, Franks and Wright all survived the war.

The following are five other men from Clacton and Walton-on-the-Naze who had enlisted into the Essex Yeomanry who unfortunately lost their lives:

John Barker, Private, service number 1261, was killed on 14 May 1915, aged 21, obviously from wounds following the cavalry charge at Frezenberg Ridge. He was the son of Charles and Katherine Baker of the Marine Hotel, Walton-on-the-Naze. Commemorated on the Ypres (Menin Gate) memorial – Panel 5.

Walter Charles Bareham, Corporal, service number 80403, was killed on 11 April 1917, aged 20, presumably one of the 135 men killed in the charge at Monchy-le-Preux. He was the son of Lydia Bareham, Worthing Villas, Page Road, Clacton-on-Sea. Commemorated on the Arras Memorial – Bay 1.

John Arthur Eade, Private, service number 1970, was killed on 15 January 1916. He was the son of Henry and Robina Eade of Cromwell House, Chapman Road, Clacton-on-Sea. Buried at Vermelles British Cemetery.

Henry Edward Botteler, Sergeant, service number 80592, was killed on 10 August 1918, two months before the end of the war, aged 22. He was the son of Edward and Dorothy Bolleter of 19 Crescent Road, Walton-on-the-Naze. Buried at Vignacourt British Cemetery.

Herbert Digby, Trooper, service number 80567, was killed 11 April 1917, aged 43, Resident of Great Holland. He was the son of James and Elizabeth Digby. Commemorated on the Arras Memorial.

The following letter from Private E. Burling of Clacton to his uncle is a little more explicit and gives us a truer idea of what it was like at the front:

> We lost two more of our men; one was killed in the trench and another from a shell from a German big gun. As far as I know only one was wounded, although I thought there would be more. My mate who was killed leaves a wife and three children, what a blow to them. Truly this is a horrible war.
>
> We are having some wet and cold weather and as we only have the clothes we stand up in, they have to dry on us. Some of the trenches we walk through are knee deep in water so we do not always have dry feet.
>
> We have dug outs in the trenches to sleep in if we can snatch the time. It would be a treat to get home for a while and lie in a warm bed at night. I do hope more Clacton men will come out and help finish this dreadful war. They certainly ought to do their bit as we are doing ours.

The Reverend Harry J. Hensman was instituted as the second Vicar of St James's, Clacton, on 20 July 1914. Just over a year later in November 1915 he was called up to serve the army in France. For the next eight months he sent home a monthly letter to be included in the parish magazine, either from 'somewhere in England' or 'somewhere in France'. One such letter in February 1916 thanked the congregation for monies raised for a portable altar with cross, candlesticks and vase, chalice and paten in a case also a large cross and material for altar cloths. By July the Reverend realized that the war would not end as quickly as people thought, so he resigned as Vicar of St James to concentrate on the troops at the front, but by August he was lying seriously ill at the London General Military Hospital suffering from a strained heart. He recovered, however, and continued serving the troops. In 1938 he became Canon of Gloucester Cathedral. He died in 1940.

As we know, throughout the war Clacton had troops stationed there or nearby and at service time the church would be packed with troops. On at least one occasion a thousand people attended. In July 1918 the church received a lovely letter from a soldier, with a gift:

Dear Sir,

When I was billeted at Clacton at the end of last year, I saw you had a new church and an amount was owing on it. I intended putting 2/6d in the box at the church but had to leave quickly one morning in January and did not do so, therefore I send you a postal order for that amount and ask you to put it towards the building fund.

'Tis better late than never. At the same time I must thank you for the enjoyable times I spent in your place for soldiers in, I believe Pier Avenue. I and the other 'boys' used to be very pleased with the puddings the helpers made for us and I must not forget, the genial old gentleman (with the dark cardigan), who was nearly always to be found there. Let us hope they are all well. I remain anon as I do not wish you to acknowledge, feeling sure it will be all right. From yours faithfully, A.A

Amazing that a soldier in the middle of a bitter war can remember and find the time to send such a letter.

Possibly our first fatal land casualty was Captain **John Norwood**, believed to be the holder of the first Victoria Cross awarded during the Boer War in 1899. He was born on 8 September 1876, in Beckenham, Kent. He had a fascinating and unbelievable pedigree that has been traced back to the marriage of the daughter of Harold Bluetooth,

King of Denmark and so of King Olaf of Sweden, in the tenth century.

He joined the 5th (Princess Charlotte of Wales's) Dragoon Guards on 6 February 1899 and was commissioned as a second lieutenant. By 30 October 1899 he was at Ladysmith in South Africa) where he led a patrol that came under heavy fire. While in retreat at full speed, Private Mouncer was shot in the throat. Norwood went back some 300 yards and picked the man up, carrying him on his back under heavy fire from the Boers. He was helped by Private Sibthorpe and later Sergeant Harris. Norwood reported the Sibthorpe's act of valour but made no mention of his role. It

Captain John Norwood VC. (Frinton War Memorial Club)

was only later that the squadron commander, Captain Hoare, learnt the truth and submitted a report of his heroic deed. Norwood tried to insist that he did not want to be recommended for an award but on 20 July 1900 the *London Gazette* reported the award of the Victoria Cross.

> On the 30 October 1899, this officer went out from Ladysmith (S. Africa) in charge of a small patrol of the 5th Dragoon Guards. They came under a heavy fire from the enemy, who were posted on a ridge in great force. The patrol, which had arrived within about 600 yards of the ridge, then retired at full speed. One man dropped and Second Lieutenant Norwood galloped back about 300 yards through heavy fire, dismounted and picking up the fallen trooper, carried him out of the fire on his back, at the same time leading his horse with one hand. The enemy kept up an incessant fire during whole time that Second Lieutenant Norwood was carrying the man until he was quite out of range.

Staying in South Africa, he was promoted to lieutenant on 27 June 1900 and served as a staff officer to Major Bulfin's column in 1902 and

Sketch of Norwood carrying the wounded trooper. (RDG Museum)

was mentioned in despatches. On 14 April 1904 he was promoted to Captain and became adjutant of the Calcutta Light Horse, returning to England in 1907 when he married Lilian Collier. They had three children, one also being named John who became a group captain in the RAF in the Second World War.

John himself was serving in the Westminster Dragoons when war broke out. He transferred back to the 5th Dragoon Guards and they were immediately sent to France. On his 36th birthday, 8 September 1914 he was in command of 3 Troop of 'B' Squadron which had been ordered to attack Sablonnières, during the Battle of Marne. He, along with Captain Robert Partridge and two other troopers, was killed when fired upon by a large force of Germans. It is believed he was trying to help a wounded sergeant in a similar manner as to when he won the VC all those years before.

He was a Freemason, and belonged to the Cavalry Club. His interests were hunting, shooting and tennis. His family owned East View (Ladywood), 15 Third Avenue, Frinton-on-Sea. He was buried at Sablonnières New Communal Cemetery. He is named on the following memorials:

- St Wilfred's Church, Haywards Heath, Sussex.
- Garrison Church, Aldershot, Hampshire.
- St Michael's Church, East Peckham, Kent.

His medals are in the Lord Ashcroft Collection at the Imperial War Museum.

Three days later on 11 September Private **Stanley Everson**, service number 8780, was killed at the Battle of the Marne. He was 27 years of age and serving in the 1st Battalion King's Own (Royal Lancaster

Norwood plaque in St Michael's Church, East Peckham.

Regiment). The majority of the records have the date of his death as 11 September but the battalion records it as being the 8th.

Stanley was born in Wix, Essex, to Frederick and Hannah, but is understood to have been a resident of Clacton on the outbreak of war. He had enlisted in the 1st Battalion King's Own at Colchester, presumably as a reservist but he found himself with the battalion in France on 23 August 1914. Initially the battalion was serving with the 12th Brigade of 4th Division which was held back in England in case of a German invasion but because of the losses suffered by the BEF and the French the decision was reversed and they proceeded to France.

The battalion was involved in the Battle of Le Cateau, the retreat from Mons, and the Battles of the Marne, the Aisne and Armentières. The battalion records read:

> A party under Lieutenant W.E.G. Statter having fought a sharp action killing two then advancing into the town of La Ferte-sons-Jarre, 'D' Company came under fire with Lieutenant L.S. Woodgate and two other ranks killed in the square. A party led by Major R.G. Parker tried to recover Lieutenant Woodgate's body. Stanley Everson was one of the volunteers. Moving into the square the party came under fire. Corporal J.C. Pike was mortally wounded, Private S. Everson killed and Major Parker wounded.

It was at the Marne that the French with the help of the reinforced BEF held the Germans and pushed them back over the river, stopping them from getting to Paris. One of the interesting points of this Battle is that 6,000 troops were transported to the front from Paris by 600 taxis, the first large-scale automotive transport of troops in the history of war. On the 10th the Germans began a general retreat that ended north of the Aisne River where they dug in, resulting in the trench warfare that was to typify the Western Front for the next three years. Stanley was awarded the British and Victory War medals alongside the 1914 Star. He is buried at Montreuil-Aux-Lions British Cemetery, Aisne France. He is commemorated on the Clacton War Memorial and in the UK, in *De Ruvigny's Roll of Honour, 1914-1919*.

One of the first Brightlingsea men to be killed was **Arthur Hawkins Goddard**, born Brightlingsea, 14 July 1895 to Thomas and Susannah

Goddard. He was educated at the London County Council School, Wapping and Raine's Foundation School, Stepney. He worked as a clerk for Girling Bros for four years; before enlisting with some fellow scouts from Toynbee Hall, Whitechapel. He enlisted in the 13th (County of London) Battalion – Princess Louise's Kensington Battalion – on 1 September 1914, rank Private, service number 2500, and after several months' training arrived in France on 10 February 1915.

The regimental/battalion headquarters was close to the home of Princess Louise, daughter of Queen Victoria. King Edward VII was approached by the regiment to ask if Princess Louise would associate her name with the regiment – his consent was given and she took considerable interest in the regiment, organizing the design and production of the regiment's colours. The colours were duly consecrated and presented to the regiment by King Edward VII at Windsor on 19 June 1909. Thereafter the regiment was referred to as the 13th London Regiment. Four years later Princess Louise consented to give her name to the regiment.

Within the month he served with the battalion in the Battle of Neuve Chapelle (10–13 March 1915). This was a surprise attack by the British which included an Indian Corps and they successfully retook the village and positions that the Germans had occupied in October 1914. The infantry advance was preceded by a concentrated 35-minute artillery bombardment by 342 British and French guns, helped by 85 reconnaissance aircraft from the RFC. Though a British success it was also costly, with 12,000 casualties out of 50,000 men involved. The German Sixth Army suffered similar losses and with the British taking 1,200 prisoners.

It is interesting to read the German report on the battle. Although they accept the fact that the British had regained the village,

Arthur Hawkins Goddard. (De Ruvigny's Roll of Honour)

they placed great emphasis on the British casualties with relative little material gain and the stern resolve of the German soldiers' efforts to repulse the attack. The report goes on to say that Indian troops deserted in sizeable numbers to the German side and that the British used German prisoners-of-war as cover for their advance. Both claims are unsubstantiated but propaganda was the name of the game. It was also claimed that 250 Englishmen in German cloaks and helmets lured a group of German soldiers towards them, only to shoot them down at short range – another unlikely story. The report finally said that although the enemy succeeded in winning a slight tactical success and in gaining territory, these successes were quite out of proportion to the enormous losses, particularly of officers, which were characterized as 'heavy' even by the enemy himself. Unsurprisingly they made no reference to their own losses.

Approximately a month later, on 9 May Arthur was wounded in the action at Festubert and died the day after, and is buried at the Military Cemetery at Rue Petillon. He was awarded the 1914-15 Star along with the British War and Victory medals. He is commemorated on the Brightlingsea War Memorial and listed in *De Ruvigny's Roll of Honour*.

James Henry Baker (De Ruvigny's Roll of Honour)

Rifleman **James Henry Baker** from Frinton died on 26 May 1915 following the Battle of Festubert. He was born on 21 August 1875, the second son of Samuel Baker of 17 Hadleigh Road, Frinton-on-Sea. His occupation was that of a postman and he had completed twenty-five years' service at Brixton when war broke out. He had initially joined the 24th Middlesex Volunteers in 1896 but later transferred to the Post Office Rifles of the London Regiment and with the rest of his battalion volunteered for foreign service.

A comrade wrote 'he was wounded severely in my company on

Wednesday night the 25th at Festubert and have just received official information that he died in Bethune Hospital on the 26th and was buried in Bethune cemetery. I knew he was terribly wounded but did not think he was dangerously wounded, as I had the sad task of attending to his wounds; the latter were in both legs, from knees downwards.' His colonel, in writing to express his sympathy to his wife Mrs Eliza Baker, spoke of the 'Many kind things he did to help one'. The above two statements and his photograph appear in *De Ruvigny's Roll of Honour*. He left behind two children, Constance Sophia born 31 December 1901 and James Alfred born 7 December 1904. He was awarded the 1914-15 Star, and the Victory and British Medals.

Ralph Norton, son of Captain John Norton of the barge *Tintara* which was interned at the beginning of the war, was another Brightlingsea boy who volunteered early on following Kitchener's call. He enlisted at Colchester on 15 September 1914. The following day he was in Winchester with the 10th Battalion Rifle Brigade (regimental number S/1489) which formed part of the Second New Army (K2). On 10 October he was appointed acting corporal of the 11th Service Battalion but at his own requested reverted back to rifleman on 6 April 1915. He had spells at Blackdown and Witley and finally at Hamilton Camp, Stonehenge before being sent to France on 21 July 1915, landing at Boulogne.

The battalion had joined 59th Brigade, 20th Light Division and initially they were concentrated in the Saint-Omer area before moving to Fleurbaix for trench experience. Ralph and the division saw their first real action at the Battle of Mount Sorrel, 2–14 June 1916. It was mainly a Canadian operation but supported by the 20th Light Division. After losing the first two phases of the battle, the Canadians regained the ground lost in the final phase but in doing so the Canadians suffered over 8,000 causalities compared to the Germans' 5,500.

Ralph had been made Acting Corporal (unpaid) on 13 March 1916, then following the battle he was promoted to Corporal. The division's next major campaign was the Battle of the Somme or, as I would prefer to refer to it, the Somme Offensive, as it was made up of a number of individual battles over a period of 141 days commencing on 1 July 1916 (or 147 days if you include the preceding six days of artillery bombardment). July 1st goes down as the biggest disaster in British military history, the artillery bombardment having only limited effect on the strong German defences, also warning the Germans that the British were coming. The British suffered 57,470 casualties on this first day which included 19,240 killed. The French suffered 7,000 casualties while the Germans in comparison only suffered 8,000. The British were not really ready for this offensive but the French were having a terrible time at the Battle of Verdun, so to help relieve them the British went on the offensive. It was to continue until 18 November, and consisted of thirteen separate battles:

1. Battle of Albert, 1–13 July.
2. Battle of Bazentin Ridge, 14–17 July.
3. Battle of Fromelles, 19–20 July.
4. Battle of Delville Wood, 14 July–15 September.
5. Battle of Pozières, 23 July–7 August.
6. Battle of Guillemont, 3–6 September.
7. Battle of Ginchy, 9 September.
8. Battle of Flers-Courcelette, 15–22 September.
9. Battle of Morval, 25–28 September.
10. Battle of Thiepval Ridge, 26–28 September.
11. Battle of the Transloy Ridges, 1 October–11 November.
12. Battle of Ancre Heights, 1 October–11 November.
13. Battle of the Ancre, 13–18 November.

In the end the final outcome was stalemate, resulting in 419,654 British casualties (95,675 killed) and 204,255 French casualties (50,756 killed). The Germans suffered just as badly with 465,000–600,000 casualties (164,055 killed) and 30,000 prisoners taken.

A significant event during the offensive was the detonation of nineteen mines under the German front line on 1 July. Those at Lochnagar and Hawthorn Ridge were the largest. At the time the joint effect amounted to the largest artificial non-nuclear explosion in history. Reports claimed that the sound was heard in London and beyond. The mine detonation was eventually surpassed, however, on 7 June 1917 at the Battle of Messines.

A second innovation was the use of tanks for the first time at the Battle of Flers-Courcelette on 15 September. Forty-nine tanks were available but only thirty-two managed to reach the front line. They did not initially have great success other than that their appearance shocked the Germans in a similar way to how those back home were

Mine explosion. (Author's collection)

shocked when Zeppelins first appeared overhead. However, as the war progressed they became more reliable and began to prove their worth.

Ralph's division does not appear to have seen action until the Battle of Deville Wood in mid-July. It was possibly his actions at this battle that resulted in the award of the Military Medal. The report of the award appeared in the *Essex Newsman* on Saturday, 16 December 1916. The paper went on to say that he had previously received the Distinguished Conduct Medal (DCM) However, by this time and well before the Somme Offensive came to an end, he was back home (on 10 September 1916) suffering from influenza and did not return to France until 3 March 1917 where on 14 March his division found themselves pursuing the Germans as they retreated to the Hindenburg Line.

The Hindenburg Line was a formidable German defensive position built between Arras and Leffaux during the winter of 1916/17, a few months before the end of the Somme Offensive. The losses the Germans had suffered at Verdun and on the Somme, together with the Austro-Hungarian armies struggling in Russia and Romania joining the Allies had forced them to fall back to a more defensible position on the Western Front. The Line was some miles behind their front line and from February 1917 they began to withdraw to it. When the

Tank on display in Trafalgar Square, 1917. (Author's collection)

British became aware of what was happening they cautiously followed up until they were brought to a standstill at the outer defences of the line. It would appear it was during one of the various skirmishes approaching the Line that Ralph lost his life on Easter Sunday, 4 April 1917. He is buried at the Neuville-Bourjonval British Cemetery, plot number A51. He was awarded the 1914-15 Star, and the Victory and British War Medals to go alongside his DCM and M.M.

Two other sons of the Norton family were in the Merchant Navy, John Leo Norton, born 1884 who became a master mariner and Edward Norton, born 1889, and both survived the war and continued to live in Brightlingsea. They were both awarded the British Medal, Mercantile Marine Medal and Ribbons to attach.

Returning to that disastrous day 1 July 1916, the start of the Somme Offensive, we find a number of men from the area who were killed.

'I Have a Rendezvous with Death'

I have a rendezvous with Death
At some disputed barricade,
When Spring comes back with rustling shade
And apple-blossoms fill the air –
I have a rendezvous with Death

When Spring brings back blue days and fair.
It may be he shall take my hand
And lead me into his dark land
And close my eyes and quench my breath –
It may be I shall pass him still.
I have a rendezvous with Death
On some scarred slope of battered hill,
When Spring comes round again this year
And the first meadow-flowers appear.
God knows 'twere better to be deep
Pillowed in silk and scented down,
Where Love throbs out in blissful sleep,
Pulse nigh to pulse, and breath to breath,
Where hushed awakenings are dear . . .
But I've a rendezvous with Death
At midnight in some flaming town,
When Spring trips north again this year,
And I to my pledged word am true,
I shall not fail that rendezvous.

By Alan Seeger

Alan was an American poet who volunteered to fight for the French Foreign Legion in 1914 and died at the Battle of the Somme on 4 July 1916. It is reported that he was cheering on the second wave of the advance as he lay dying from his wounds. The poem was published posthumously.

Edgar Lulham Block was born in Holloway in 1892 to William and Kate Block. Edgar enlisted into the 2nd Battalion, Essex Regiment at Walthamstow, appointed lance corporal, service number 15971. The battalion was in the Mailly-Maillet area near the Serre Road and some 1,200m away to the south-west were the Germans. At 8.35 am the battalion advanced into No Man's Land, their objective being the enemy trenches on the Grandcourt Pusieux Ridge. They came under heavy fire from artillery and machine guns and though they initially occupied some German trenches they soon had to abandon them, losing 22 officers and 414 other ranks of which Edgar was one. He is buried at the Serre Road Cemetery and though he is commemorated on the Clacton's memorial, his actual connection to Clacton is unknown.

Private **Sidney Jennings**, service number 23281, was of the 2nd Battalion, King's Own Yorkshire Light Infantry. He was born in Clacton-on-Sea and originally enlisted in the 12th Hussars as Private No 22752 at Colchester. The 2nd Battalion was part of the 97th Brigade, 32nd Division. They went up the line on 1 July in support and went over the top at 7.30 am. They immediately came under heavy machine-gun fire from Thiepval. They made slow progress into the front trench at Leipzig Salient and positions opposite Fort Hindenburg. Hand-to-hand fighting ensued with attack and counter-attack before the battalion retired the following day to Crucifix Corner. It was some time on the first day that Sidney lost his life. His body has never been found. He is commemorated on the Thiepval Memorial but surprisingly he does not appear on the Clacton War Memorial.

Ernest Claude Horton, son of the Reverend E.V. Horton, vicar of Bude, Cornwall and husband of Adele Horton (née Cox) enlisted into the 14th (County of London) Battalion of the London Regiment (London Scottish) as a private, service number 5320. He was living at the time in Westminster, but the 1901 census has him living at Clacton-on-Sea and working as a clerk in the gas works. The battalion was detailed for the attack on Gommecourt, suffering heavy casualties and though they reached the German front line they had to retreat to their start line. It was during this attack that Ernest lost his life and is buried at Thiepval. He is commemorated on the Thiepval Memorial and also on the Clacton Memorial.

Sidney Duncan Grellier Hardie was born in Holloway, Middlesex but was living at Clacton at the start of the Great War. He enlisted as a private, service number 15367, in 'D' Company, 7th Battalion of the Bedfordshire Regiment but later was promoted to corporal. The 7th Bedfordshires were part of 54th Brigade, 18th Division and along with the 11th Battalion Royal Fusiliers they took part in the successful attack on Pommiers Redoubt. The battalion took and held the Redoubt, Beetle Alley and New Trench though on the way they lost nearly all their officers and the total casualties were 321 of which Sidney was one. He, like Ernest above, is buried at Thiepval and is commemorated on both the Thiepval Memorial and the Clacton Memorial.

Lionel Robert Last, was born in Woking, Surrey in 1897. The 1911 census has the family living at Powis Lodge, Edith Road, Clacton-on-Sea and his father William Henry, at the young age of 52, was a retired Cheese Manager. On 7 September 1914, at the age of 19 years and 2 months, he enlisted at St James Street, London, as a private in 'C' Company, 16th Battalion Middlesex (Duke of Cambridge's Own) Regiment. It was known as the Public Schools Battalion, hence the 'PS' prefix to his service number PS462. His occupation at the time was that of a journalist. The Public Schools Battalions were 'Pals' battalions of the British army and were raised as part of Kitchener's Army, originally they were made up of former public schoolboys but later numbers were made up from ordinary volunteers. The question is was our Lionel a public schoolboy? He arrived in Boulogne, on 17 November 1915 and was soon promoted to lance corporal and then to sergeant on 1 May 1916. The battalion joined up with the 86th Brigade of the 29th Division. The battalion saw its first action on 1 July in support of 86th Brigade's attack on Beaumont Hamel. Despite the previous six days of heavy bombardment most of the German wire was intact and the few passages through it were clogged with the dead and dying. The casualties for the battalion were 524 and when Beaumont Hamel was finally taken in November an observer reported that 180 Middlesex soldiers killed on that day were found along with their pay books and personal effects in the sunken road in No Man's Land. Lionel's body has never been found. He is commemorated on the Thiepval and Clacton Memorials. He was awarded the 1914/15 Star, and the British and Victory Medals. His elder brother **Harold Haile Last** had enlisted a month earlier in August 1914 in the 1st Battalion, Honourable Artillery Company as a private, service number 1012. He had died of wounds on 26 April 1915.

James Neil Large, born in 1893 to James and Grace Large of 106, Sydney St. Brightlingsea. He also enlisted in the 16th Battalion Middlesex (Duke of Cambridge's Own) Regiment. He is commemorated on the Thiepval Memorial and the Brightlingsea Memorial. I wonder if he knew Lionel Last.

Percy Graham Simmonds was born at Southend-on-Sea in 1886. The 1911 census has him living with his parents at 'Hillside' Holland Road, Great Clacton. He enlisted into the 9th (County of London) Battalion (Queen Victoria's Rifles) (QVR). The battalion was formed on 1 April 1908 when the volunteer regiments were reorganized into the new Territorial Force. It arrived in Le Havre, on 5 November

1914. It is possible that Percy was with them and therefore involved in the attack to capture Hill 60 which overlooked the Ypres Salient on 17 April 1915. The hill was captured but as expected the Germans counter-attacked and the QVRs had to hold the line. The company commanders were killed and Lieutenant G. Harold Woolley took command, rallying the troops. Woolley helped to repulse the counter-attack, which won him the Victoria Cross.

The QVR's next major offensive was at the Battle of Gommecourt on 1 July 1916. Gommecourt was no more than a number of hamlets dotted amongst rolling farmland. It was the site of a secondary operation with two aims, one to draw some German reserves away from the main Somme offensive further south and the other to try and eliminate a German salient which was centred on the nearby wood. An anonymous soldier of the QVRs wrote: 'We left our trenches under cover of a terrific artillery fire from our own guns and a barrage of fire from German trenches and guns and also machine gun fire from them and also under cover of a tremendous cloud of smoke which we threw out. At 7.30 in the morning we went over in waves at about 40-yard intervals. We walked to the German trenches as if on parade. Several of my pals got hit going over.' At some point in the battle Percy lost his life at the age of 30. The attack was not successful, in fact you could say it was a German victory. The British suffered 6,769 casualties compared to German casualties of 1,241. The few remaining QVRs and others eventually retreated and escaped back into their trenches. Percy is commemorated on the Thiepval Memorial and Clacton Memorial.

William Sterry was born at Lowestoft in 1897 and the 1911 census has him still living there, his occupation being Errand Boy. He enlisted at Lowestoft into the 10th Battalion, Essex Regiment. The battalion commenced their advance at 7.30 am just after the Casino Point mine was blown, the debris from the mine actually injuring a number of the men. They followed up with an attack on Pommiers Redoubt at around 8.30 am and cleared a number of trenches in the vicinity. William was killed some time during the day south-west of Montauban. His body has never been found but he is commemorated on the Thiepval Memorial and the Clacton War Memorial but like a number of others his actual connection to Clacton cannot be established.

The last person presumably from the Clacton area we have a record of losing his life on 1 July 1916 is **Arthur James Wood**. He is commemorated on the Clacton War Memorial, though we cannot find any connection to the area. We can only assume that at the time of the declaration of war he was somewhere in the area, possibly working, because he was only a young man of around 17 or 18 years of age. Arthur was born in Sheffield in 1899 and enlisted as a private, service number 13387, in the 8th Battalion, King's Own Yorkshire Light Infantry (KOYLI). The battalion attacked Authuille Wood in the early hours of the morning and though they had early success they lost 50 per cent of the battalion by early afternoon through machine-gun fire while crossing No Man's Land. They retreated back to the British lines, with only the medical officer and 110 other ranks surviving. Arthur was not among them.

Many families lost more than one son and today it is difficult to imagine what that must have been like but the shock of hearing that you had lost two sons who were in the same regiment on the same day must have been devastating. Charles and Dinah Roper of 'Kenwood', Harold Road, Frinton-on-Sea, lost both their sons, Arthur aged 24 and Frederick aged 25, on 5 August 1915, killed in action at Gallipoli. One can only guess at the anguish suffered by Charles and Dinah.

The *Chelmsford Chronicle* reported on Friday 17 September 1915 that Mrs Roper, of Rush Green, Clacton had received official notification that her two sons Lance Corporal **Arthur Roper** and Private **Frederick Roper**, both 1st Essex, had been posted as missing after fighting on the Gallipoli Peninsula on August 6th.

The 1911 census has Frederick a private, service number 8868 with the 1st Battalion, Essex Regiment. His age is given as 24: it would appear then that he had lied about his age when enlisting because in 1911 he would have only been 19. At the outbreak of war the battalion was stationed in Mauritius: the question is was his younger brother Arthur with him as he had also enlisted into the 1st Battalion, service number 9359.

By December the battalion had returned to Harwich, then in January 1915 moved to Banbury and joined the 88th Brigade of the 29th Division. On the 21 March they embarked for Gallipoli from Avonmouth, arriving at Cape Helles on 25 April 1915. From the outset they found themselves in action in the First, Second and Third Battles of Krithia, the Battle of Gully Ravine and finally where the boys lost their lives on the first day of the Battle of Krithia Vineyard.

The battle against the Turkish forces was intended as a diversion at Helles to divert attention from the imminent launch of what was to be a major August offensive. Because of the shortage of artillery, the attack was split in two with the 88th Brigade attacking on the afternoon of 6 August while brigades of the 42nd (East Lancashire) Division attacked the following day. Although the 88th Brigade initially managed to capture some Turkish trenches they were driven back. Several more attempts were made by the British but they failed to hold any ground other than a small area known as 'The Vineyard'. The 88th Brigade though was effectively destroyed as a fighting force. Both Arthur and Frederick were awarded the 1914-15 Star, and the British and Victory medals. They are buried at the Twelve Tree Copse Cemetery, Gallipoli, Turkey and remembered on the Clacton War Memorial.

The first St Osyth man to be killed appears to have been Lance Corporal **George Emmerson** on 14 September 1914. He was just 20 years of age but had been in the army for three years. He first enlisted on 14 September 1911, still only 17, in the 3rd Battalion, Norfolk Regiment, Special Reserves. Then on 16 January 1912 he re-enlisted at Colchester into the 1st Battalion, Norfolk Regiment. His occupation at the time of enlistment was stated as Gardener and his religion, Wesleyan. On 23 December 1912 he was promoted to lance corporal.

He was born in 1894 to Samuel and Eliza at St Osyth. The 1911 census has the family, which at the time also included his three sisters Florence, Edith and Violet, living at Mill Street, St Osyth. His occupation was listed as Farm Labourer. He had an elder brother Samuel who was already in the army. This was probably the reason that George was so eager to join up.

It would appear that he was a bit of a lad as he found himself in trouble for minor offences such as being absent from parade, slackness on parade and neglect of duty and was punished with either three days CB (Confined to Barracks) or reprimands. These misdemeanours all occurred while he was with the 3rd Battalion. On signing up for the regular army as his record says he transferred first to Aldershot then onto Holywood in Belfast in November 1912 where they became part of the 15th Brigade, 5th Division. The regiment stayed there until it sailed to France as part of the BEF, landing on 14 August 1914 at Le Havre.

British soldiers in retreat. (Author's collection)

On 23 August 1914 the 5th Division and the rest of the BEF faced the Germans at the Mons Canal, the first British battle on European soil since the Battle of Waterloo in 1815. The German guns had opened fire on the British positions, focusing on the northernmost point of a salient formed by a loop in the canal. The Germans enjoyed a two-to-one numerical advantages along with 600 guns but thanks to the rapid fire of their bolt-action Lee-Enfield rifles the Germans at one point believed that the British had massed numbers of machine guns. The selection of positions by the 5th Division was a matter of the greatest difficulty, the ground being a wilderness of deep ditches, straggling buildings, rough roads and tracks, and high slag heaps. Fortunately on the enemy side the conditions were almost identical. Although the British were holding their own they were slowly being pushed back but at around 8 pm the Germans had had enough so withdrew for the day. British casualties after nine hours of fighting were 1,600. The Germans casualties were closer to 5,000.

The BEF were elated and expected more success the following day. However, due to the general retreat of the French Fifth Army, which left the BEF in danger of being surrounded, the decision was made to retreat also. The Great Retreat, also known as the Retreat from Mons, is the name given to the long withdrawal to the River Marne. For some 200 miles, the BEF was followed by the German First Army and fought a series of rearguard actions in order to protect the retreat.

The long retreat from Mons can only be described as a miracle and, as already mentioned, ended at the river Marne just north of Paris, where the BEF turned to help the French defeat the Germans at the Battle of the Marne (5–12 September). One despondent German commander told the Kaiser that the war was lost but as we know it was going to take another four years of trench warfare to prove him right.

Not only did the Allies halt the Germans at the Marne but they were also in retreat, but unfortunately the Allied forces were slow to exploit this owing to fatigue etc, and the Germans eventually dug in on the north bank of the River Aisne. So on the evening of the 12th the Battle of Aisne commenced. Fighting was eventually abandoned on the 28th once it became clear to the Allies that they would not be able to mount a frontal attack upon the well-entrenched German positions. However, as we now know it was too late for George: he had lost his life on the 14th presumably in this battle. The *Essex Newsman* reported him missing on the 31 October 1914: 'Lance-Corpl. G Emmerson, of the 1st Norfolk Regt, whose home is at St Osyth is reported by the War Office as wounded and missing since the 14 September.' He is buried at the La Ferté-sous-Jouarre Memorial Cemetery. He would have been awarded the 1914 Star, British War Medal and the Victory Medal.

Samuel Emmerson was approximately two years older than George. He had enlisted into the Royal Field Artillery and the 1911 census has him stationed at the Louisberg Barracks, Bordon, Hampshire, with the 134th Battery, rank bombardier, service number 59093 (bombardier is the equivalent of corporal). Unfortunately like many others I have been unable to find his service records and therefore have not been able to trace his military career other than the circumstances of his death. He appears to have been with the 29th Division Ammunition Column, Royal Field Artillery, who boarded the SS *Marquette* when she set sail from Alexandria in Egypt to Salonika in Greece on 19 October 1915. On board were 22 officers and 588 other ranks of the 29th Division Ammunition Column with its vehicles and animals. Also on board were eight officers, nine NCOs and seventy-seven other ranks of the New Zealand Medical Corps and equipment and stores of No.1 New Zealand Stationary Hospital, including thirty-six nurses, plus the ship's crew of ninety-five, giving a total of 741 personnel aboard

Marquette was being escorted for the first four days of her voyage by the French destroyer *Tirailleur*. At 9 am the day after the destroyer left her she was hit by a torpedo from the German submarine *U-35*. Those not killed in the explosion moved quickly to put on lifebelts and moved to lifeboat stations but chaos reigned, one of the lifeboats fell on another, others got tipped over as they were being lowered with the survivors falling into the sea. The ship went down within ten minutes. Many died from exposure and exhaustion while others were picked up by the British destroyer *Lynn* and the French destroyers *Tirailleur* and *Mortier*. One hundred and sixty-seven men and women (nurses) died including our Samuel. Eliza and Samuel Emmerson had lost their second son. One group miraculously survived by reaching Greece by themselves six days later on 29 October. *U-35* had been sent to the eastern Mediterranean to support the struggling Austrians and Turks. She became one of the most successful U-boats of the First World War, sinking 224 ships, some using her deck gun after the crew had been allowed to abandon ship. Samuel's body was never found. He is commemorated not only on the St Osyth war memorial but also on the Mikra Memorial, Thessaloniki, Greece. He was awarded the 1914-15 Star, and the British War Medal and Victory Medal.

Approximately 41 per cent of the men of the village of St Osyth joined up, so you can imagine that for a time it must have been very quiet, perhaps even a little eerie but it was not long before all this changed with the 1st Royal Devon Yeomanry with their horses and gun carriages. The officers occupied the Priory main house and the troops initially slept under canvas on Jubilee Piece, off Mill Street but later wooden barracks were erected. The horses were stabled around the village at the various farms, with veterinary stables being set up in the Priory stables.

The commanding officer was Captain Edward Hain, who was so taken by the village that he rented a cottage on Spring Hill for his wife, household and dogs. Edward was born in 1887 in St Ives, Cornwall to Sir Edward Hain, Chairman of the Hain Steamship Company

Captain Hain with his dogs. (Phyllis M. Hendy)

Ltd, also MP for West Cornwall and Catherine Seward. He was educated at Twyford School, Winchester College and New College, Oxford. While at Oxford he was secretary of the University Dramatic Society and he performed the part of Puck in a production of *A Midsummer Night's Dream* in 1908. The previous year he performed in *Henry IV Part 1* as both Bardolph and Mistress Quickly during the scene in which the two are arguing – with each other! He was a keen footballer and cricketer and in 1906 he headed the Winchester averages with 67.66 which included a forceful innings against Eton, he also represented Cornwall and while at university he scored 26 in the Oxford Freshmen's match. He was also fond of hunting and while living in St Ives formed the Porthia Beagles Hunt.

His first year at work was at Readhead's shipbuilding yards at South Shields to obtain practical experience in construction of steamships and marine engineering. Then he went travelling, working for a few months in one of the largest shipping offices on the Continent. On his return he joined his father's firm, became a partner in E. Hain & Sons and then a director of Hain's Steamship Company.

On 8 June 1912 he joined the 1st Royal Devon Yeomanry as a lieutenant and on 8 August 1914 was promoted to captain. He was often referred to as Teddy and in 1913 he married Judith Wogan-Brown the daughter of former Lieutenant Colonel F.W.N. Wogan-Brown, formerly of the Hussars.

The 1st Royal Devon Yeomanry were part of the Army Reserve. By the outbreak of war the regiment were equipped as Hussars and consisted of four squadrons – 'A', 'B', 'C' and 'D' – and were known as the Cornish Squadron. On the outbreak of war many members including Teddy volunteered for

Hain on horseback.

overseas service. The Yeomanry were mobilized as part of the 2nd South Western Mounted Brigade but as the war on the Western Front had reached a stalemate, there was little need for cavalry, so in September 1915 the unit was dismounted and got ready for their deployment to Gallipoli as Infantry.

On 9 October 1915 Teddy, now commander of 'A' Squadron, landed at Suvla Bay, approximately five miles north of Anzac Cove. They were set to work in an area west of Karakol Dagh in digging trenches, and constructing and reinforcing dugouts. Then on 30 October the regiment spent their first three hours in the front line before spending the next three days constructing dugouts and trenches in the second line south of Karakol Dagh.

On 3 November the regiment moved into the trenches at Jephson's Post, a relatively quiet spot, the only threat being the odd Turkish sniper and a very occasional shell but on 11 November, just a few hours before the regiment was due to leave Jephson's Post for a well-earned rest, Hain was killed when his dugout suffered a direct hit. At the time he was discussing the hand-over of his section with the incoming officer. The regimental war diary records the event: 'November 11th Suvla-at 10.45 hours D43 was shelled. Captain

Edward Hain was killed in his dug-out and two men wounded, one dangerously.'

Lord Vivian, commanding officer of the Cornish Squadron, in a letter to Hain's family had this to say: 'Words fail me to say how deeply we all feel the loss of our gallant comrade and friend and he had proved himself to be a very brilliant officer . . .' all ranks of which would have followed him everywhere . . .' He went on to say that on one occasion when Hain had heard that one of Hain Line's ships, the SS *Trewellard*, was in Suvla Bay, he went on board and persuaded the captain to part with some of the ship's stores which he distributed – not only to his own men but to his former troopers in the Cornish Squadron. Corporal Pearce who attended Teddy's funeral, wrote; 'It's a terrible affair and it has cast quite a gloom over the whole regiment, we could not spare him, not only on account of his being so popular with all ranks but because he was really a clever soldier.' He continued, 'He was in his dugout when a shell pitched right on top, killing him instantly.'

Back home during the November meeting at the Masonic Hall at St Ives, the Secretary of Tregenna Lodge No. 1272 reported that one of its members, Captain Edward (Teddy) Hain of the 1st Royal Yeomanry had been killed at Gallipoli on 11 November. The family were hit hard on the news of his death and his father Sir Edward Hain never really recovered from his death and two years later he suffered a severe breakdown and died on 20 September 1917. A memorial fund was set up by the Hain Steamship Company and with Lady Hain contributing, an attached property overlooking St Ives Bay was purchased and a new hospital in 1920 was opened by the Mayor in honour of Captain Edward Hain and has been in operation ever since – The Edward Hain Memorial Hospital. Lady Hain also donated land near the parish church for the erection of a war memorial which she unveiled in November 1922.

Just prior to the 1st Royal Devons leaving St Osyth they had taken up a collection in appreciation of their reception in the village. Two silver-topped cruets for wine and water and a solid silver box for wafers were presented to the Church. The box bears the inscription:

A Thank offering to St Osyth Church from the Officers and men
of the Royal 1st Devon Yeomanry Sept. 1915.

On 26 November 1915 the *Exeter and Plymouth Gazette* reported that the ladies of St Osyth had raised funds to send cigarettes out to the 1st Royal Devon Yeomanry: I wonder if this was prompted by the death of Captain Hain.

> The people of St Osyth, Essex, where the 1st Royal Devon, Yeomanry were stationed for a year before their departure for the Mediterranean, have this week sent a Christmas present and reminder of the good feeling that existed between them and the regiment. Some ladies of the village organized a whist drive and with the proceeds and other subscriptions, were enabled to send a parcel of 5,000 cigarettes to the Colonel for distribution among the men. A letter from the Vicar of St Osyth, on behalf of the parish, was enclosed with the parcel, conveying the best wishes and kind remembrances of all.

The village were as dismayed as if the unit was one of their own as news filtered through of the dreadful losses being sustained by the Devons at Gallipoli, including the death of Sergeant Harris who appears to have become the sweetheart of a Miss Ann Ramplings. The final chapter of the Devons' involvement at St Osyth's was the village watching with compassion as the widowed Mrs Judith Hains, packed up her home and returned to the West Country.

In November 1915 a new chapter opened in the village as the Gloucester and Worcester Regiment arrived to continue their cycle of twelve months' training, though possibly due to the experience with the Devons the community became a little more reserved. **Arthur Anderson Dean** was born in 1893, in Berkhamsted, Hertfordshire, but by 1901 his family had moved to Hadleigh Road, Frinton-on-Sea. The 1911 census has Arthur stationed at Warley Barrack, Brentwood. He had enlisted into the 1st Battalion of the Essex Regiment, service number 98(6)42. He was just 18 years of age and his occupation was given as Gardener.

It would appear that he was in Mauritius with the regiment when war broke out. They returned to England in December and on 18 January the regiment moved to Banbury to join the 88th Brigade, 29th Division. They were training for France when orders were received that they were going to Gallipoli. On 1 March they set of from Avonmouth via Malta to Alexandria then on to Mudros. They reached Cape Helles, Gallipoli, on 25 April 1915, arriving at 9.30 am. They came under fire immediately and it took them until 2 pm to get a small foothold by taking Hill 138 and the first enemy defensive position. Over the next few days they made slow progress under very heavy fire and on 2 May they managed to take another defensive position but it was costing them heavy casualties.

On 5 May the division attacked Fir Tree Wood which was fiercely defended and were finally beaten back. The division lost nearly half its strength, although the 1st Essex were comparatively lucky with 15 men killed and 142 wounded but one of the dead was our Arthur. He is commemorated on the Helles Memorial, Turkey and Frinton War Memorial and he was awarded the 1914-15 Star, and the British War Medal and Victory Medal.

We are not sure when he enlisted but **Adolphus Joy** of 45 Cambridge Road, Clacton-on-Sea' joined the 1st Battalion of the Grenadier Guards, service number 13690, and appears to have been stationed with them at Warley, Essex. The battalion joined up with the 20th Brigade of the 7th Division and moved to Lyndhurst. They left for the front on 7 October 1914, landing at Zeebrugge.

A month later, on 13 November, the *Chelmsford Chronicle* printed the letter he sent to his mother in Clacton:

> Just a line to relieve your mind and to let you know I am safe so far after a week's hard fighting in the trenches. We have lost a lot of our battalion and I have had some narrow escapes. We get plenty of food when we do have a chance to have it. The Germans tried to rush our trenches the other night but they met with a warm reception. I cannot stop to write much as we are on the move again. We had a wash this morning – first one for three days. Should be very pleased if you could manage to send some fags on.

I wonder if he ever received his fags, as he was killed on 26 October 1914, midway through the First Battle of Ypres. During a night attack on the 25 October a German raiding party were heard to shout 'Don't shoot we are the South Staffords'. The eagled-eyed sentries, however, spotted their distinctive Pickelhaube helmets and open fired on the party, killing several and scattering the rest. Then on the 26th heavy shelling rained down on the 1st Grenadier Guards, burying and suffocating many of them under three feet or more of earth. It is possible this is how Adolphus lost his life. However, it would appear from the *Chelmsford Chronicle* report of Friday, 1 December 1916 that he had been taken prisoner after the Battle of Ypres and died while in German hands. The paper went on to say that Mrs Joy had four other sons in the Army. He is buried at Tyne Cot Cemetery, Passchendaele. He was awarded the 1914 Star, and the Victory and British War Medals and is commemorated on the Clacton War Memorial.

This battle took place after the Battle of Marne in late September 1914. The so called 'Race to the Sea' began. Germany only had a small coastline so they were desperate to extend it. The race, however, ended in mid-October at Ypres, the ancient Flemish city with fortifications guarding the ports to the English Channel and access to the North Sea. Fighting commenced on 19 October 1914 and only ceased on 22 November 1914 with the arrival of the winter weather which brought the battle to an end.

Although a critical victory for the Allies both sides suffered heavy losses. The 1st Battalion, for example, were left with only 4 officers and 200 men. This defence of Ypres ensured that the war in the West would not be over as quickly as the Germans had hoped. Fighting around the Ypres Salient, as it became known, would resume again in April 1915 with the Second Battle of Ypres and again with the Third, also known as the Battle of Passchendaele, from 31 July to 10 November 1917. The Fourth Battle of Ypres, also known as the Battle of Lys, followed between 9 and 19 April 1918, and then finally the Fifth Battle of Ypres, from 28 September to 2 October 1918.

On Thursday, 21 January 1915 the *Gloucestershire Echo* reported that Lieutenant **Anson Lloyd Silvester** of the 2nd Battalion Royal Sussex Regiment had been killed in action

Lieutenant Anson L. Silvester. (Great Clacton Church collection)

on 3 January. Anson was the son of the Reverend James Silvester of Great Clacton. The family had only just received a cheery letter from him on Christmas Day. He was born on 11 December 1888 in Walcot Bath to Constance and James, James being the local senior curate. Because of his job the family had moved several times, to Cublington in Buckinghamshire, to Stonehouse in Gloucestershire and then to Nympsfield in the Cotswolds before the family eventually settled in Great Clacton where his father became the rector of St Johns. By now Anson had learnt how to play the piano and organ, so at the Wednesday and Sunday evening services he would play the organ. He became a pupil at Ascham College, Clacton from where he gained a place at Jesus College Oxford to study History. In the meantime in 1905 he joined the Officers' Training Corps (OTC). His brother joined him at Oxford in 1910. He graduated in 1912 with a 2nd Class honours degree. Anson was quite an accomplish sportsman and during the summer holidays he and his brother would help out at children's holiday clubs. As member of the OTC he was one of the guards of honour at the funeral of King Edward VII and at the coronation of King George V.

On 6 September 1913 he enlisted in the 9th Royal Sussex Regiment Special Reserves as a second lieutenant. He spent time in Germany in the spring of 1914 to improve his German, having also studied French. He was helping out at a YMCA camp when war broke out. His intention was to join the consular service for which he had received the necessary nomination. However, on mobilization he was recalled to his regiment at Chichester and for a short time was stationed at Dover.

On 26 September 1914, the day before Anson set sail from Southampton for Calais, his father held at Farewell service at Church.

Trust in God
Spiritual Counsel for these days

'Trust in the Lord and do good.'
Psalm xxxvii, 3.
'Trust in God and even if anything should happen we will meet in the realms above . . . . God be with you till we meet again'
A.L.S., Sept.26th, 1914.

Along with seven other officers and 124 men, on 8 October he joined the 2nd Battalion in the front line just north of the River Aisne.

He was given command of the 9th Platoon of 'C' Company with W. Smethurst as his platoon sergeant. The battalion HQ was based in a tiny hamlet called Troyon, just below the Chemin des Dames. Although this part of the line saw little activity it was still fairly dangerous due to heavy artillery fire. Then on Fifteen October they were relieved by French troops and they joined up with the rest of the BEF and moved further north to the area of Ypres. He boarded a train with his battalion at Fismes, after a night march of fifteen miles. A three-day train journey took them to Cassel where they were billeted in the town. On 20 October, the battalion was again on the march, this time into Belgium. As they marched they could hear heavy artillery fire: the First Battle of Ypres had begun.

They were billeted at Elverdinghe, moving on to Boesinghe where they remained for a few days before finally marching to Ypres. The battalion was still being held in reserve when on the 26th they moved east of Ypres to the area of Haalte. Then the following day they relocated several kilometres away to Chateau Wood. On the 28th they were off again crossing, the Menin Road and taking up a position in Polygon Wood but the next day they found themselves back at Chateau Wood. During all this to-ing and fro-ing, and though not involved in any fighting they lost two officers, a horse and a man, and three others wounded, to shelling.

On the 30th the Germans started shelling Chateau Wood; the battalion was immediately ordered to move round south towards Zandevoorde where they took up position in Sanctuary Wood. Though not in the thick of the fighting, which was going on around Gheluvelt to the east and Zandevoorde to the south, they still lost 5 officers killed and 394 men killed, wounded or missing. By 3 November the British somehow held the various sectors under attack, although many of the men had not had water or food for forty-eight hours. On the 9th the battalion was relieved and they retired to Hooge but continued to face constant shelling and low-level attacks, but they held on.

It would have been during this period that Anson would have written home and an extract from his letter was printed in the *Chelmsford Chronicle* on Friday, 6 November 1914, a complete contrast to many of the letters that were received from the soldiers at the front:

The innkeeper used to get very nervous when he heard of the firing of the guns and often asked me to tell him confidently when I thought it was necessary for safety to depart. His wife and family and many of the women of the village had already gone. One day we got a little shrapnel over and you should have seen the excitement everywhere. People began to push off everywhere and we saw a huge cart, full of women and children, going to safety. When the shells began to burst just over the village he solemnly dressed himself in his best and almost with tears in his eyes, entrusted his house to us to be at our disposal and pushed off some miles back. The soldiers had the run of everything in the inn; not a thing was locked up. Next day, as things were quieter, Monsieur turned up quite early with a beaming face, expecting to find half his things gone. He couldn't make it out, as he went up and down and found not a thing touched and yet the soldiers had been there all the time. Finally he came to us and expressed his entire admiration for the British Tommy and for the excellent discipline which prevailed.

A couple more letters that were printed in the local press at this time do not really give you an idea of what it was really like; one can only assume they did not want to worry their loved ones.

Six days later the 1st Division, of which the battalion was part, were on their way for a well-earned rest arriving six days later in a blizzard at Hazebrouck, where the officers were granted ninety-six hours' leave. Anson took advantage of this, since because of the terrible conditions he had developed a persistent cough, and he went back home to Great Clacton to recuperate but was back at the front with his regiment on the 23rd, although he had not completely recovered. A couple of days later he received a letter from his mother to say she was in Boulogne and whether he could get time off to meet her at the Hotel Boulogne. Whether this meeting took place is not known but a further letter home on 5 December stated that he was feeling much better.

Anson and the battalion stayed behind the lines for the next couple of weeks during which Field Marshal Sir John French thanked them for their efforts around Ypres. The King also visited the battalion. Training continued until 20 December when they received orders to move south to Cambrin. This time part of the journey was made in buses followed by a march on foot that took a couple of days and between 21 and 23 December they were involved in a number of skirmishes during which one officer was killed and two wounded and twenty-eight other ranks killed, wounded or missing.

The battalion rested over Christmas but it is doubtful if Anson was aware of the Christmas Truce that was taking place in parts of the front line. On Boxing Day they took up a position on the right of the British line, north of the La Bassée canal just south of Givenchy. Due to ninety of its men being hospitalized, 'C' Company had effectively ceased to exist so men from the Northants Regiment had been sent to reinforce the battalion. Anson took command of one of the platoons that was held back in reserve.

On the evening of 30 December the Germans captured an observation position and machine-gun post on the south bank of the canal. A counter-attack was planned for later that night involving Anson commanding 9th Platoon and 'B' Company. They crossed the bridge and with 9th Platoon leading got within 30m of the Germans who opened up with heavy machine-gun and rifle fire. Anson and eleven of his men were hit immediately.

Later his platoon sergeant, W.R. Smethurst, wrote to the family:

> We had some very rough times together, shared each other's rations and always the same dug out during that awful time we had last October at Ypres. About that time he contracted that bad cough that he had and I tried many a time to get him to go to hospital but he would not. When he went on leave I never expected that he would come back to us again as he really was not fit . . . we crept up to 30 yards of them [the Germans] when they opened on us a terrific fire both from machine guns and rifles. Your son fell practically at the first shot and so did 11 men out of 20. I spoke to Mr. Silvester and asked him if he was badly hit. He did not answer my question but ordered me to take the men away and retire back to our old position. He must have expired almost immediately.

His parents were informed of his death by telegram received at the vicarage on 4 January 1915, but his body was not located until 11 January. He was buried in the Communal Cemetery at Cuinchy, just behind where he fell. He was awarded the 1914 Star, and the Victory and British War Medals. He is commemorated at Cuinchy Communal Cemetery in France, on Great Clacton's Roll of Honour as well as a memorial to him on a communion rail in St John's Church, on Clacton-on-Sea's Roll of Honour, on the Roll of Honour in the Chapel of Jesus College, Oxford and in *De Ruvigny's Roll of Honour*.

Anson's father in addition to his Christian work was also a very good poet and a number of his works appeared in the local paper. The following, *A Hero's Death*, appeared in the *Chelmsford Chronicle* on Friday, 25 December 1914:

> Boldly he led the vanguard
> Through pine wood dark and high,
> While the load rifle rattle
> Told of the foemen nigh.
>
> Then many of his company
> Did round about him fall,
> And he for reinforcements
> Made pressing instant call.
>
> But he by swift misfortune
> Was sorely struck and bled
> Till his kind sergeant comrade
> Bound up his wounded head.
>
> Then with a draught of water
> He felt refreshed for fight;
> Nor would turn back for shelter
> He while he safely might.
>
> He said, of invitation
> As given by his friend,
> 'First I must see this business
> Through to the very end.'
>
> But when he thus had spoken,
> Ere he command could tell,
> He once again was smitten,
> And to earth he fell.
>
> And so he died for Britain,
> His duty bravely done –
> A noble Christian warrior,
> His crown of victory won.

His men will not forget him,
To them a brother dear.
Though they by death have lost him
No more to meet him here.

O brave, heroic spirit,
Be ours to follow thee.
That so we may inherit,
Thine immortality.

The poem was to commemorate Lieutenant Leslie Robert Croft of the 10th Platoon, 'C' Company, 2nd Battalion Royal Sussex Regiment who fell in action on 31 October 1914. He was born in Farnham and had no connection to the Clacton region other than being a close friend of Anson (9th Platoon, 'C' Company) and it is possible that he was one of the five officers killed in the fighting around Gheluvelt. Leslie was shot in the head but refused to leave the men and get to safety. He was then shot through the neck, dying instantaneously.

A letter from a man who had served with Leslie and saw him die was printed in the Farnham Grammar School magazine, where he had been a pupil:

> Mr Croft, finding the enemy too strong for us, sent for assistance. A few minutes after, he was wounded in the head. I bandaged his wound, having done this, I selected the best way for him to get safely away. To my great surprise he refused to leave, his only answer to my suggestion was, 'I must see this job finished first.' These happened to be his last words of our officer and hero, for he just raised his head to give some command when a bullet passed through his neck. In conclusion allow me to say that we all realized we had lost not only an officer and a leader but a great friend. For Lieutenant Croft was a great a hero as anyone who has fallen or who will fall in this great campaign, he remained at his post when thousands would have left.

So like many other officers and men, his short but gallant military career came to an end. It was also the end of the original BEF.

The Christmas Truce of 1914 has become one of the most famous episodes of the First World War. It is amazing considering the world was in the middle of the most devastatingly violent war it had ever known. As the decades have passed with the story being told time and time again we have come to believe that for a short period men from both sides emerged from the trenches and met in No Man's Land to exchange greetings, gifts and play football. The following letter from an unidentified lieutenant, first published in the *Daily Mail* in late December, lends credence to the idea that such events did take place:

> An extraordinary thing happened between us and the Germans yesterday. We are so close in our trenches that we can talk to the Germans, and yesterday we got quite friendly. After a lot of talking and shouting to each other, we arranged that one of our men should go out half way and meet a German and that there was to be no shooting meanwhile. Both men got up at the same time and went out, everyone in the opposing trenches looking out over the tops of them. The men met and shook hands amid cheers from both trenches. Our man gave the German some cigarettes and received in return some chocolate. Then I went out and met a German and did the same, and so did a few others. I went right up and stood on the parapet of their trench and talked to them. Several spoke English quite well. They said they were very sick of it, and added, 'Hurry up and finish this cursed war'. They told us they were in a bad state as regards water in the trenches but were fed fairly well and got letters about every five days. We had quite a long talk, and then one of their superior officers came along, so they said, 'Get back'. So back we got, and then they fired very high over our heads just to warn us that they were going on as before, evidently to satisfy their superior officers. They were very sporting, and played the game perfectly. We asked them whey the sniped such a lot, and said 'Why don't you chuck it? It's a terrible nuisance'. Funnily enough, they never fired a shot while we were relieving last night.

From further reports from brigades, regimental war diaries and veterans, there is no doubt that at some places along the front unauthorized truces did actually take place but it was far from the mass event that we have been led to believe.

Back home the people were becoming only too aware of the conditions their loved ones in France were putting up with and that they would not be home by Christmas. So throughout the month, 460,000 parcels and 2.5 million letters were sent to British soldiers in France. King George V sent a card to every soldier, and his daughter, Princess Mary, lent her name to a fund which sent a small brass tin of gifts, including tobacco or writing sets, to serving soldiers. General Haig even records in his diary for 24 December: 'Tomorrow being Xmas day, I ordered no reliefs to be carried out and troops to be given as easy a time as possible.'

The Germans too received small gift boxes – along with tabletop Christmas trees and festive wreaths with which to celebrate the season – and it would appear it was them that made the first move by placing the small Christmas trees etc on the top of their trenches and singing 'Stille Nacht' ('Silent Night'). The British a little surprised responded with the 'The First Noel' with both sides finally singing 'O Come all ye faithful'. Then slowly, along parts of the front, some men responded by tentatively emerging from their trenches into No Man's Land. In addition to exchanging greetings etc, it gave either side the opportunity to remove their dead and injured. There is no doubt that small-scale kickabouts took place but not the organized football matches we have been led to believe, although one unknown soldier wrote 'We sent a cyclist back to find a football and on his return we played them a match winning easily 4-1.'

It would appear that it was only the British that joined in with this Christmas spirit. The Belgian, Indian and French troops who witnessed episodes of fraternization were at best puzzled and at worst furious that British troops were being friendly towards the Germans.

The Christmas Truce

Been up the front for hours,
The day is getting old,
Fighting in winter showers,
My boots are filled with mould.

It's Christmas Eve this evening,
I wish I was at home,
To see my children waiting,
Till Christmas day has come.

And as I start to ponder,
That this war would never end,
I see a sort of wonder,
But it's hard to comprehend.

Are the 'Fritz' surrendering?
Or is it a sign?
Is a Christmas miracle happening?
Will we all be fine?

Oh wait, now I hear singing,
Coming from their side,
I find a sense of feeling,
Which I'd be shot just to abide.

'Merry Christmas' I say willingly,
'Frohliche Weihnachten' he replies,
He's almost as scared as me,
I see it in his eyes.
But that isn't all I see there,
A kind and friendly soul,
He doesn't want to be here,
Like me, he's wet and cold.

All the soldiers with their meals,
All look at us in awe,
As we shake hands on the battlefield,
Never seen before.

So that one Christmas morning,
We paused the dreadful war,
For peace and love and caring,
Until the very next morn'.

And then we're back to fighting,
Until this war is through,
But we'll always be recounting,
The wonderful Christmas.

By Kayleigh Porter (13 years old – the author's
granddaughter)

However, in other parts of front, bloody battles were still taking place and those that dared to stick their heads above the parapet of the trench were met not by gifts but by gunfire.

Not only on the Western Front, but also at sea and in the air. Albert Perks, RNAS took part in an AGE UK Essex memories project in 1966 and was living at Holland-on-Sea at the time recorded his memories of how he spent Christmas 1914. He was an air mechanic serving aboard a seaplane carrier, the converted Channel steamer HMS *Empress*:

> After waiting at Harwich about a month for the Air Raid that we were to make, we started under way about 4 am on the morning of December 24th. I could not sleep after we started but stayed in bed until 6.30 am. Directly I got up I felt sea-sick but unfortunately I could not be sick and was doing nothing but heaving until dinner time, when I was advised to eat as much as I could. This I did after a struggle and began to feel better in the afternoon when I went up on deck and had a good look around.
>
> I found we were being escorted by eight destroyers, four on either side with the *Arethusa* leading, followed by the *Engadine*, *Rivers* and *Undaunted* with the *Empress* last. After staying on deck during which time we passed several mines, I went down to my cabin and went to bed as I felt better lying down.
>
> At 7 that evening an order was given out that all Air Mechanics were to be on deck at 5 in the morning (Christmas Day).
>
> We were all on deck at the arranged time and found that we were about ten to twenty miles off the German Coast, having passed through the Bight of Heligoland and the principal German minefields. We at once got to work launching our three Seaplanes which we accomplished in about half an hour. In the meantime the destroyers were circling round keeping a sharp look out for submarines etc. Then the signal came from the Flagship for the planes to start. Unfortunately one of them piloted by Lieut. Bone failed to start and had to be brought on board.
>
> Of course this delayed us as the other ships began to steam off to the appointed place where we were to pick up the Seaplanes after they had accomplished their task. When we got under way again we were about two miles astern of the other ships. While we were on deck admiring the sunrise, as the day was beginning to break, we were suddenly surprised to see on the horizon

a Zeppelin and a German Seaplane, which, according to the estimate of our officers were thirty miles away.

The Seaplane at once began to make for the boats ahead of us and dropped two or three bombs at the destroyers which luckily missed. Then we observed another Seaplane on the port side of us and we all got our rifles but were ordered not to fire as they were not certain whether it was one of ours. Later it was observed that it was a German plane and we began firing.

By this time the Zeppelin had got astern of us and seemed to be drifting away when all of a sudden it made a dash for us and was very soon directly over the top and dropped three bombs but owing to the magnificent handling of the ship by the Captain not one of the bombs hit us, although they only missed by a few yards.

It is impossible for me to describe my feelings. When I looked up it seemed to cover the whole length of the ship. While this was happening, needless to say, we all had our lifebelts on and best part of the officers and Air Mechanics were firing at the Zeppelin with our rifles. Then we signalled to *Arethusa* and *Undaunted* that we were being attacked. All this time we were still about two or three miles behind and seemed to be absolutely at the mercy of the Zeppelin, as we had no aircraft guns on board. When *Arethusa* and *Undaunted* slowed down they at once put their guns on her.

The Zeppelin, disappointed at not having hit us, turned their Maxims on us and started to clear off, much to the relief of all on board.

What a Christmas! No wonder he could remember the incident so clearly.

The *Chelmsford Chronicle* reported on Friday, 7 April 1916 that young **Jack Linder**, a private in the Middlesex Regiment, had been killed in action. His full name was John Magner Linder, his parents were John and Ann Linder and the 1911 census states that they were living at 137 Sydney Street, Brightlingsea and that his father was a river policeman. The paper goes on to say that he was the first Brightlingsea boy to enlist after the commencement of war at the tender age of just 18. At the outbreak of war he was working as a mariner.

His war record, of which there is very little, has him signing up on 17 August 1914. I believe he did so following Lord Kitchener's appeal in early August. Kitchener. unlike the rest of the country, did not believe the war would be over by Christmas. In fact he was concerned that if our forces were not increased we would be in a very bad state. He managed to persuade the Cabinet and Parliament of the need to enlarge the army, initially by 500,000 men. The first recruitment poster came out on 11 August with those famous words 'Your Country Needs You' and within two weeks 100,000 men enlisted. The new divisions created were called 'Kitchener's Army' or K1. Men continued to volunteer which also saw the establishment of K2, K3 and K4. Later divisions were created as Fifth New Army etc. Between August 1914 and December 1915 2,466,719 men volunteered but even this was insufficient and on 27 January 1916 the first Military Service Act was passed, introducing conscription of single men of military age for the first time.

Jack enlisted at Mill Hill in the 11th Battalion of the Duke of Cambridge's Own (Middlesex) Regiment, service number G/458. which formed part of the 36th Brigade, 12th (Eastern) Division in K1. His records show he was 19 years 3 months old when he enlisted although in fact he was only 18. Their initial training was at Colchester before moving on to Shorncliffe in November and then to Ramillies Barracks at Aldershot. He left for France with his battalion on 1 May 1915, landing at Boulogne, and by 7 June they was in Fleurbaix. After a short period of instruction they took over a section of the front line at Ploegsteert Wood on 23 June 1915. However, the 11th Battalion's first real taste of action was at the Battle of Loos which commenced on 30 September 1915. The battle was the first genuine large-scale British offensive, launched to support the French who were having a hard time in the Third Battle of Artois. It was also the first time the British had used poison gas. It included six divisions and at the time was referred to as the 'Big Push'.

At that time the British were planning to play a defensive role until 1916 when the army had grown to a sufficient size, along with the necessary equipment and munitions. But the British suggestion to postpone the offensive until 1916 was rejected by the French and, with the problems the Russians were having on the Eastern Front, Kitchener expressed the view that he felt the Allies must act vigorously in order to take some pressure off Russia.

The 11th Battalion took over a section of the trenches under heavy artillery fire. Then on 8 October they repelled a heavy Germany infantry attack and on the 13th were involved in the action at the Hohenzollern Redoubt where they captured a gun trench and the south-western face of the Hulluch Quarries but two days later the battle, as usual, fizzled out with the Germans regaining most of the ground that they had lost. It was considered a Germany victory with the British casualties totalling 59,247 and the Germans approximately 26,000.

So it was back to both sides holding defensive positions and on the 21st the 11th went back behind the lines to Fouquières-lès-Béthune for a short rest before moving back to the front line until 15 November when they went into reserve for a well-earned rest at Lillers. For a short period they supported the 9th Royal Fusiliers in rounding-up spies and suspicious characters in the streets of Bethune. On 10 December they took over a section of the front line north of the La Bassée canal at Givenchy. In the New Year they began a period of training in open warfare at Busnes, followed by a move back to the front-line trenches at Loos at the Quarries on 12–13 February and by the 15th held the line from there to Hohenzollern Redoubt. It would have possibly been here that Jack was killed on 3 March 1916. He is commemorated on the Brightlingsea War Memorial and the Loos memorial. His family eventually received his 1914-15 Star and British War Medal in 1920.

An interesting and upsetting footnote to the 11th's involvement at the Battle of Loos is that Private Abraham Beverstain was executed for desertion on 20 March 1916 and is buried at Labourne Military Cemetery, Pas-de-Calais. He had no legal representative and it appears that it was his own words that condemned him: 'I felt nervous and lost my head, I thought I'd stay at the farm for a few days and go back to the company when they came out of the trenches.' The court was convinced he had intended to desert.

The *Chelmsford Chronicle* reported on Friday, 23 February 1917 that William Bailey Durrands of the Suffolk Regiment, whose wife and daughter were living in Dudley Road, Clacton, had been award the Military Cross. He already held the DCM and the Russian Cross of the Order of St George, 4th Class and had been in the regular army for sixteen years. William was born in 1879 to James and Mary at

Croxton Kerrial, Grantham, and he would have been approximately 21 when he enlisted. By the time the war broke out, William was with the 1st Battalion of the Lincolnshire Regiment as part of the 9th Brigade of the 3rd Division, stationed at Portsmouth. His service number was 5754 and his rank with the Lincolnshire Regiment was that of company quartermaster sergeant. The regiment was mobilized and landed at Le Havre on 14 August 1914 as part of the original BEF.

They were soon in the thick of it, being involved in the Battle of Mons. the Battle of Le Cateau, the Battle of the Marne, and the Battle of the Aisne, followed by the Battles of La Bassée and Messines from 12 October to 2 November 1914. It was at Hooge, during the First Battle of Ypres, that William was awarded his DCM: 'For gallantry on 14 November at Hooge, when he rallied his men in an emergency, although wounded. Has done consistently good work throughout the campaign.' It would appear that his actions were during a withdrawal. Major General C.R. Simpson in his book *The History of the Lincolnshire Regiment 1914-1918* has this to say about the 14 November:

> On the 14th the Lincolnshires, the enemy having gained ground on the left, were ordered to take up a line about two hundred yards in rear of the one held, which had become untenable. As soon as it was dark the withdrawal was carried out and the battalion occupied a line which the Diary describes as 'a remarkably ill-chosen position.' A series of very small strong points had been constructed in support. One was allotted to the Lincolnshire. It would no doubt have been useful in the event of a breakthrough but owing to its restricted space extremely unpleasant during heavy shelling.

They were fighting from trenches, ankle-deep in mud and water, an extremely unpleasant experience but one they were going to suffer from time and time again.

The Regiment next saw action at the First and Second Battles of Bellewaarde. Very little is written of these engagements which took place during June and September 1915 but at the first battle 1,000 men died within a twelve-hour period. We assume that William took part, having recovered from his wound. During this period he was awarded the Russian Cross of the Order of St George 4th Class.

Notification of the award appeared in the *Nottinghamshire Evening Post* on 26 August 1915:

Decorations for Local Territorial Heroes

His Imperial Majesty the Emperor of Russia has been graciously pleased to confer, with the approval of his Majesty the King, the undermentioned rewards for gallantry and distinguished service in the field.

Cross of the Order of St George, 4th Class

5754 Company-Sergeant-Major, William Bailey Durrands, 1st Battalion Lincolnshire Regiment.

Unfortunately I have not been able to establish why he was awarded this decoration.

Then on 14 October 1915 he was transferred to the 1st Battalion, Suffolk Regiment, initial rank of second lieutenant. A day later he was promoted to major. The regiment then went off to Salonika, via Egypt, from Marseilles on 24 October 1915 where they would engage the Bulgarian army. They arrived in Greece on 22 November 2015 and reached Salonika on 4 January 1916.

During the first four months of 1916 the British force spent most of the time building up its defences with large amounts of barbed wire, linking the city with the Vardar marshes to the west and Lakes Langaza and Beshik to the east and so to the Gulf of Orfano and the Aegean Sea. The area was known the 'Birdcage' due to the amount of barbed wire used. The main offensive that the 1st Battalion was involved in during 1916 was the occupation of Mazirko and the capture of Barakli Jum'a. In May 1917 the regiment was involved in the capture of Ferdie and Essex Trenches (near Barakli Jum'a), followed up with the capture of Barakli and Kumli in October 1917.

It would appear that William received his Military Cross just prior to the Ferdie and Essex Trenches attack while out on patrol. The citation reads: 'For conspicuous gallantry and skill when in common of a screen of scouts leading a night march. He handled his command with great ability and overcome the opposition of all the enemy outposts. He set a splendid example throughout.' It would also appear that William saw his time out in the Salonika area (also known as Macedonia). The last battle that the British were involved in was the Battle of Doiran in September 1918. Although the British casualties were high, the French and Greeks were progressing well and had achieved a breakthrough at Dobro Pole. Although the Bulgarian army was not routed, many of its retreating troops mutinied. It is understood that between 4,000–5,000 rebellious troops threatened Sofia, forcing a Bulgarian government delegation to ask for an armistice. On 29 September 1918 the Armistice of Thessaloniki was signed by the Allied commander General Franchet d'Esperey which ended the war against the Bulgarians. The Macedonian campaign was brought to an end at noon on 30 September 1918 when the ceasefire came into effect. The soldiers' uprising was finally put down by 2 October and Tsar Ferdinand I of Bulgaria abdicated and went into exile the next day. William's war was at last over, one of the few of the original BEF to have survived the war to be known later as one of the 'Old Contemptibles'. In addition to his gallantry medals he also received the 1914 Star, British War Medal and Victory Medal. What a soldier!

Vivian John Woodward, who had a close connection to Clacton, also survived the war. He joined the 17th (Service) Battalion of the Middlesex Regiment in December 1914, accepting a commission as lieutenant and rising to captain as the war progressed. He was born in Kennington, Surrey on 3 June 1879 to John and Anna Woodward. He attended Ascham College, Clacton, while staying with family at Silver-Cloud, which still stands today in Pier Avenue. He was an outstanding sportsman, excelling at cricket, tennis and football.

Although his father wanted him to concentrate on cricket and tennis he eventually relented and at the age of 16 he was playing centre forward

Vivian Woodward.

for Clacton Town and continued to play for them until 1901. He had no intention of becoming a professional, however, and became a quantity surveyor like his father. He did agree to play on amateur terms for Tottenham Hotspur (Spurs) in the Southern League. Spurs were at the time considered one of the best teams in the country, having won the 1901 FA Cup Final against Sheffield United.

He played for Spurs from 1901 to 1909 making 132 appearance and scoring 63 goals. When he signed as an amateur it was on the understanding that he played for them whenever it was 'convenient for him to play' as he had other commitments to the Spencer Cricket & Lawn Tennis Club. He was at the time one of England's best tennis players, reaching the Lawn Tennis Championships twice. He also played cricket for the Essex second eleven in 1902 and 1903, though he was not considered quite good enough for county championship matches.

He won his first full football international cap for England against Ireland on 14 February 1903 and scored two goals in England's 4-0 victory. He set a record in 1908 when he scored eight of England's fifteen goals against France. He went on to play twenty-three times for England and forty-four times for England Amateurs and competed as Captain and winning gold on both occasions for Great Britain in the 1908 (London) and 1912 (Stockholm) Olympics. Abroad, he was worshipped – 'Vich ees Woodward?'. In addition to his sporting prowess, being a surveyor and architect he was responsible for designing of the main stadium in Antwerp which was used for the 1920 Olympic Games.

He initially retired from football in July 1909 but he returned and signed for Chelsea in November of that year. Even the *Dundee Courier* announced his return: 'The football world will be startled by the announcement that Vivian J Woodward England's International captain, an amateur and one of the best players that ever toed a ball, has returned to league Football and will give his services to Chelsea.'

He went on to play well over 100 games for Chelsea. In the early months of 1915 he still played the odd game for them but ceased as training took priority. However, the battalion, as one would expect, formed its own football team of which he became captain and played throughout 1915.

The 17th was formed as a 'Pals' battalion and its core was a group of professional footballers and became known as the 'First Football

Battalion'. It was formed in December 1914 by William Joynson-Hicks, later Home Secretary after the war. There was initially a slow uptake of recruits amongst the professionals. Contracts were said to be part of the problem, with the clubs keen to keep playing to offer a release for the general public from the daily horrific tales from the front line. Sir Arthur Conan Doyle stepped in with an appeal: 'If a footballer has strength of limb, let them serve and march in the field of battle.' It had the desired effect and by March 1915, 122 professional footballers had joined the regiment. Vivian had been playing for Chelsea when he enlisted and it would appear that his presence persuaded many Chelsea (Blues) supporters to enlist.

The *Birmingham Daily Post* report on Monday, 1 November 1915 that the Footballers' Battalion which included Vivian played a match against Birmingham. There was a crowd of 10,000 and the primary object of the match was to obtain recruits for the battalion from the spectators. Speeches were made during the intervals with recruiting sergeants mingling with the crowd. A few young men came forward and were heartily cheered by the crowd. The proceeds of the match were to be divided between various charities and the battalion funds.

Although there was no major battle going on at the time, Vivian was wounded while on the Western Front in January 1916. He was hit by shrapnel in both legs, although a letter to his brother in late January confirmed that the injuries were not serious. While in France he was Mentioned in Despatches and at some later date awarded the OBE. On returning from the war he was expected to return and continue his football career although he was approaching the ripe old age of 40. The *Daily Mirror* had this to say in December 1918: 'I suppose Woodward will come back to Chelsea but for my own part all the best memories of the international are bound up with his football life at Tottenham. When Woodward left Hotspur it was like old "W.G" forsaking the home and county of the Graces to play for London County.' Well, he did not return to Chelsea but played a few more games for Clacton before retiring for good. He bought a farm at Chisbon Heath near Weeley, just outside Clacton and a dairy business in Frinton-on-Sea. He was also interested in pigeon-racing and fishing. During the Second World War he was an Air Raid Warden. He was awarded the British War and Victory Medals. He suffered a nervous breakdown and died in an Ealing nursing home on 31 January 1954 aged 74, a forgotten man. Maybe it's time that Clacton recognized in some way their wartime and footballing hero.

> **A GALLANT ESSEX OFFICER** – Lieutenant Denis Patrick Joseph Kelly of the Connaught Rangers, has been awarded the Military Cross, is the only son of Mr and Mrs Kelly, of Kingscote Saville Street, Walton-on-the-Naze. The London Gazette Issue 29713 page 8225 18th August 1916 – 2nd Lt. (temp. Lt.) Denis Patrick Joseph Kelly, Conn. Rang. For valuable service on reconnaissance work and for gallantry in action subsequently. (*Essex Newsman* – Saturday, 2 September 1916)

Denis was born in 1887, in Wood Green, Middlesex to Matthew and Catherine Kelly. By the beginning of the war the family were living in Walton-on-the-Naze. In 1906 Denis had enrolled at Downing College, Cambridge, coming out with a Bachelor of Arts (BA) degree and was employed thereafter by the War Office. Following his enlistment and training either in Ireland or England with the 5th Service Battalion Connaught Rangers, he found himself on his way to Gallipoli via Mudros, Greece. The battalion was part of the 29th Brigade attached to the ANZAC (Australian and New Zealand) force that landed at Anzac Cove in the early hours of 6 August 1915. They had arrived aboard HMS *Clacton*.

In February/March 1915 an Anglo-French naval task force attempted to break through the Dardanelles to open up a sea route so they could supply their Russian allies fighting on the Eastern Front. This failed so it was decided to launch a land invasion of Turkey's back door, the Gallipoli Peninsula, to enable them to capture the Turkish capital of Constantinople. The invasion took place on 25 April 1915 with British, French and Commonwealth Troops including Australians, New Zealanders and Gurkhas. The British made a fatal mistake, believing the peninsula to be lightly defended. The invasion failed and the troops were trapped along a thin stretch of coastline by entrenched Turkish Troops.

So the Rangers, along with other battalions, were part of a second offensive to break the stalemate and get the Allied troops off the beaches and inland. The Rangers endured the heat and misery for seven weeks but they fought desperately with tragic consequences in the Battles of Suvia, Sari Bair and Hill 60. The Australians described the attack of the Irishmen on Hill 60 as the finest they had ever seen in the war. They had 400m of open ground to cover. The Turks opened fire from wells and from Hill 60 immediately. None of the Irishmen fired a shot: they ran silently. The Turks withstood the wild charge for a minute, but then they either ran in panic or were killed. On the hillside the dead, Irish and Anzac troops lay so thickly that it looked as though they had fallen under a magic spell of sleep. They were buried a week later when the hill was finally captured. The 5th Battalion had suffered heavy casualties and on 29 September they were withdrawn to the Greek Island of Lemnos. The Gallipoli campaign ended in total failure and the Peninsula was evacuated in late December 1915.

In October 1915 an expeditionary force of French and British troops, which included the 10th Irish Division and the 5th Connaught Rangers, was sent to northern Greece in an attempt to assist Serbia. On 6 October a combined German and Austro-Hungarian army had launched a full-scale invasion of Serbia from the north. The Bulgarian army also assisted the invasion by attacking Serbia from the east. Tsar Ferdinand of Bulgaria had opted to join the war on the side of the Central Powers. The Serbian army was no match for the combined invasion force and were soon in full retreat.

Greece, still officially neutral, allowed the Allies to use Salonika as a base from which to prepare their operations to cross into Serbia. The 5th Battalion Connaught Rangers arrived at Salonika from the island of Mudros on 10 October. After a month's training in atrocious weather conditions, the Rangers crossed the Greek frontier into the snow-covered mountains of southern Serbia.

At 10.30 am on 20 November the 5th Connaught Rangers received orders to go to Tatarli. After a long delay due to the ammunition column cutting in front of them, they eventually reached Tatarli at 1.20 pm where they got ready to settle down for the night. All the villages in the area had been cleared of its inhabitants by the French, a very necessary precaution. The following day after morning service by the chaplains, Captain Kelly and Second Lieutenant D.J. Cowan were sent out on reconnaissance patrol at 10 am. Kelly was commended for his excellent results.

From early December, light shelling and sniping were obvious signs that the Bulgarians were preparing for an offensive. By 3 and

4 December the Bulgarians' firing increased on the lines at Kajali and Krivolak being held by the French and at the same time the bombardment of the Rangers' trench line grew heavier and more intense. December 5th was much quieter, apart from a few shells earlier on the Rangers line. By the evening everybody was warned to be ready for an expected attack, information having been gained from Bulgarian prisoners. As the Rangers had been in the trenches for seven days instead of seventy-two hours, they were given the opportunity to retire but all the officers decided to stay put.

On the morning of 6 December the Bulgarian and possibly German guns from Kosturino opened up on the part of the line held by the Rangers. The Battle of Kosturino had begun. The enemy offensive and murderous fire continued all day. The noise of the rifle fire and machine guns from the Rangers was staggering and the enemy was mown down, but they continued to surge forward. The enemies attack continued the following day and at one point over 5,000 Bulgarians attacked the Rangers' trenches and managed to get into some of them but Captain Kelly and his men gallantly stood their ground. The huge Bulgarian army gradually overran the frozen trenches and it was reported that the enemy began to shoot those who resisted and bayoneted even those lying wounded in the trenches or behind the lines. As the Rangers slowly retreated the majority (twenty-six in number) of the survivors of 'A' Company under Captain Kelly fought their way back to Crete Simonet. The Bulgarians later took Crete Simonet, forcing the British to retreat back to Greece.

On 21 December, names of officers and men of the 5th Battalion, Connaught Rangers were submitted for their good service during the actions of 6 and 7 December: 'Lieut. and Temp-Captain D.P.J. Kelly 5th Battalion, Connaught Rangers for gallant service on the 6 and 7 December, when commanding the right Company, when he held his position although the Company on his left had been driven by the enemy, who were in overwhelming force.'

It was therefore for this action that Kelly was to receive his Military Cross which was awarded on 21 August 1916 although it was not reported in the papers until September 1916 (*Chelmsford Chronicle*, 1 September 1916):

He went into training as soon as the war broke out and a month or two later he received his commission. He first saw active service in Mudros but was soon after fighting with the Irish Brigade in covering the retreat of the Serbian Army. It was during this activity that the incident occurred in which Lieut. Kelly distinguished himself, although the award was also made in recognition of his general ability as a soldier. He was, as acting Captain, in command of a company of 200 men whom he took into action as part of the Irish Brigade against a sudden deadly onslaught of the Bulgars, before which the British had to retire. Lieut. Kelly and his brave company fought against enormous odds of about eight to one and surrounded on three sides until it seemed impossible that they could ever get away. Three times they were driven back and three times they hacked their way forward and did not retire until only 26 men of the gallant 200 were left to return. But the British troops were successful in their object, viz., securing the retreat of the Serbian Army.

The 5th Battalion Connaught Rangers remained at the Salonika front for a further two years with little progress made by either side. The Allied presence in northern Greece prevented the Bulgarian army invading Greece but the inhospitable mountainous terrain and adverse weather, unbearable heat and malaria in the summer and ice and snow in the winter, made an offensive almost impossible. It also meant that huge numbers of Allied troops were tied up in a 'sideshow'.

On 10 September 1917 the battalion was transferred to the Palestine/Egyptian Front, and saw action at the Third Battle of Gaza (the capture of the Hareira Redoubt), and the capture of Jerusalem. Then on 30 April 1918 they sailed from Port Said to Marseilles, France and on the 8th October pursued the German army from the Hindenburg Line at Cambrai to Selle in Picardy. On Armistice Day, 11 November 1918, the 5th was the only Connaught battalion still on the Western Front.

On returning to England Kelly joined the Army Education Corps and was promoted to General Staff Officer, 3rd Grade, then temporary captain, then captain in June 1920. By the late 1920s he was in India as Chief Instructor, Army School of Education. In November 1935 he was promoted to major and also received the OBE. Promoted in 1940 to lieutenant colonel, he returned home after eleven years' service in India and was appointed Command Education Officer in Scottish

Command. He was appointed colonel in 1944 and in 1945 became Deputy Director and Controller of the Royal Army Education Corps.

Although he appears to have had a successful career and survived a devastating war, his heart was broken by the loss of his son Dermot Daly Aloysius Kelly who had joined the RAF. He reached the rank of Squadron Leader and was mentioned in Despatches three times but was killed while piloting a Wellington bomber on a raid on Duisburg on 17 June 1941. The aircraft crashed at Hamont (Belgium), and all the crew were killed. They were initially laid to rest at the local cemetery but after the war transferred to Heverlee War Cemetery. Kelly himself was promoted to Brigadier before he retired in 1947 and the records state that he was also awarded the Belgian Croix de Guerre in addition to the 1914/15 Star, British and Victory Medals. He passed away on 24 August 1950 age 63.

While most Germans in Britain were being interned, we had one German fighting for our cause. Captain **Adolf Frederick Wittkugel**, a naturalized British citizen of German stock, who lived with his wife Margaret at 'Waverley', Harold Road, Frinton-on-Sea. Adolf had been born in Karachi, Bombay, India on 18 June 1876 to Johann Friedrich Theodore and Eleanor Wittkugel. Johann retired in 1889 and was receiving a pension from the British government following a career as Chief Mechanician of the Persian Gulf Section of the Indo-European Telegraph Department. This department was a branch of the Government of India, based in London, which managed a series of telegraph lines in Persia (Iran). He applied for and received a Certificate of Naturalization on 4 October 1889. Adolf was 13 years old at the time. It's not surprising then that prior to the outbreak of war Adolf was himself employed by the Indo-European Telegraph Department. With the outbreak of war the Telegraph Department were having problems. The Bushire-Teheran line fell into enemy hands but a third line connecting India with Teheran via Meshed and Seistan was maintained for the duration of the war.

Most of the focus on the land war is around the Western Front and Gallipoli but there were other areas of conflict such as Persia and at some point during the war Adolf joined the Special List and the South Persia Rifles. He may have been one of the many interpreters. The South Persia Rifles (SPR) was a Persian military force formed in 1916 in response to German influence in southern Persia. Most of the recruits came from pro-British tribes, and the force was run along the lines of an Indian Army regiment under British officers.

The newly-commissioned Wittkugel and Colonel Fraser Hunter joined a force sent to Bushire. To get there they had to travel through Kazerun, a territory between Shiraz and Bushire that was committed to the German cause. On Christmas Day, 1916, the Kazerunis fired on the advancing force. For about an hour and half, a company of the Baluchis and an SPR company had been moving to the high ground in order to guard the right flank of the main column. At 10 am the Kazerunis began firing heavily on them and they were forced to take cover. Hunter and some of his Persians manhandled two old 7-pounder mountain guns to where they hoped to be able to fire on the Kazerunis, but not only was the range too great but they also discovered that many of the shells were defective. The flank guard had to return to the main column since their commander Captain Weldon was unable to get his troops to advance into the Kazeruni fire.

At this point Captains Wittkugel and Weldon volunteered to make another attempt to secure higher ground and defend the right flank of the main column. The Persians went forward again in two sections, one led by Hunter with Weldon at his side, the other led by Wittkugel. The mountainside was steep, there were precipitous drops and the ground was covered by dense undergrowth. The Persian infantry, who had only a couple of weeks training, had little stomach for the heavy fire that was poured down on them by the Kazerunis at the summit and very soon, Hunter found his force reduced to a mere twelve men and a machine-gun crew. Despite this they continued to make an attempt to reach the summit.

News now reached them that Wittkugel had been wounded and several Persian infantrymen with him killed. Sunset was about 5 pm and Hunter realized that it would be impossible to take the summit before dark. He told Weldon that he would take three Persians and try to rescue Wittkugel who had got to within a hundred yards of the enemy before being hit. Under intense fire Hunter reached the spot were Wittkugel lay wounded: he was still alive though clearly he was dying. He told Hunter that his back was broken and there was no hope of him surviving. He asked Hunter to request Sykes to ensure his wife was looked after. They were his last words. Hunter tried to move him but he was too heavy and as soon as Hunter's Persian companion moved closer to assist he was shot. He struggled closer only to be shot again. At the point the SPR machine gun giving Hunter supporting fire ran out of ammunition and the crew shouted the news to Hunter. Unfortunately, the Kazerunis heard the message as well! Keeping up rifle fire to protect the dying Wittkugel and the Persian soldier, Hunter withdrew and got a message to Weldon. Within an hour relief had arrived with more ammunition for the machine gun. The relief poured heavy fire into the enemy's positions and managed to drag Wittkugel to cover. Adolf succumbed to his wounds and died on 15 February 1917 aged 40 and is buried in Tehran War Cemetery, Iran. His wife Margaret died in 1942. He was awarded the Victory and British Medals

On 30 November 1917 the British attacked the Hindenburg Line in the Battle of Cambrai. It was yet another bloody but pointless offensive on the Western Front. The most spectacular part of the battle is that the British used 476 tanks, a far cry from the 30-odd used at the Battle of Flers-Courcelette in September 1916. Mind you 179 were destroyed along with 44,000 casualties which included 6,000 prisoners, while the Germans took 45,000 casualties which included 10,000 prisoners, The reason Cambrai was chosen for the offensive is because the town had one of the principal railway intersections and German garrisons on the Western Front, it also appeared to be ideal terrain for the tank. The idea of using tanks was so that an initial bombardment was not necessary, increasing the element of surprise. The British also used Livens projectors to shower poison gas on various parts of the 10km-wide front. Although the British made head way the heavy congestion on the road meant the delay of reinforcements in fact at one point it took fifteen hours for reinforcements to cover the final 5km to the front. The Germans were initially going to retreat but instead went on the offensive and within two hours they had advanced 5km and by the time the fighting finished around 4–6 December they had regained all the ground lost, so it was stalemate once again. It was at this battle on the 6 December that **William Victor Grigson**, brother of George Grigson, coxswain of the Clacton lifeboat, was killed. He had enlisted into the 2/1st Buckinghamshire Battalion of the Oxfordshire and Buckinghamshire Light Infantry, rank private.

Sidney Aldrich was born in Dickleburgh, Norwich, in 1891 to Walter and Maria Aldrich. By the start of the war his mother was living at Home Cottage, Clacton Road, St Osyth, Sidney had enlisted several years earlier in Colchester in the 'G' Company, 2nd Battalion West Yorkshire Regiment, service number 9167. The 1911 census has him stationed at The Royal Artillery Barracks and the Cavalry Barracks, Butt Road, Colchester.

At the outbreak of war the regiment was stationed in Malta. It arrived back in England on 14 September and the regiment joined up with 23rd Brigade part of the 8th Division. It had previously been in the Balkans and India, so returning to England gave the men a chance to visit their families whom they had obviously not seen for years. They landed at Le Havre in France on 5 November 1914 and by 12 December the 2nd Battalion were in the front line near the village of Neuve Chapelle. Part of the German front line included a fortified farmhouse, surrounded by a moat; on maps it is known as 'Ferme Vanbesian' the British would call it the 'Moated Grange'. It was a snipers' den and was creating a steady stream of casualties. The British decided that they had to put a stop to this activity. On the 18th they attacked. The assault was led by the 2nd Devonshire Regiment, supported by the 2nd West Yorkshire Regiment and the Royal Engineers. The objective was initially achieved with a number of German prisoners being taken. The captured German trench was being controlled by the West Yorkshire men and being used as a communication trench.

Then around 7.30 am troops of the German 13th Infantry Regiment counter-attacked, armed with sacksful of grenades. Although the mixture of West Yorkshires and Royal Engineers in the area also had grenades at their disposal, it proved to be a largely one-sided fight: the British had no really effective weapon with which to reply. Their home-made grenades proved to be very difficult to light, being fiddly and slow to use and prone to the fuse failing to light in the wet conditions. Most men simply did not know how to use them. Within the confines of a trench the German grenades proved to be devastating. They appeared to have no fuse to light and could be thrown up to 40 yards. In this desperate close-in fighting, a platoon of the West Yorkshires was nearly wiped out. To make matters worse, their trench and the recently-dug saps were rapidly filling with flood water. Saps were short trenches dug across No Man's Land towards the enemy trenches and enabled soldiers to move forward without exposure to enemy fire. They were often joined together at their far ends to create a new trench.

Lieutenant Philip Neame of the Royal Engineers, who knew how to light the grenades by holding a match-head on the end of the fuse and then striking a matchbox across it, clambered up onto the parapet and began to calmly fight off the enemy with the stock of grenades. This extraordinarily brave young man held the enemy at bay for forty-five minutes, causing them a good many casualties, whilst the West Yorkshires evacuated the captured trench and carried their wounded back to the original front line. He was awarded the Victoria Cross for his part in this action.

The West Yorkshire lost at least five officers and ninety-five men and our Lance Corporal Sidney Aldrich was one of them. He was awarded the 1914 Star, and the Victory and British War Medals and is commemorated on Le Tourlet Memorial and the St Osyth war memorial.

Passchendaele

Like the Somme Offensive in 1916 the Third Battle of Ypres (31 July – 10 November 1917), or 'Passchendaele' (as it is more often referred to), has come to symbolize the Great War. Although referred to as a battle it was similar to the Somme in that it was an Allied offensive staged over sixteen weeks with a number of major battles interspersed with minor skirmishes. The major battles were:

1. Battle of Pilcken Ridge, 31 July – 2 August.
2. Battle of Hill 70, 15–25 August.
3. Battle of Langemarck, 16–18 August.
4. Battle of Menin Road Ridge, 20–25 September.
5. Battle of Polygon Wood, 25 September – 3 October.
6. Battle of Broodseinde, 4 October.
7. Battle of Poelcappelle, 9 October.
8. First Battle of Passchendaele, 12 October.
9. Battle of Malmaison, 17–23 October.
10. Second Battle of Passchendaele, 6 October – 10 November.

Passchendaele was a small rural village situated on a hill ridge close to Ypres. The main reason for the campaign was to control the ridges south and east of the City and be in a position to disrupt German lines of communication. It was a controversial decision for the Allies to go on the offensive and today it is still debated how successful the campaign was considering the massive loss of life. The Allies are estimated to have lost at least 370,000 and the Germans 217,000, though it is believed that the losses were much higher and bodies are still being discovered today. Similarly to the Somme offensive the weather had a considerable effect on the various battles, as it varied from rain and mud to hot and dry. In the end the Allies only managed to advance five miles and the campaign has gone down in history not as a victory but a campaign which troops and tanks endured appalling conditions in a period of unprecedented weather.

As you would expect the Clacton area lost quite a number of men in this particular campaign. The following are those that killed on the first day.

Bertram Arthur Bennett was born in Ipswich in Suffolk but was living at Clacton when war broke out. He enlisted in the 1st Battalion Welsh Guards at Clacton, as Private 3188. The 1st Battalion left for France on 17 August 1915 and joined up with the 3rd Guards Brigade. Though only young, it is possible that Bertram was with them, and if so he would have seen action at the Battle of Loos in 1915, and the Battle of Flers-Courcelette (part of the Somme Offensive) and the Battle of Morval in 1916 before being involved in the attack at Pilckem Ridge on the opening day of the Passchendaele Campaign.

On 31 July the battalion was in the Boesinghe sector of the front line waiting for zero hour. The following report by its commander is from the battalion's war diary:

> The morning was dark and inclined to be wet; rain had fallen and the ground was distinctly heavy. Zero hour was 3.50 am but the Guards and French Divisions could not move till zero + 30 am – The Barrage commenced at zero + 34 and this was inclined to make me nervous as had the Bosch but given his Barrage on our advanced lines our men would have been unable to move for 38 minutes.
>
> The sight was one never to be forgotten. During the night for 6 hours incessantly the enemy batteries and lines were dealt with by Gas Shells never for one moment did other shelling cease and

when the actual zero hour came, boiling oil was poured on the enemy and the place became a perfect inferno.

One of the outstanding features of the attack, the Battalion did quite splendidly in every way and no words of praise can be too high for all ranks. At 5 pm the Battalion was relieved by 1st Battalion Grenadier Guards and now it is in rest about 1000 yards behind Zommerbloom Cabaret on the south west side of the western Elverdringle Road.

Somewhere along the line of the attack Bertram was killed and his body was lost forever in the mud of Ypres. In addition to being remembered on the Clacton memorial he is also commemorated on the Menin Gate (Ypres) Memorial.

George Butcher was also born in Ipswich, the son of Mr and Mrs S. Butcher who at the time of the Great War were living at Rush Green, Clacton. He enlisted at Colchester into the 1/1st Battalion Hertfordshire Regiment as Private No 270188. The battalion had spent the first half of 1917 holding the line near Ypres but in July it began training for the Passchendaele offensive and they were employed in the third phase of the Pilckem operation, advancing through Steenbeek towards the Langemarck line. They suffered heavy casualties from enemy machine-gun fire and on reaching the enemy wire it was found to have been undamaged by the artillery bombardment and the battalion was forced to fall back, suffering further casualties as the Germans counter-attacked. It was at this point that George lost his life. His body has never been found. He is commemorated on the Clacton and Menin Gate War Memorials.

Frederick William Peck was a native of Clacton and was living there at the outbreak of war. He enlisted initially as a private in the Essex Regiment before transferring to the 1st/8th Battalion, The King's (Liverpool) Regiment as Private No 325016. The battalion transferred to the 164th Brigade and in their attack at Pilckem Ridge they advanced in support of the 2/5th Lancashire Fusiliers, successfully capturing five batteries of 77mm guns, enabling them to consolidate their line, but it was in this attack that Frederick lost his life. He was 30 years of age. His body has never been found. He is commemorated on the Clacton and Menin Gate Memorials.

The following is a communiqué from the commanding officer issued the day before the Battalion went into action:

A. B. C. D. & Details.

1/8 IRISH/OFFE/988.

In sending out to the Battalion the attached letters of the Divisional and Brigade Commanders, I desire once more to remind all ranks that they are fighting not only to break down the vaunted might of Germany and the militarism of Prussia, which have brought so much trouble on the world during the past three years, but that each one is also fighting for the freedom of mankind, for the security of his home, for the future safety of his mother, sister, sweetheart, wife, daughter and of all else that he holds dear and sacred.

That the fighting spirit of the Battalion is excellent I am fully convinced. Your good work in the trenches, your able construction of defences, your valuable patrolling, your steadiness under frequent heavy bombardments from front and flanks, in the most dangerous and difficult part of the whole Army front and your patience and cheerfulness through all the trials and hardships of the Winter, are proof that your spirit is excellent and your heart in the right place.

Let each one go forward with the feeling and knowledge that he is winning, determined to play his part to the utmost of his ability, doing his level best to obey all orders implicitly, and, by his good work and splendid example of courage and devotion to duty, helping all to victory.

Let the name of the "Liverpool Irish" go down to posterity as a glorious and imperishable name, the name of aregiment in which each one nobly did his duty on this great occasion.

To every Officer, Warrant Officer, Non-Commissioned Officer and Private of the Battalion who is taking part in this, the first great engagement that you have been in since I have had the honour to Command you, I wish God Speed and Good Luck.

Lieut. Colonel.
Commdg. 1/8th(Irish)Batt.K.L.R.

In the Field.
29/7/17.

The following men who had connections to the Clacton area were also killed on 31 July 1917 at Pilckem Ridge. Very little information can be found about them and they do not appear on the Clacton War Memorial but are commemorated on the Menin Gate Memorial.

Albert Charles Southgate, Private 43354 of the 10th Battalion Essex Regiment. The son of Matilda Southgate of 2 Lower Kirby, Clacton-on-Sea.

Samuel Walter Gray, Private 235246 in the 8th Battalion Lincolnshire Regiment. The husband of Caroline Susan of Kirby Cross, Clacton-on-Sea.

George Sidney Rix born Great Holland was also a private, 235207 in the 8th Battalion Lincolnshire Regiment. He had originally enlisted in Colchester in the Cambridge Regiment. At the time of the Great War he was resident of Lower Kirby. He was only 22 when he died: I wonder if he knew Albert and Stanley. George is also commemorated on the memorial plaque in All Saints' Church, Great Holland.

Stanley Edward Barker, a native of Walton-on-the-Naze initially enlisted in the London Regiment but later transferred to the 15th Battalion Royal Welsh Fusiliers. This battalion was formed in London on 20 October 1914, arriving in France in December 1915 and saw its first action at the Battle of Albert (1– 13 July 1916), the first major battle of the Somme offensive. The battalion suffered heavy casualties and had the rest of the year off while its strength was built up again. This is possibly when Stanley transferred to it. The battalion's next engagement was the Battle of Pilckem Ridge.

They went over the top at Zero hour 3.50 am and their war diary states that they experienced great difficulty in keeping direction because of the darkness of the hour but after encountering considerable opposition they eventually passed Pilckem village and reached their objective, the Iron Cross Ridge. By this time they had lost all their officers so they were ordered to consolidate and hold their position and beat back any counter-attacks. Somewhere along the way Stanley lost his life, age just 19. He is commemorated on the Menin Gate Memorial.

Thomas Cecil Adams, son of Thomas and Charlotte, 1 Nelson Street, Brightlingsea, enlisted into the 1st/5th Battalion, King's Own (Royal Lancaster Regiment) as Private 260013. He was killed on

Stained-glass window, St James' Church, Clacton. (Author's collection)

31 July 1917 aged 23 but unlike the others he is buried at the New Irish Farm Cemetery.

The *Chelmsford Chronicle* reported on Friday, 14 December 1917 that Lieutenant Colonel James Nicholson unveiled a stained-glass window in the Lady Chapel of St James's Church, Clacton in memorial to his mother, Annie Morris Nicholson. The window is next to another in memory of his son who was killed at the Battle of the Somme. The citation with a quotation reads:

> In loving memory of **Charles Stanley Nicholson** killed in action 15th September 1916
>
> 'Be thou faithful unto death I will give thee a crown of life'.

Charles is depicted in the window in a full suit of armour and being held by an angel. This window is the only confirmation that is

Charles Nicholson plaque beneath the window. (Author's collection)

currently to be found that connects Charles Stanley to Clacton. He does not appear on any of the Roll of Honour lists.

Charles was born on 31 August 1887 in Gibraltar. The 1901 census has the family living on the Isle of Man. The 1911 census has his parents still living there but no Charles it appears that he had immigrated to New Zealand because we find that he enlisted at Wellington in the New Zealand Machine Gun Corps, 3 Company of the 1st Battalion New Zealand Rifle Brigade, and his address at the time was Inglewood, Taranaki, North Island, New Zealand. On 9 October 1915 he embarked on a New Zealand troopship for Cairo, arriving on 14 November. They were there to counter a Senussi invasion from Libya. The 1st Battalion fought two actions with others at Matruh, one on Christmas Day, the other on 23 January 1916. Both actions were successful and the back of the invasion was broken.

Then in mid-February the battalion met with the 3rd and 4th Battalions at Moascor, in the Suez Canal area. After a period of reorganization they left Egypt for France. Their first major offensive was the Battle of Flers-Courcelette on 15 September 1916. It was on this day that Charles met his death. He is buried in the Caterpillar Valley New Zealand Memorial at Albert, Department de la Somme, Picardie, France.

Winchester Cathedral plaque. (David Rymill, Cathedral archivist)

The question remains why did James dedicate two windows to his mother and son in St James Church, Clacton. He had risen to the rank of lieutenant colonel in the Royal Army Medical Corps (RAMC) after serving in the South African War (Boer War) of 1899–1901. It is just possible that he joined Dr Thomas Carlyle Beatty who had married his second cousin Marion Williams and had set up his practice in Clacton-on-Sea. For the period of the war the doctor had been appointed honorary anaesthetist to the Middlesex Hospital. Did James join him here?

There is another plaque to Charles in Winchester Cathedral: again the question is why? The Winchester Cathedral archivist, David Rymill, kindly checked the minutes of meetings of the Dean and Chapter of Winchester Cathedral and confirmed that at a meeting of 28 November 1916 the Dean read out a letter from Colonel Nicholson, SMO (Senior Medical Officer) at Winchester, asking for permission to erect a memorial in memory of his son, killed in action. Also, in a minute of 27 March 1917, it is reported that Colonel Nicholson had made a donation of £5.5s.0d for the purchase of something useful for the Cathedral. It would therefore appear that Colonel Nicholson was stationed at Winchester for part of the war in his role as a medical officer.

Lieutenant H.T. Culliford. (Daily Mail, *1917*)

On Saturday, 4 August 1917 the *Daily Mirror* reported with a photograph that Lieutenant Henry Thomas Culliford of Clacton-on-Sea had been awarded the Military Cross. The *London Gazette* also announced the award on 6 July 1918. All I have managed to discovered and this is from his medal card is that he was an officer with the Royal Army Service Corps. When he join it was known as Army Service Corps (ASC), referred to jokingly as 'Ally Sloper's Cavalry' ('Royal' was not added until 1918). They were, however, the unsung heroes of the British Army. The army need food, equipment, ammunition etc.

and it was these boys that provided the movement of these supplies by horse-drawn and motor vehicles, railways and waterways. There is no doubt they performed prodigious feats and were one of the great strengths of the organization that helped win the war. It would appear that Henry survived the war.

Well, our last hero has to be **Herbert George Columbine** VC, a native of Walton-on-the-Naze. He lost his life on 22 March 1918 the second day of the 1918 Battle of the Somme at Hervilly Woods. A few days later his mother Emma received the Army notification form B104-82:

> Madam
>
> It is my painful duty to inform you that a report has been received from the War Office notifying the death of No. 50720 Private Herbert George Columbine of 9 Squadron Machine Gun Corps (Cavalry) at Hervilly Woods on the 22nd March 1918.
>
> The report is to the effect that he was killed in action. By his Majesty's command I am to forward the enclosed message of sympathy from Their Gracious Majesties the King and Queen. I am at the same time to express the regret of the Army Council at the soldier's death in his country's service . . .

Not long afterwards Emma received a second letter this time from Lieutenant Eade, 9th Squadron, Machine Gun Corps:

> Dear Mrs Columbine,
>
> You will no doubt have been informed by the War Office that No 50720 Private Columbine H. G. is wounded and missing. He was in my sub-section and although I had not the luck to be with him on 22nd March. I heard what happened from those who were there. He kept his gun firing to the last, although the Germans had got into the trench on both sides of him and were throwing bombs at him. In the end, he was seen to be hit by a bomb and very badly wounded. He was one of my best gun numbers and is a great loss to the Squadron. I deeply sympathise with you but it may be some consolation to you to know that he has been recommended for a medal in token of his bravery. It is the bravest deed I have ever heard of.

These were letters that Emma was dreading as it was the second such notification she had received. Her husband, also Herbert, who was with the 2nd Battalion (10th Foot), Lincolnshire Regiment had been killed, on 1 July 1900 at the Battle of Zilikaats Nek during the Boer War.

In fact Emma was to receive a further two letters from France, both on the same day. The first she opened was from Captain MacAndrews, commanding 9th Squadron, Machine Gun Corps informing her that the King had the pleasure of granting her son the Victoria Cross, the highest honour he could bestow. The second was from one of his comrades, Private F.H. Burke, who was close to the action.

On 4 May 1918 the *Daily Mail* reported the posthumous award of the Victoria Cross to Private Herbert Columbine 'for holding back an enemy attack and saving a threatened flank from what might have been a disaster. He saved the situation by his self-sacrifice and was killed at his post. He showed the highest valour and determination.'

Local papers as far north as Aberdeen also reported the full citation:

> For most conspicuous bravery and self-sacrifice displayed, when, owing to casualties, Private Columbine took over command of a gun and kept firing it from 9.00 am till 1.00 pm in an isolated position with no wire in front. During this time, wave after wave of the enemy failed to get up to him. Owing to his being attacked by a low flying aeroplane, the enemy at last gained a strong footing in the trench on either side. The position being untenable, he ordered the two remaining men to get away and though being bombed from either side, he kept his gun firing and inflicted tremendous losses. He was eventually killed by a bomb which blew up him and his gun. He showed throughout the highest valour, determination and self-sacrifice.

Herbert, or Bertie as he was known, was born in November 1893 and from an early age was determined to join the army like his father. In 1905 Emma was 50 and Bertie 12 and about to leave school. Emma decided to leave Lambeth in London for a quieter and cheaper place to live. Her husband's pension plus proceeds from her furniture business and the wages Bertie could now earn would be enough for them to live on. Remembering the good times she had spent at seaside resorts as a child, she decided to move to Walton-on-the-Naze.

However. five years later Bertie returned from Colchester to inform his mother that he had enlisted in the 19th (Queen Alexandra's Own Royal) Hussars, service number 5780. Why not his father's old regiment is unknown. I can imagine how upset she must have been, bringing back memories of her husband. The 1911 census has Columbine stationed at Aldershot and Emma still carrying on her business at Walton.

There was a considerable amount of varied training, they were taught to ride, muck out and groom the horses and though as cavalrymen they were trained to use the sword they were also trained to use the rifle and Maxim machine gun. In addition to mounted training they also spent time crawling across the ground on their stomachs with rifles. Academic education also went on in the classroom and they were all expected to pass the Army First-Class Certificate of Education. Bertie became very proficient on the machine gun.

By July 1914 the 19th Hussars were in Hounslow until the outbreak of war, a number of changes were taking place and Columbine found himself with 'A' Squadron and attached to the 5th Division. They arrived in France in August as part of the original BEF and were to be involved in many of the major Battles of the War, 1914 saw them at:

- Battle of Mons.
- Retreat from Mons.
- Battle of Le Cateau.
- Battle of the Marne
- Battle of the Aisne.
- Battle of La Bassée and Messines 1914.
- The First Battle of Ypres.

By the end of 1914, although having put up a tremendous fight, the BEF were close to being wiped out. Reinforcements were urgently required and in time these would come but the newly-trained volunteers naturally lacked the experience of their predecessors. Columbine was one of the lucky ones to survive this first four months of ferocious fighting.

We read a lot about the 1914 Christmas truce but we are not sure whether Columbine took part in it. The Hussars appeared to have taken a rest and were not called on again until the Second Battle of Ypres and the capture of Hill 60 in April/May 1915. Just prior to this they had been reorganized again and were now part of the 9th

Cavalry Brigade of the 1st Cavalry Division. The rest of the year was relatively quiet other than the occasional skirmish.

In 1916 the Machine Gun Corps (MGC) was established and in June Columbine was transferred to the 9th Squadron MGC and allocated a new service number, 50720. It was here that he met who was to become his best friend, the Australian Francis Burke who had won the Distinguished Conduct Medal earlier in the year.

The pair of them spent a considerable amount of time in reserve but eventually went into action on 15 September 1916 at the Battle of Flers-Courcelette on the Somme, the day the British used tanks for the first time. It was on this day and at this battle that the author's grandfather was injured and invalided home.

By August the Germans were losing ground at the Somme and Verdun and had suffered nearly a quarter of a million casualties. In addition the Allied naval blockade of the North and Adriatic Sea was causing food shortages in Germany, resulting in rationing. Morale was low and many German leaders believed the battle was lost. The Germans therefore decided to employ new tactics: they were to concede ground in order to inflict the maximum number of casualties on the Allies. Captain von Hentig of the Guards Reserve Division commented that the Somme was the muddy grave of the German Army.

Haig wanted to deploy the tank, but it was not until 15 September when they were ready to take part in the last major offensive of the Somme campaign. Forty-nine tanks were ready to take part but only thirty-two made it to the start line, and eventually only eighteen went into action. The rest had either suffered mechanical failure or became trapped in shell holes or trenches. The tanks made slow progress due to the landscape being dotted with shell holes. It was like riding the waves in a rough sea, however they could plough through barbed wire, cross trenches and gave the infantry some protection as they followed up behind. There is no doubt that initially they caused considerable fear in the Germans.

After the battle, the British press reported:

> When the German outposts crept out of their dugouts in the mist of the morning of 15 September and stretched to look for the English, their blood was chilled to their veins.

Monument of a British soldier (Royal (London) Fusiliers) at the Village of Flers, his rifle pointing in the direction the tanks came. There is a replica monument in High Holborn, London. (Dawn Knox)

Two mysterious monsters were crawling towards them over the craters. Stunned as if an earthquake had burst around them they all rubbed their eyes, which were fascinated by the fabulous creatures.

The Press Association correspondent at the front reported:

The topic of the moment, both with our soldiers and the German prisoners, is the new 'tank' or mobile turrets which have done such valuable work. Indeed, without claiming too much for this latest addition to our war machinery, it really looks as though a good means of effectively dealing with the enemy's machine-guns has been devised. The prisoners admit that the sight of these weird monsters creeping towards them, spitting fire as they came, was one of the most demoralising experiences they have yet met. The whole tone of the prisoners is one of great depression. They say that they had been told our offensive was spent, which the lull of the preceding few days led them to believe was true. The answer that the British Army is but beginning and that what is happening now-a-days is as a fleabite to what may be expected when we develop our full strength is not particularly comforting.

The *Liverpool Echo* reported a number of stories from the front, this is one of them:

OFFICER WHO WENT INTO FLERS VILLAGE

The officer who did what the soldiers called the great 'stunt' in Flers told me his story. He went into Flers before the infantry and followed by them, cheering in high spirits and knocked out a machine gun which began to play on him. The town was not much damaged by shell fire, so that the tank could walk about real streets and the garrison, which was hiding about in dugouts, surrendered in small, searing groups. Three other tanks came into Flers and together they lolloped around town in a free and easy manner before going further afield

We have to be very careful with regards to press coverage: you could get the impression that the tank was a massive success but they only had a modest impact. A gunner had this to say:

> Our tank commander was 2nd Lt. Macherson, a fine and likeable fellow but he like all of us had never been on a battlefield or in action before. Indeed that was the position of practically the whole of the 32 tanks which took part in this first action. The briefing and instructions regarding objectives were quite inadequate and there was little or no co-operation between the infantry and the tanks.

As a result of the day's action the villages of Flers and Courcelette were captured but the advance was limited to 2,500 yards on a three-mile front. However, despite the lack of real progress Haig expressed his faith in the tank, stating: 'Wherever the tanks advanced, we took our objectives and where they did not advance, we failed to take our objectives. Go back and make as many more tanks as you can.'

A few more minor actions took place but with torturous winter weather setting in, the British stopped their offensive officially on 11 November, with Haig intending to restart it in February 1917. Over one million Allied and Central Powers men were wounded or killed and we were no further forward.

1917 started with the Battle of Arras in April 1917 followed by a number of minor battles that were part of the Arras offensive. Then later in the year was the Third Battle of Ypres, more commonly known as Passchendaele. Whether Columbine was involved I am not sure but I would be surprised if he was not involved in some of the smaller battles that made up this offensive.

Finally we come to 1918, the year that peace at last would arrive and after four years of fighting, Columbine was one of the very few original men of the BEF to have made it this far. On 21 March the Germans launched their long-awaited Spring Offensive. It was their last attempt to win the war, and they had been strengthened by 500,000 troops from the Russian Front. The German General Erich Ludendorff had said: 'We must strike at the earliest moment before the Americans can throw strong forces into the scale. We must beat the British.'

As we know it was Columbine's last fight and the following two eyewitness accounts give a clear indication of the heroic fight that he put up at Hervilly Wood. The first is the letter received by his mother from Private F.H. Burke:

Dear Mrs Columbine,

I do hope you will excuse me for taking the liberty of writing to you. But I feel I must write to you to sympathise with you for the terrible loss of your son and to tell you how bravely he died. As I am the only one who got away alive, I feel sure you would like me to tell you about it. I am a very poor hand at writing but if it were possible for anyone else to see and feel as I do, they would understand how I feel about your son. He was the bravest man I have even seen in my life and no man on earth could possibly have given his life more bravely than he did, he never thought once of retiring when others were doing so and if he had chosen he could have got away. But we had lost both the Officer and Sergeant in charge of us and no one else was left to give us orders so he stayed.

Well this is just what happened. He was No 1 on one gun and I was No 1 gun on the other, we were both in the same section and we were ordered to take up a certain position with our guns and gun teams which consisted of 5 men each gun, we were given to understand that there were some of our own men in front of us. This however, was unfortunately not so, for at about 8.30 am we espied the Germans advancing to attack our trench. It is to be noted that we had no artillery support whatever. Bert saw them before I did and he shouted to me and we both opened fire and were able to hold them until about 1.30 although in front of Bert's gun there was no wire. I had wire in front of mine so I had a better chance than he. We had lost our Sergeant in the first rush and our Officer was killed shortly after. Just after 10'clock we were repeatedly attacked by low flying aeroplanes which fired machine guns at us and the Germans also attacked at the same time. About 1.30 they made a very strong attack against us and as your son had no wire in front of him they were able to gain a strong footing in his trench on each side of him. I managed to check them, helped considerably by the wire round me.

Bert's position being now quite hopeless, he sent away the only two men who were left alive with him, both these men were severely wounded in getting way.

When I had, by continuous firing, somewhat checked the attack in front of my immediate position. I looked round to see how things were faring with your son. With the exception of a few yards in front of his gun, he was absolutely surrounded by

Germans. He was firing furiously and inflicting terrible losses among the oncoming enemy and there were piles of dead and wounded all round him and in front. He kept working his gun until, suddenly, the inevitable happened; a bomb exploded with terrific force right in front of him and blew up both Bert and his gun.

Mad with rage at the death of my dearly beloved pal, I swung my machine gun round and rapidly fired the remainder of my ammunition into the masses of Germans around him and under cover of this temporary check, managed by great good fortune, to get clear away.

Oh! You have reason to be proud of your son dear Mrs Columbine, a braver man never lived than he; I could not have stopped there had it not been for his example. Through sticking there I have been awarded a Bar to my DCM. I have just told what happened regarding your dear son and he has been recommended for the VC and if ever a man on this earth deserved it, he did, he refused to retire when he might have done so and by his devotion to duty and his example to the rest of us, he was the means of holding up a large number of the enemy for about six hours and he died like a brave gunner should, with his gun and face towards the enemy.

Words fail me dear Mrs Columbine, to express the sorrow I feel for you in your terrible loss. I too miss him for he was my friend but he left us an example which I for one, will never forget. I have a wallet with a letter and a post card that belonged to him, these I will send on to you. My address is 50773 F H Burke, 3rd Section, 9th MGS, BEF France.

I remain
Yours sincerely
F.H. Burke.

Dr P.G.C. Atkinson witnessed the last few hours of Bertie's life:

Nothing I have seen or heard of could be finer than the heroism of this soldier. The enemy attacked suddenly in great force. They made considerable headway and from 'vantage ground' on either side they started to enfilade our trenches, causing severe casualties amongst the men. Part of our defence system included a machine gun post somewhere in advance of the main trench.

The men working this were all knocked out. Running the gauntlet of very heavy fire Private Columbine rushed forward and took charge of this gun. He was followed by some comrades and in spite of the fact that the whole of the enemy machine guns in the immediate neighbourhood concentrated their heaviest fire upon the post, which was almost unprotected by any devices commonly used, Columbine kept the machine gun going for over four hours.

At that time the enemy had been working round the position with strong forces and actually had the post cut off, save one narrow gap by which it was possible to communicate with the main position. For the whole of the time, save when he went across the fire swept ground to bring ammunition, the brave chap remained at his post and despite frequent rushes, he kept the enemy at bay. In the course of the fight, a German Officer appeared and repeatedly urged his men to attack on the isolated post, but every rush of the Germans was stopped in a few yards by the deadly fire from this brave gunner who was actually wounded but continued to work the gun in spite of that.

Early in the afternoon it became obvious that the position was hopeless and Columbine told the only two unwounded comrades left that it was folly for them to remain there. 'Save yourselves, I'll carry on' was what he said. They were reluctant to go but he insisted and in the end they came to see the force of his contention that there was no point in sacrificing three lives where one was enough. He shouted a few words of farewell and that was the last his comrades heard of him.

From where we lay, we could see the fight going on, the swarms of grey-blue infantry around the position, the machine gun manned by the wounded hero, spitting out death. In the course of the hour, from noon to one, the enemy made eight attempts to rush the post. Each one was brought to a standstill. Therefore new tactics were necessary. Retiring to their positions, the enemy concentrated heavy rifle and machine gun fire on the hero and his gun. At the same time a number of hostile aeroplanes appeared overhead. They were promptly engaged by our machines but one detached itself from the fighting group and came down to about a hundred feet or so above the machine gun position, circling above for a few seconds like a great vulture ready to pounce on its prey.

We saw Columbine elevate his gun to attack his new enemy. The fight could only have one ending. A bomb was launched from the aeroplane and there was a sharp report, gun and gunner blown up. The heroic fight of Columbine was not without its value, for the way in which he delayed the enemy attack gave us time to consolidate our position in the immediate neighbourhood and when the enemy attacked, they found that the four hours' stand by one man had put the Germans' plans hopelessly out of gear so far as capture of that series of positions was concerned. The comrades of the dead hero speak highly of him.

It is difficult to comprehend what was going through his mind as he manned his machine gun. Did he think he was indestructible or was he thinking of his brave father or had he decided he would not get out of the scrap alive so he might as well take as many of the enemy with him? Amazing courage.

One could say that his effort was not in vain: the fighting went on until June when Ludendorff called off the offensive. Although the Germans had advanced many miles, their losses were huge, approaching a million men and they had overstretched their supply lines. Then in August the Allies hit back with the final Hundred Days offensive which would end the war.

In addition to his VC he was awarded the 1914 Star, and the British and Victory Medals. He is commemorated on the Pozières Memorial but he has no known grave. At home in Walton he is remembered and honoured with a statue and a bust plus the local leisure centre is named after him – Columbine Centre.

To our Fallen Heroes

For heroes lost in field and flood,
Who for their country shed their blood;
In Belgium, France & Italy,
In Serbia and Gallipoli;
For these, O God, we lift our prayer;
And leave them sleeping 'Neath thy care,
To thy safe keeping we entrust,
Their quiet graves and splendid dust.
Their comrades shall march home one day;
But they'll be sleeping far away.

Theirs wars are o'er; their sun is set,
But England never shall forget,
And through the long, long years to be,
Their deeds shall live eternally

By W Williams (M.A. Oxon)

It is very difficult to explain and to fully understand the grief of losing a love one many miles from home but in some cases it was too much to bear. Joseph Jowers, aged 63, a labourer of Park Gate Farm in Little Clacton, who had lost one son to the war and had another badly wounded, hung himself in a shed.

CHAPTER 10

Peace at Last

❧

1917 was in many ways a continuation of the previous two years with various successes by both the Allies and the Central Powers but there were a number of important events which eventually affect the outcome of the war in 1918.

The first of these was on 16 January when the German government proposed a military alliance with Mexico. Germany was planning unrestricted submarine warfare to try to starve Britain into surrender. This would mean sinking American shipping and almost certainly force America to declare war on Germany.

The following is the decoded telegram sent by the German Foreign Secretary Arthur Zimmerman to the Mexican government:

> We intend to begin on the first of February unrestricted submarine warfare. We shall endeavour in spite of this to keep the United States of America neutral. In the event of this not succeeding, we make Mexico a proposal of alliance on the following basis: make war together, make peace together, generous financial support and an understanding on our part that Mexico is to re-conquer the lost territory in Texas, New Mexico, and Arizona. The settlement in detail is left to you. You will inform the President of the above most secretly as soon as the outbreak of war with the United States of America is certain and add the suggestion that he should, on his own initiative, invite Japan to immediate adherence and at the same time mediate between Japan and ourselves. Please call the President's attention to the fact that the ruthless employment of our submarines now offers the prospect of compelling England in a few months to make peace.' Signed, ZIMMERMANN

The idea was that if America did declare war on Germany its forces would be tied down dealing with Mexico therefore restricting the help that they could give to the Allies. Fortunately, for a number of reasons Mexico turned down Germany's offer.

It did not stop Germany declaring unrestricted submarine warfare on 1 February 1917. Then on 3 February America broke off diplomatic relations with Germany following the sinking of the US ship *Housatonic* off Sicily but it was not until 6 April before America actually declared war on Germany following President Wilson's request to the American Congress on 2 April with the plea, 'Make the world safe for democracy'.

In the meantime there was a revolution going on in Russia which resulted in the overthrow of the Imperial Government resulting in the abdication of Tsar Nicholas II who with his family was eventually executed on 17 July 1918, an event that was to have worldwide consequences for generations to come.

In 1917 the following countries either declared war on Germany or broke off diplomatic relations:

- 14 March 1917 – Chinese government breaks off diplomatic relations with Germany.
- 7 April 1917 – Cuba declares war on Germany.
- 8 April 1917 – Panama declares war on Germany.
- 4 June 1917 – Brazil declares war on Germany.
- 5 October 1917 – Peru beaks off diplomatic relations with Germany.
- 7 October 1917 – Uruguay breaks off diplomatic relations with Germany.

Passchendaele was the final battle of the year but was by no means the breakthrough that the Allies expected and such gains as were made came at a great human cost. Also during November Russia started peace talks with Germany which resulted in the signing of a humiliating peace treaty on 3 March 1918.

So what did our troops expect on the dawn of a new year? Peace must have been the furthest thing from their minds after three years of fighting in conditions that today we cannot even imagine.

In March the New Military Service Bill raised the maximum conscription age to 50 years and introduced conscription in Ireland:

things were looking desperate. The situation was not helped by Germany's Western Front troops being reinforced by troops released from the Eastern Front, enabling Germany on 31 March to launch its Spring Offensive before the Americans could join in the fighting, in the hope of breaking the Allied lines in France and forcing the Allies to sue for peace. They advanced some 40 miles, even threatening Paris again, taking approximately 80,000 prisoners as they did so.

The German tactics, although successful at first, were in the end their downfall, since the fast-moving stormtroopers leading the attacks could not carry enough food and ammunition to sustain themselves for long periods and by middle of July their offensive had petered out, in part through lack of supplies but also due to their massive casualties of around 1,000,000. And by now the Americans had joined in with 250,000 men.

Discipline in the German Army was beginning to break down and the Allies decided to take advantage and go on the offensive, what has become known as the 'The Hundred Days Offensive' or the Advance to Victory (95 days in fact). Like previous campaigns it was a series of major battles that took place between August and November.

- The Battles of the Marne – 20 July–2 August.
- The Battle of the Soissonals and of the Ourcq – 23 July–2 August.
- The Battle of Tardenois – 20–31 July.
- The Battle of Amiens – 8–11 August.
- The Second Battles of the Somme – 21 August–3 September.
- The Battle of Albert – 21–23 August.
- The Second Battle of Bapaume – 31 August–3 September.
- The Second Battles of Arras – 26 August–3 September.
- The Battle of the Scarpe – 26–30 August.
- The Battle of Drocourt-Queant – 2–3 September.
- The Battles of the Hindenburg Line – 12 September–9 October.
- The Battle of Havrincourt – 12 September.
- The Battle of Ephey – 18 September.
- The Battle of the Canal Du Nord – 27 September–2 October.
- The Battle of the St Quentin Canal – 29 September–2 October.
- The Battle of Beaurevoir – 3–5 October.

The railway carriage in which the Armistice was signed in the Forest of Compiègne. (Author's collection)

- The Battle of Cambrai – 8–9 October.
- The Battle of Ypres – 28 September–2 October.
- The Battle of Courtral – 14–19 October.
- The Battle of Valenciennes – 1–2 November.
- The Battle of the Sambre – 4 November.
- The capture of Mons – 11 November.

In between these battles there were several other operations that also played a part in the final defeat of the Central Powers.

Bulgaria was the first of the Central Powers to surrender on 30 September 1918, followed by Turkey on 30 October and Austria on 3 November, then eight days later Germany signed an armistice at 5 am on 11 November – peace at last. However, in the hours between the announcement of the armistice and its enforcement of 11 am (French time) fighting continued and almost 3,000 men died. Fortunately I have not be able to trace anybody from Clacton or the surrounding seaside resorts who was killed during this period, although there were many in the months leading up to the Armistice.

Everyone Sang

Everyone suddenly burst out singing;
And I was filled with such delight
As prisoned birds must find in freedom,
Winging wildly across the white

Orchards and dark-green fields; on – on – and out of sight.

Everyone's voice was suddenly lifted;
And beauty came like the setting sun:
My heart was shaken with tears; and horror
Drifted away ... O, but Everyone
Was a bird; and the song was wordless; the singing will never be
done.

By Siegfried Sassoon

While all this was going on, what was happening back on the home front? Military Service Tribunals were still being held and though many applications failed, it appears that in most cases they were given three to six months' exemption. There were many such examples in the Clacton and surrounding villages where this happened so the chances of them being conscripted reduced as the months slipped by.

In March 1917 at the County of London Appeal Tribunal Mr Alfred Gerhold of St Clere's Hall, St Osyth, was refused any further exemption and was arrested as an absentee. The main evidence against him was based on a letter presented to the Tribunal by Mr Maurice Baker, the agricultural representative of Tendering Tribunal, in which it alleged that Mr Gerhold was an incompetent farmer, and that his farm was practically derelict, and that it had been decided to take the farm away from him and have it farmed for the benefit of the country. One can understand this decision because all available land was required for food production. However, Mr Gerhold was not happy with the decision and obviously believed he was not incompetent so in June 1918 he took what seems an unusual step and brought a libel case against Mr Baker for the malicious content of the letter. The defendant pleaded that the letter was published on a privileged occasion without malice. The judge in his summing-up pointed out that the question of whether the occasion was privileged was for him to decide. However, it was down to the jury to decide whether the letter was malicious. The jury found that there was libel and that the words were malicious and the judge also found in Mr Gerhold's favour stating that the letter was not written on a privileged occasion. He awarded Mr Gerhold £100 damages plus costs. We can only assume he was allowed back on his farm

Reports were also still coming in of those that had been killed, taken prisoner or received gallantry awards. For example, in January 1918 it was reported that Private J. Barnes, son of W. Barnes of Grove Cottage,

Brightlingsea, who had previously been reported missing presumed killed, was in fact a prisoner in Germany. Private E.H. Barrell of the Middlesex Regiment, a citizen of Brightlingsea again believed missing was also in fact a prisoner. Another, Captain Handley, son of Mrs Handley of New Street, Brightlingsea, also reported missing, wrote home informing his mother that he was a prisoner in Germany and that he had been promoted to his present rank for gallantry in the field. Mrs W. Beare of Spring Hill, St Osyth, received a card from her eldest son, Private William Beare of the East Surreys Regiment, who had been reported missing that he is quite well and a prisoner in Germany.

Also in January it was reported that Sergeant W.J. Goodwin of the Rifle Brigade had been awarded the Distinguished Conduct Medal and Private Godfrey Welham of the Canadian Contingent of St Osyth had been awarded the Military Medal for bravery as a 'runner'. A runner was somebody who took on the dangerous task of carrying messages back and forth on the front.

In July we have a report that A. Rampling of the Royal Engineers from St Osyth had been awarded the Military Medal. Then as late as September we have a report that another Brightlingsea man Private Edward Ernest Hodges of the Essex Regiment was awarded the French Croix de Guerre for helping wounded men under heavy fire but at the time he was in hospital in France suffering from the effects of gas. He was well known in Brightlingsea and prior to his enlistment was an agent for the Prudential Assurance Company.

It is obvious that the German prisoners in England were not receiving any reports on the state of the war otherwise I do not think that the following two prisoners would have attempted to make their escape as late as October if they had realized the war would be over within a month. They had escaped from Foxborough Farm, Chigwell Row, and managed to steal a boat at Maldon and set sail but were picked up several miles out at sea by a patrol boat after being spotted by an Ipswich captain who was in command of a trading vessel that regularly sailed between England and France. The prisoners were brought back to Brightlingsea.

In addition to the war news being reported in the local papers, life appeared to be going on as normal with reports on criminal activities, marriages, drownings, elections, sporting and entertainment activities etc, Frinton-on-Sea seemed to be a favourite venue for newlyweds' honeymoons. Like today Frinton seemed to be the most exclusive of the seaside resorts along this Sunshine Coast.

Armistice Day Parade, Brightlingsea. (Brightlingsea Museum)

When the Armistice was finally announced bells in London burst forth into joyful chimes, bands paraded the streets followed by cheering crowds of soldiers and civilians.

On Tuesday, 12 November 1918, Brightlingsea celebrated the signing of the Armistice with a service at All Saints' Church. This followed a large procession to the church which was led by the Australian engineers. The congregation was so large they could not all get in the Church so an overflow service was held outside.

There is no doubt that celebrations took place in the Clacton area but very little about the events were published in the local papers; it appears that they waited for the peace treaty to be officially signed some eight months later. The Treaty of Versailles was finally signed on 28 June 1919, exactly five years after the assassination of Archduke Franz Ferdinand, and so it was on Saturday, 19 July 1919 that the country officially celebrated the peace and our seaside resorts wholeheartedly joined in.

At Brightlingsea Commander Mahon of the Royal Navy and his bluejackets entertained all the local children, their relatives and friends to a big tea party on St Osyth Point. Various forms of amusements were made available by the Naval officers, even a tank was

Peace Day parade, Clacton 1919. (Author's collection)

on display, climbing a 10-foot obstacle and performing a number of remarkable manoeuvres. Mr Howard of the Station Hotel entertained a large company of sailors and others at the Picture House, followed afterwards by public entertainment and during these entertainments he presented a house, 22 Park Road, to the town for use as an institute and £100 for the future War Memorial. A Whippet tank was the centre of interest in the street procession and over 4,000 flags, many bearing the arms of the Cinque Ports, decorated the town. The Salvation Army and town bands played a selection of music. In the evening there was a fancy dress carnival and a further procession through the principal streets and a bonfire on West Marsh with fireworks.

In Clacton the streets were ablaze with flags with thousands parading through the town following the carnival procession with scenes of extraordinary enthusiasm. In the afternoon there was children's entertainment at the Band Pavilion.

At Frinton the proceedings commenced with a carnival procession of decorated vehicles from the railway station followed by a programme of sports and fairground entertainment. Music was played by the Frinton Ladies' Orchestra. Tea was also provided for the residents followed by a torchlight procession and a huge bonfire.

The local papers do not report any celebrations at Walton-on-the-Naze, Holland-on-Sea or St Osyth, but one can only assume they took place or they were incorporated with the others.

> I cannot imagine
> The horrors they saw,
> Their constant fear
> To win the war.
>
> The heavy bombardment
> Of enemy fire,
> Endless rolls
> Of lethal barbed wire.
>
> Ignoring the rats
> And the terrible stench
> They shiver and curse
> In their sodden trench.
>
> The stink of bodies
> Living and dying
> Sightless eyes
> No longer crying.
>
> Across the years
> We echo their cry
> Our bitter despair
> For those who die.
>
> For death brings such
> Tremendous sorrow
> 'They gave their today
> For our tomorrow.'
>
> So do not pine
> Or shed more tears
> But remember their bravery
> Amid their fears.
>
> By Sue Radford

At this point one must give a thought to those families that lost love ones. Did they join in or stay quietly in their homes with their memories.

CHAPTER 11

The War Memorials

ల~ఎ

The War Memorial

A war memorial, standing straight
And proud against the sky
Issues this challenge, demanding still
Of those who pass it by
Do you recall men went to war?
These bodies that I guard?
Did you learn the lesson that they left?
Or legacy discard?
Most men fought and some men died
Some wounded, some remain
By ignoring that, you're not saving lives
You're killing them again!
They suffered long-in trench and pit
For principles they believed-
That sacrifice prevents repeat
And were they all deceived?
I am not here to glorify war
Or justify its right;
I am just here because men believed
Their death could make your future bright.

By S.J. Robinson

For the next fifteen years or so, war memorials sprang up across the country to honour those who had lost their lives. The names that appear on the Rolls of Honour are from the war memorials, church plaques, local casualty lists, newspapers and Geoff's

Brightlingsea War Memorial. (Author's collection)

Search Engine (where dates cannot be found, the space has been left blank).

The Brightlingsea War Memorial was unveiled in 1921, with Brigadier General F.W. Towsy attending. The memorial was designed by Richard Reginald Goulden and is constructed of white granite with bronze plaques. It consists of a cenotaph and towards the top of the west and east faces are rectangular bronze plaques, each with a relief design representing the heads of three servicemen and at the top is a carved inscription which reads: '**IN MEMORY OF THOSE WHO GAVE THEIR LIVES IN THE GREAT WAR**'. On the north and south side surmounted by wreaths are inscribe the names of those who died. There is now an additional plaque with the names of those who lost their lives in the Second World War.

Richard Goulden was born in Dover on 30 August 1876. He was educated at Dover College, then Dover School of Art where he won a scholarship to the Royal College of Art in London. He studied architecture then sculpture. During the war he served with the Royal Engineers in France. He was mention in despatches and given the temporary rank of captain. Following an injury he was sent back to England and spent time at Brightlingsea where he was appointed adjutant to the Australian Engineers. It therefore seemed fitting with his connection with Brightlingsea that he designed the memorial.

Brightlingsea Roll of Honour

Name	Died
Adams, T. Cecil	31 July 1917
Aldous, Sydney	19 December 1914
Aldous, Thomas B.	
Aldous, Walter Robert	15 September 1916
Aldrich, George Richard	4 December 1917
Alexander, G.	4 November 1918
Almond, Albert Rouse	28 September 1915
Andrews, Thomas	10 February 1919
Aunis, Alfred	
Austin, Chris	1 April 1918
Austin, Chris J.	
Bagley, Thomas W.	
Baker, Wilfred	8 August 1917
Barnes, Arthur Hector	16 September 1917
Barnes, Basil Willie	5 October 1918
Barnes, H. Reginald	29 September 1915
Barnes, James	
Barnes, T. Aubrey	14 July 1916
Beales, Arthur	23 June 1917
Bishop, Arthur	
Bowdell, George Major	14 February 1917
Bowdell, Jack Godfrey	15 November 1916
Bowers, William George	25 May 1916

Bragg, Ridgeway Alfred	24 February 1917
Bragg, Ted	15 December 1919
Branch, William J.	13 June 1918
Brooks, Harry	3 July 1916
Brown, Hartley	
Bush, C F	
Butcher, Wilfred J.	15 October 1919
Butler, E.W.G.	15 April 1917
Bye, George Alfred	10 November 1917
Cant, G.E.	24 January 1917
Cardy, W.G.	30 September 1917
Chaplin, Benjamin	6 July 1918
Chaplin, Geoffrey Fred	29 April 1917
Clark, William	25 September 1916
Cook, Thomas William	20 December 1918
Cook, William	14 March 1918
Coppin, Albert	
Cross, Eustace	25 March 1918
Dines, Walter B.	25 August 1915
Doyle (Dople), Harry Thomas	24 February 1917
Dowling, G.A.	26 July 1916
Draper, Charles J.	
Eade, Edward H	15 October 1917
Ellis, Leonard G	1 February1915
Evans, Llewellyn L.M.	
Everett, J Burgess	25 September 1915
Every, Walter	12 January 1917
Farrington, Isaac K.	10 July 1916
Forrow, T.	29 March 1918
Francis, Walter H.	
French, Harry	28 June 1915
French, Harry	28 December 1917
French, William	

Frost, Henry	
Gant, Henry	9 November 1915
Gilbert, William	8 May 1917
Goddard, Arthur Hawkins	10 May 1915
Godfrey, Ernest	21 February 1917
Goff, John M.	
Goodwin, John H.	
Gosling, Clara B.	7 November 1918
Gould, Frederick	27 March 1918
Gould, Luther R.	
Greenland, Frederick John	22 September 1914
Gunn, Noble	1 October 1916
Hammond, Harry	18 August 1916
Hardingham, Jack	18 May 1915
Hardman, Harold E.	4 February 1919
Herbert, Edgar James	27 October 1920
Herbert, Jacob T.	23 January 1919
Horlock, William James	24 March 1921
Howard, J. Henry	26 July 1916
Ingate, Walter William	22 September 1914
Ivimy, Donald Delf	20 October 1917
Jacobs, Frederick W.	30 June 1918
Jacobs, William	30 June 1915
Jarrett, George J.	14 August 1917
Jones, Bertie Edward	10 June 1915
Kerry, Thomas	8 January 1919
King, A. Bertie	
King, Edward G.	
King, Jabez W.	
King, Stanley H.	9 August 1916
Laflin, William	
Lambert, Allan	6 September 1917
Large, James N.	1 July 1916

Lewes, Arthur	
Linder, John Magner	3 March 1916
March, Horace H.	
Marsh, William	22 March 1918
Martin, Frederick A.	
Mercer. William Richard	28 February 1916
McMillan, John Casely	6 February 1917
Mills, Frank H.	31 May 1916
Moulton, Thomas H.	15 October 1916
Norfolk, Arthur George	14 October 1915
Norton, Frederick	
Norton, Ralph (MM)	4 April 1917
Nurse, Rochford	
Oliver, Horace Percy	17 April 1917
Osborn, William Hugh	30 December 1915
Ost, Arthur Edward	29 July 1915
Oxborrow, L.G.H.	28 May 1917
Patrick, Frederick	
Porter, William Arthur	27 April 1919
Richardson, Joseph Walter	7 May 1918
Riches, Arthur G.	5 December 1915
Rose, Ernest Frederick	11 April 1917
Rose, Ernest J.	
Rose, Frederick	23 October 1915
Rowley, Charles	3 November 1917
Ruffell, William	11 November 1916
Salmon, George	24 February 1917
Sparling, Bertie	5 May 1918
Sparling, Walter	
Steady, Albert	24 December 1916
Steady, Bertie	6 March 1917
Steady, William John	24 February 1917
Steward, G.	17 October 1917

Studd, Bertie W.	26 February 1917
Tatum, George E.	
Tatum, Robert William	2 April 1918
Tavner, Clifford Mortimer	12 April 1917
Taylor, Reginald Robertson	11 April 1918
Taylor, Thomas C.	14 May 1918
Watkins, Williams A.	
Went, Clifford	27 March 1918
Westall, Albert	2 January 1919
Wheeler, James W.	26 September 1915
Wickham, Charles Edward	30 December 1917
Wringe, Arthur George	12 February 1916
Yell, Walter	

From August 1918 the Anglican church of St Peter and St Paul, St Osyth, had been putting its collection money to one side to fund a war memorial. By 1919 the church had raised £200 and on Friday, 24 December 1920 the St Osyth War Memorial was unveiled by Colonel T. Gibbons DSO and dedicated at the church in the presence of a large congregation. The memorial is in the form of a cross and stands 17ft high, made of Cotswold Stone and closely resembled the sacrificial crosses that had been erected in the vast French war cemeteries.

The Reverend Croft had decided to refer it to as the Churchyard Cross, but this caused a considerable amount of unrest, then outright opposition within the local community. Also because the list of those that had died was finalised prematurely in 1919, there were a considerable number of errors and omissions such as incorrect Christian names, missing names and names of those that survived.

In an attempt to pacify the community Mrs Cowley who owned the Priory gave two fields in Mill Street to the village for recreational purposes. She made it clear that this was to honour the men who had laid down their lives and those that returned. This did not appear to satisfy the community so a second scheme was set up and on 15 May 1921 a second war memorial was erected by public subscription in a corner of the new Cowley Park. This memorial was a much more ornate design but it still had a number of mistakes similar to the Churchyard Cross.

St Peter and St Paul Memorial Cross, St Osyth. (Author's collection)

St Osyth War Memorial in Cowley Park. (Author's collection)

St Osyth Roll of Honour

Name	Died
Aldrich, Sidney	19 December 1914
Almond, Albert R.	28 September 1915
Almond, George	
Almond, John	
Austin, William G.	26 March 1917
Bancroft, John	22 September 1917
Beere, Ernest	26 March 1917
Beale, Edward V.	12 October 1918
Biswell, Jack	19 July 1916
Bullard, Herbert	1 July 1917
Butcher, Albert (Herbert)	
Carrington, Clifton	28 October 1916
Clements, John	29 August 1916
Cook, William A.*	22 October 1918
Copsey, Frederick W.	7 May 1915
Dunlop, Edgar Arthur	November 1920
Eggleton, Wilfred Leslie	9 July 1917
Emmerson, Alfred	20 September 1917
Emmerson, George	14 September 1914
Emmerson, Philip	16 July 1916
Emmerson, Samuel	23 October 1915
Evans, William H.	2 November 1917
Fearis, W.	27 February 1917
Florey, George Arthur	27 July 1918
German, Albert Edward	24 March 1918
Gibson, Frank	23 April 1917
Gibson, William H.	5 August 1917
Goodrick, William A.	12 December 1914
Gosling, Walter	22 March 1918
Gray, Charles	15 February 1916
Gray, William Charles	26 March 1917

Kent, George	
Last, Frank	
Last, Frederick (MM)	
London, William J.	28 March 1918
Maskell, Abraham	27 May 19178
Mayes, Frederick G.	1 January 1915
Mills, Charles R.	12 March 1916
Munson, Harry	2 November 1917
Munson, Raymond	6 July 1917
Newcomb, Robert James	29 April 1918
Newman, Ernest F.	11 October 1916
Osburn, Francis Cecil Trousdale	17 May 1917
Partridge, Ernest P.	26 November 1914
Partridge, Frederick	
Planten, Ernest William	28 March 1918
Rampling, Albert (MM)	6 January 1921
Scotney, Arthur	26 March 1917
Seaman, Arthur Georg	19 April 1916
Sharman-Coates, George A.W.	8 October 1915
Simpkin, Raymond A. R.	5 May 1916
Smith, Bert	11 April 1917
Smith, Charles	26 September 1915
Smith, Harry	18 May 1915
Smith, John	25 May 1915
Snowden, Victor	9 August 1917
Tatum, George E.	9 May 1915
Tatum, Robert W.	2 April 1918
Vincent, Reginald M.	31 August 1918
Warvill, Walter	5 November 1915
Whittaker, Harry P.	30 September 1917`
Wildney, Ernest E.	9 September 1916
Wildney, George	3 April 1917
Wildney, Urban	16 August 1915
Woods, Sydney George	5 October 1917

Woodward, Walter J.	6 May 1915
Wright, Frank	26 March 1917
Young, Ernest	11 April 1917
Young, Walter A.	8 May 1918
Young, William	

*William Cook, died in captivity at Munster, Westfalen.

In addition to Frederick Last and Albert Rampling, who were killed, the following St Osyth men were awarded the Military Medal: Lance Corporal John Bruce, Private Frederick German and Private William Pratt.

The unveiling of the Clacton-on-Sea Memorial took place on Sunday 6 April 1924 in front of thousands of people. It was unveiled by Lord Lambourne, CVO, PC, Lord-Lieutenant of Essex and dedicated by the Bishop of Colchester. The memorial stands on the sea front. It consists of a base of Cornish granite, surmounted by a life-sized bronze 'Angel of Victory.' On the three sides of the base are panels inscribed with 216 names of those who never returned, while the side facing the sea bears the date '1914-18' with the following inscription 'To the memory of the brave men of Clacton who lost their lives during the Great War.' The memorial stands 18ft in height and is the work of Mr C.L. Hartwell, ARA, who was assisted by Mr D.J. Bowe, surveyor to the Clacton Urban Council, the total cost being £1,500.

In his speech Lord Lambourne, who was accompanied by Brigadier General Kincaid-Smith, Brigadier General R.B. Colvin, Colonel Brad-bridge and Colonel Eustace Hill, said:

Second Lieutenant William Pratt. (Phyllis M. Hendy)

Lance Corporal Frederick Last.
(Phyllis M. Hendry)

Lance Corporal John Bruce. (Phyllis
M. Hendry)

It was an honour to unveil the memorial to those great men who suffered and died for their country. Such a monument was an honour to the place in which it was erected and he wished every town and village had a similar one so that 'they who run can read.' He asked them to remember that it was a monument to the living as well as to the dead. Could not they remember when they looked upon it and take into their daily life something of its meaning. The men for whom it was raised had their battles to fight and their hosts to overcome. All had daily battles to engage in and hosts of enemies to overcome. What was more beautiful in life than gratitude? Surely it was the anodyne sent to smooth the rough parts of life and enable them to enjoy that sympathy which was more common in affliction than was generally believed. Those who had passed through the shadows of life could tell how grateful it was to receive the sympathy of the world. Should they not render to God that which was due to him for all his mercies, which they so often did not deny to their fellow creatures? Life

1014–1918

TO THE GLORIOUS MEMORY OF
THOSE BRAVE MEN OF CLACTON
WHO SACRIFICED THEIR LIVES
IN THE GREAT WAR

Clacton War Memorial. (Author's collection)

and health and the many other mercies they daily enjoyed, should ever be remembered. He asked them to remember the sacrifices and trials of the men whom they commemorated and remember that a gracious God overlooked them. Every time they passed that monument let them recall what it stood for.

Take the memories of the cross with them into Life and business, remembering the Lord's saying 'My presence shall go with you and I will give you rest.'

The Bishop of Colchester said:

He hoped that what Lord Lambourne had said might help many of his brothers and sisters, who, while they have heavy hearts for those who had been taken from them, were proud to be there. It was not length of years but in fullness of life that the perfect life existed. They thanked God for those who died for them. They would never forget them and they were proud that they answered the call so readily.

Wreaths were placed by relatives and others around the memorial and the ceremony ended with first the 'Reveille' then the National Anthem.

Clacton Roll of Honour

Over 1,000 men from Clacton served in the armed forces during the Great War: the following are the 311 that lost their lives.

Name	Died
Abbot, Victor	13 November 1916
Aldis, Stanley Simeon	24 March 1917
Allen, Edwin William	3 October 1917
Allen, Harry	30 July 1916
Almond, Owen Edmund	29 September 1915
Aney, William Robert	30 July 1916
Argent, Edward Harry	10 October 1918
Armstead, Sydney James	31 August 1916
Armstrong, David	15 July 1918
Atkins, Oswald Clarence	31 October 1918
Baker, Charles	15 April 1918
Baker, John Harry Dennis	30 March 1918
Balls, W.A.	1 November 1918

Bancroft, John	22 September 1917
Bareham, Frederick Charles	17 October 1918
Bareham, George	13 August 1916
Bareham, Walter Charles	11 April 1917
Barker, George	30 April 1917
Barker, John	14 May 1915
Barker, Reginald Harold	20 October 1918
Barnard, Leonard William	31 August 1918
Barrett, Chester	10 December 1915
Barry, W.M.	25 February 1918
Bates, George	21 September 1918
Bayman, Frederick William	11 April 1917
Bayman, Henry Thomas	8 June 1917
Bear, Henry Denys	12 November 1915
Beckwith, Charles Edward	3 July 1916
Bedwell, Charles Theodore	12 April 1918
Bennett, Bertram A.	31 July 1917
Bennett, Sidney George	21 November 1914
Bedwell, George William	12 March 1915
Benton, Edwin George	26 August 1918
Bescoby, Jack	2 May 1915
Bigsby, Edgar Arthur	25 September 1915
Block, Edgar Lulham	1 July 1916
Bridges, Arthur George	4 August 1915
Brown, William Douglas	
Brooks, Edward	31 July 1917
Brownlie, Bruce	1 July 1916
Bullman, Haddon R. Horsley	30 November 1917
Burgess, C	
Burton, E G	
Burwood, Norman	14 March 1915
Burwood, Rene Martin	23 October 1916
Butcher, George	31 July 1917
Butterworth, Stanley Woodall	19 January 1918

Buxton, Robert Victor	28 September 1916
Canham, Harold	31 July 1917
Canler, Frederick George	14 September 1918
Cardy, William George	30 September1917
Carpenter, Frederick James	15 October 1916
Carrington, Frank Lewis	12 September 1916
Carrington, J.V.	18 July 1919
Carrington, Rufus	23 October 1916
Cattermole, William George	13 October 1916
Chatten, James Samuel	27 March 1918
Claridge, William Herbert	12 September 1916
Clarke, Albert Buxton	1 February 1918
Clarke, David	28 July 1917
Clarke, H.P.	
Clarke, Reginald James	26 April 1915
Clarke, Roger Arthur	9 May 1917
Coates, Charles Edward	15 April 1917
Cole, Harold William	24 March 1917
Coleman, Fred Creighton	23 April 1917
Cook, Charles Frederick	11 November 1914
Cook, Robert	4 November 1918
Cook, Robert George	9 May 1915
Crosby, Ernest Leonard	29 October 1918
Curtis, Bertie	22 April 1917
Curtis, George Oliver Stanley	23 July 1918
Cutter, Francis Martin	26 March 1917
Cutter, Frederick	19 September 1918
Dacre, R.	
Danby, Frederick William Leopold	23 October 1918
David, Henry	26 March 1917
Day, Loftus George Boley	4 February 1918
Day, Percy William	11 August 1918
Day, T.	
Denton, Walter	31 December 1918

Digby, Herbert	11 April 1917
Dorey, William E.	1 April 1917
Drake, Percy Clarence	2 December 1917
Dunn, Lionel Eric	25 August 1918
Eade, Francis George	19 July 1916
Egan, Michael	1 November 1914
Ellis, Frederick	25 April 1915
Evans, Leonard Horace	28 December 1916
Everitt, Walter	24 May 1915
Everson, Stanley	11 September 1914
Fairclough, Charles Harry	6 April 1918
Fairhead Alfred Scovell	27 March 1919
Fairweather, Frederick (MM)	2 June 1918
Fenn, Alfred John Wallace	18 January 1918
Fenn, William George	14 April 1917
Finer, Horace James	27 April 1917
Fisk, Arthur Jack	18 October 1918
Flanagan, Lionel Christopher	20 November 1917
Fuller, Edward William James	22 October 1917
Garnham, Henry Frederick	18 August 1915
Gladwell, A.E.	3 September 1917
Godbeer, G.A.	
Gower, J.	
Green, Samuel William	28 April 1916
Gregg, Gordon	4 May 1916
Gibson, William Harold	5 August 1917
Grigson, Mabel Edith	3 October 1918
Grigson, William	6 December 1917
Growns, Charles John	26 October 1918
Gunn, Arthur	5 May 1915
Hammond, Frederick	22 September 1914
Hammond, P.	
Hammond, Sidney George	12 August 1917
Hardie, Sidney Duncan Grellier	1 July 1916

Harrington, John William	3 August 1917
Harrington, Leonard	10 April 1917
Harvey, George	28 April 1917
Hatcher, George Ernest	22 September 1914
Herbert, L.	
Herman, Walter	27 August 1918
Hoare, Percy Edward	25 July 1918
Hobbs, Arthur Frederick	31 May 1916
Hollox, Frank Robert,	8 October 1916
Hooper, Henry John Edward	26 October 1917
Horton, Ernest Claude	1 July 1916
Howard, Archibald	13 April 1918
Howard, Ralph Gorman	10 November 1915
Howick, Henry	26 September 1918
Huggins, Douglas Frank	29 August 1916
Huggins, Stanley	14 October 1915
Ivimy, Donald	20 October 1917
Janes, G. E.	13 August 1918
Jarry, O.	
Jeffers, Claude Herbert	31 October 1914
Jenkins, Francis Henry	3 September 1916
Jennings, Bertie	15 October 1916
Jennings, Sidney	1 July 1916
Johnson, Cecil Noble (MM)	30 March 1918
Johnson, Henry	8 May 1916
Joy, Adolphus	27 October 1914
Joy, Thomas Victor	26 March 1917
Kenyon, James Henry	11 August 1917
King, Evelyn George	3 September 1916
King, Charles	10 May 1917
King, G.	
Kirkness, Gordon	29 June 1917
Kitchen, Alfred Edward	13 July 1915
Kittle, Joseph Benjamin	18 March 1917

Kittle, William George	3 October 1916
Laitt, George	27 April 1916
Last, Harold Haile	26 April 1915
Last, Lionel Robert	1 July 1916
Lee, J.H.	
Legerton, Jack	15 July 1916
Levy, Alkin Cameron	9 August 1915
Levy, Reginald C.	
Lewer, George Henry	20 May 1916
Lewitt, Benjamin	6 or 16 October 1918
Lloyd, Arthur Felix	1 September 1917
Lockwood, Stanley Clifford	23 March 1915
Londy, F.W.	18 June 1919
Lucas, Joseph	6 December 1917
Maclaren, James Mackenzie	21 January 1916
Malnick, George	16 May 1915
Mann, Cecil Augustus	16 April 1918
Manning, Cyril Harold	10 July 1916
Manning, Walter	
Marrington, Arthur William	26 December 1915
Martin, Arthur	
Martin, Fred	23 March 1918
Mash, Harry	5 December 1917
Mayhew, George	24 April 1915
Meden, Geoffrey	5 October 1917
Mills, Albert	13 October 1915
Mills, Claud	30 July 1915
Mills, Frank	23 March 1918
Mills, Sydney George Mills	13 June 1918
Moring, Bernard Walton	6 April 1916
Muldary, Cyril Joseph	11 December 1917
Munday, Edwin George Stanislaus	20 February 1917
Newman, M.G.	26 November 1916
Nicholson, Charles Stanley	15 September 1916

Osborn, Philip William	25 July 1917
Page, Arthur Henry	26 September 1915
Page, Eric John	28 August 1916
Page, Frank James	26 October 1918
Page, Stanley	30 November 1915
Page, Walter Wallace	6 August 1915
Page, William Henry	17 August 1916
Page, William Willie	22 September 1914
Parietti, Bernard	14 December 1915
Parsons, W.O.	
Partridge, Charles William	26 March 1917
Paxman, George William	30 November 1917
Peachey, B.R.	
Pearce, Sydney Edward	18 August 1917
Peartree, Craine	23 April 1917
Peartree, Fred	27 March 1915
Peck, Frederick William	31 July 1917
Perkins, W.M.F.	26 November 1918
Petch, James	7 April 1917
Pettit, George	27 October 1917
Phillibrown, Cyril George	15 November 1917
Philpot, Frederick	16 July 1916
Playfair, Victor Hamilton	26 February 1917
Polson, John Henry	15 October 1916
Pooley, Ralph James	17 September 1918
Porley, George	2 March 1916
Potter, Frederick William	18 April 1918
Prew, Wesley D.	25 September 1917
Prince, Gilbert Carlyle Mason	24 August 1918
Pryke, F.	
Pryke, Frederick J.	4 July 1916
Pulford, Arthur Louis	9 October 1916
Pulham, William Newman	27 March 1918
Pullen, Oscar Albert	2 April 1916

Quick, Stuart Henry	6 May 1916
Rand, Henry William	7 November 1918
Randall, Thomas Percy	5 March 1917
Ranson, George	25 March 1918
Rawlings, Thomas	09 October 1916
Reed, Cecil	14 June 1917
Revett, Stanley John	3 August 1917
Ridgeon, Nelson	18 July 1916
Ridgeon, Walter	10 October 1917
Ridgeon, Walter William	4 January 1917
Riley, George Harold	21 August 1918
Robinson, Arthur	10 October 1915
Roper, Arthur	6 August 1915
Roper, Frederick	6 August 1915
Rush, Frederick Robert	10 April 1918
Russell, Harry	1 May 1917
Samuel, Felix Leopold	7 October 1917
Saunders, Reginald George	13 November 1916
Sawyer, Alfred	12 April 1917
Sayer, Frank Joseph	30 October 1914
Schneider, Arthur Frederick	25 April 1917
Scott, Ernest	27 September 1915
Seager, Frank Owen	13 March 1915
Seaman, William Arthur	26 March 1917
Sergant, G.P.	14 April 1917
Shears, Herbert Charles	18 October 1916
Silvester, Anson Lloyd	31 December 1914
Simmonds, Percy Graham	1 July 1916
Simpkin, Raymond Alic Risley	5 May 1916
Smith, Allen	30 July 1917
Smith, Arthur John	25 September 1915
Smith, Cecil William	23 December 1917
Smith, David Henry	4 September 1916
Smith, Harold	28 March 1918

Smith, John	11 April 1917
Snart, George W.	22 March 1918
Stacey, Arthur	12 July 1915
Starling, W F	21 September 1918
Stebbing, Charles	17 August 1918
Stebbing, Edward John	8 July 1916
Sterry, William	1 July 1916
Stroulger, Laurence	19 September 1917
Strutt, Francis	13 May 1916
Suffling, James	18 October 1918
Sully, Percy Reece	17 July 1917
Summers, Albert	10 May 1915
Talbot, Cecil Melliar	27 September 1915
Tavner, Clifford Mortimer	12 April 1917
Taylor, A.	13 November 1915
Taylor, Charles William	21 September 1916
Taylor, George Francis Woodland	4 May 1917
Taylor, Percival John	26 February 1918
Terry, John Arthur	13 December 1915
Thorn, Edgar William	23 March 1918
Tolhurst, Alfred Wilfred	6 October 1917
Townsend, Frederick Charles	27 July 1917
Turner, Septimus Reynolds	9 February 1918
Ungless, Henry James	6 August 1915
Urry, James Suffling	
Valentine, Henry Edgar	14 February 1917
Varrow, George Ernest	18 February 1917
Vinson, Alexander	30 September 1915
Wade, Cecil Murrell (MM)	1 September 1916
Wade-Smith, Robert Charles	28 March 1918
Walford, Jabez James	06 April 1915
Walton, Robert	29 May 1915
Watton, William H.	28 April 1917
Watton, Arthur	14 April 1917

Watson, William H	28 April 1917
Watts, Graham Reginald	1 August 1916
Wearne, Cecil Aubrey	30 December 1917
Weatherhead, Henry Kenneth	10 September 1916
Webb, A.	
Webster, Colin Ailesbury	25 November 1914
Wells, Bertram T.	30 April 1916
White, A.W.	13 April 1919
White, William Reginald	26 September 1917
Widney, Ernest Edgar	9 September 1916
Wilden, John Stanley	1 December 1917
Willett, Frank Alfred	30 May 1917
Williams, Walter	04 November 1918
Williamson, Ernest	27 September 1918
Williamson, Harold	18 May 1917
Wolton, Robert	19 October 1917
Wood, Arthur James	1 July 1916
Woodman, Douglas	11 March 1918
Worledge, Frederick	22 April 1917
Wright, Cecil George	25 August 1918
Wright, Wesley William	7 July 1917
Wyles, Chester	01 November 1914
Young, Colin Turner	24 April 1917
Young, Ernest	3 July 1916
Young, Ernest	9 October 1917
Young, E.F.	
Young, L.T.	
Youngs, Leonard James	19 April 1918

St James Church's Clacton Calvary was erected on the external wall of the chancel behind the High Altar and dedicated as a war memorial on 2 October 1921. Then in June 1922 the War Memorial Steps were built and dedicated.

The War Memorial at Great Holland is in the form of a drinking fountain which is situated opposite the Church School and was bombed in the Second World War. It was a gift from Mr and Mrs

Samuel James, who were already well known for their generosity to the village.

It bears an inscription but not the names of those from the village who lost their lives these are on a brass tablet in All Saints' Church. The inscription reads:

This Drinking Fountain was
Erected as a memorial of the Great War 1914-1918
And in memory of all who fought
and worked to obtain
Victory.
A Bronze Tablet in the parish Church
Records the Names of the Men of
this Village who gave their lives
for their Country
Peace was signed June 28th 1919.

The following Roll of Honour lists the names of those from Great Holland but also from the Holland-on-Sea (Little Holland) area.

Great Holland War Memorial. (Author's collection)

Holland-on-Sea Roll of Honour

Name	Died
Bath, A.	8 May 1917
Beckworth, Samuel	21 July 1915
Borley, Frederick George	16 August 1917
Bridges, Alfred John	2 April 1917
Bridges, Arthur George	4 August 1915
Byford, Harry	18 October 1916
Davis, Reginald	20 October 1916
Day, Percy William	11 August 1918
Digby, Herbert	11 April 1917
Easey, Robert	15 August 1918
Garner-Watts, Graham Reginald	1 August 1916
Gray, Reginald Claude	6 October 1918
Hales, Osborne	14 October 1917
Harding, Alfred Stephen	5 November 1918
Harvey, George	28 April 1917
Hobbs, Arthur Frederick	31 May 1916
Howard, William	26 March 1917
Leonard, Martin	9 May 1915
Lott, Horace	30 September 1916
Pamment, Frank	22 December 1917
Partridge, Charles William	26 March 1917
Rainbird, Frederick	16 August 1917
Rix, George Sidney	31 July 1917
Rix, Henry James	26 October 1918
Rouse, Robert	26 March 1917
Sadler, William Henry	22 November 1918
Sharp, Thomas Alfred	30 September 1915
Wolton, Robert	19 October 1917

The inscription on the brass plaque in the church reads:

Great Holland
This Memorial is consecrated
To The
Glory of God
In Loving Memory of
The men of Great Holland
Who dies for Their Country
In The Great War 1914-1918
They Triumphed
In The Power of The Cross

Also in the church is a set of four stained-glass windows with an inscription across the base of the windows:

To the Glory of God and in memory of
Valiant Dead Sailors, Soldiers and Airmen
Who helped save this Country
From ruin and Desolation in the great War 1914-1918

After several months of deliberation the council unanimously agreed that the memorial should be in a form of a club. Frinton-on-Sea War Memorial is part of the front elevation of the Frinton-on-Sea War Memorial Club building in Fourth Avenue. Two separate but connected organizations were involved in the formation of the Club. Frietuna Hall is the building, and a Masonic lodge was the hall, subsequently purchased at a cost of £3,300. The money was raised by donations, notably Lord Byng of Vimy, Sir Richard Cooper £500 and the club's first President £500.

The club was officially opened and memorial plaque unveiled on 8 October 1921 by Sir Richard Cooper, who with a closing remark noted: 'whether he be a man of riches or a workman all would unite as one under that roof'. Included in the club's charter are the following words:

A lasting memorial raised to the Frinton men who made the supreme sacrifice, to be a place where those who served in the Great War might meet together and spend a social hour, joining good fellowship with the younger men and inclining their own hearts and the hearts of all who find entrance here to keep the lamp of remembrance burning.

Front entrance of the Frinton War Memorial Club. (Author's collection)

Frinton-on-Sea Roll of Honour

Name	Died
Almond, Charles Percy	5 April 1917
Baker, James Henry	26 May 1915
Barnes, Thomas Aubrey	14 July 1916
Bayfield, Henry Frederick	25 May 1919
Beckton, Harry	23 September 1919
Chaplin, William	27 August 1918
Churchill, Charles Percy	18 July 1917
Clarke, Herbert Palmer	1 October 1918
Conway, Alfred	14 October 1916
Darvell, Alfred	13 March 1917
Davidson, Ernest George William	6 October 1918

Dean, Arthur Anderson	8 May 1915
Fenn, Arthur Richard	15 June 1916
Hallum, E.J.	17 February 1917
Hazell, Dudley Howard	27 September 1918
Herbert, William Robert	17 July 1916
Horton, Robert Edmund	13 August 1918
Jackson, Charles	23 November 1917
Mann, Louis George	2 September 1917
Marker, Raymond John	13 November 1914
Moss, William Charles	22 April 1918
Norwood, John (VC: Boer War)	8 September 1914
Prince, Gilbert Carlyle Mason	24 August 1918
Ranson, Joseph William	1 September 1918
Rix, Frederick	23 August 1918
Robinson, Ronald Joseph	21 March 1917
Roper, Arthur	6 August 1915
Roper, Frederick	6 August 1915
Saunders, William George	26 March 1918
Strain, Michael Richard Dean	11 April 1917
Viney, Taunton Elliott	21 May 1916
Whittingham, Howard Shadwell	17 July 1916
Wittkugel, Adolf Frederick	15 February 1917

On Sunday, 21 November 1920 at 3.15 pm, General Lord Byng of Vimy GCB, KCMG, MVO, former commander of the Third Army, inspected local ex-servicemen at Walton-on-the-Naze. This was followed by a procession involving every organization in the town (Coast Guards, ex-servicemen, council members, Girl Guides, lifeboat men, Freemasons, Buffalos and children from the elementary school etc) from the local church to the Marine Gardens to pay tribute to Herbert G. Columbine, the town's VC hero, at his War memorial.

A hymn, 'Fight the good fight with all thy might' was sung followed by a prayer, a reading from the Scriptures and another hymn 'God of our fathers'. The chairman of the War Memorial Committee said a few words which was followed by the unveiling of the Memorial by Lord Byng.

Frinton War Memorial. (Author's collection)

The memorial had been designed and built by Mr N.A. Trent of London, and was a simple bronze bust, its likeness taken from a photograph. It rests on a stone pillar. Under the bust a plaque bore the words:

> Pte H G Columbine V.C.
> Killed in action 22nd March 1918
> He refused to retire
> When he might have done so

A second plaque below simply stated 'Erected by his Friends and Countrymen in ever grateful memory in the year 1920'. A prayer followed and then the hymn 'For all the saints'. Silence then fell on the 2,000-strong crowd as the Last Post was played, the ceremony finished with a rousing chorus of 'God Save the King'.

Emma, Herbert's mother, then laid a wreath with the words 'To my darling son from his mother'. In a short time the whole area was

Memorial to H.G. Columbine VC on the seafront. (Author's collection)

covered with wreaths to the fallen. Many shook Emma's hand and congratulated her on having such a brave son.

During the week following the unveiling a public meeting had been held to discuss the possibility of a War Memorial to honour

Bust of H.G. Columbine VC in the churchyard. (Author's collection)

all those men from Walton who had lost their lives. A memorial was eventually erected within the Garden Park, churchyard enclosure next to the church in Church Road with the names of those who lost their lives followed by the inscription:

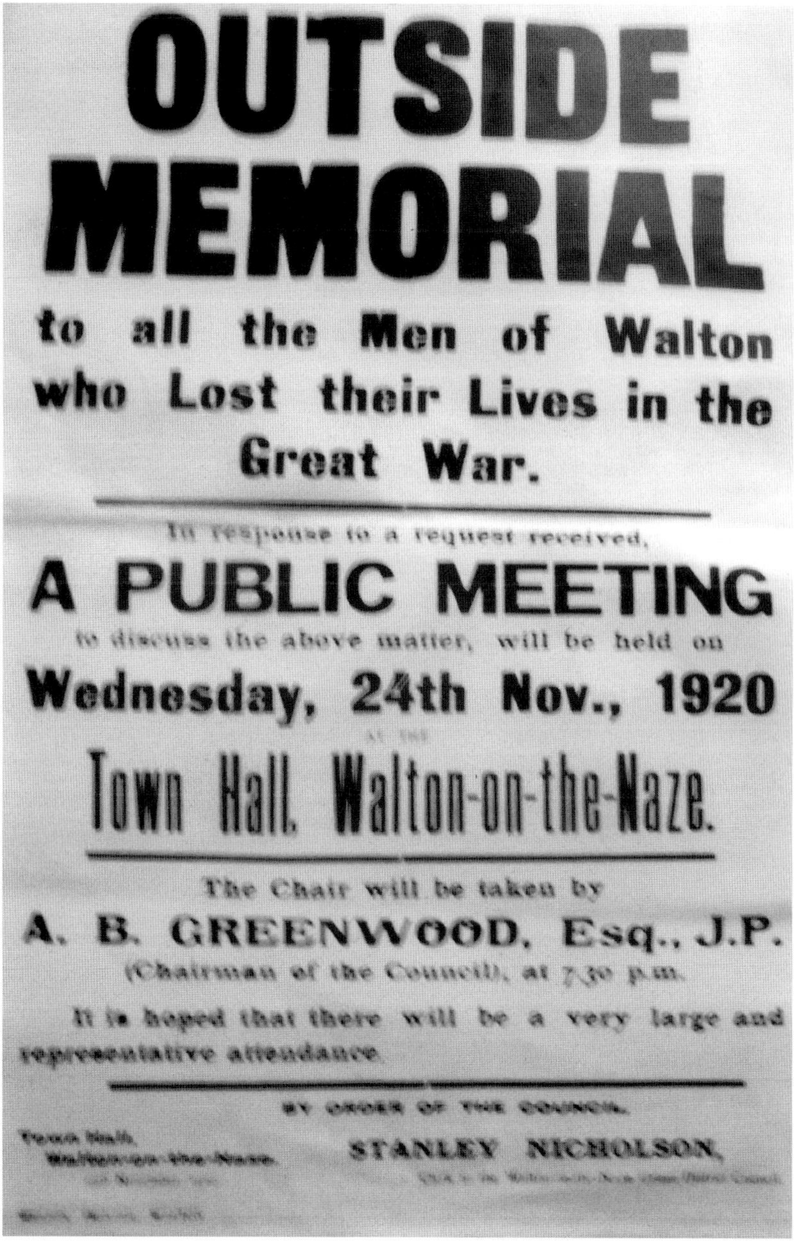

Public meeting poster.

Walton-on-the-Naze War Memorial. (Author's collection)

Of Walton-on-the-Naze
Who gave their lives in the
Great War 1914-1918
'Lest we forget'

Walton-on-the-Naze Roll of Honour

Name	Died
Austin, Claude	
Austin, Sydney	9 July 1917
Bailey, Albert	
Balls, Frederick Arthur	18 October 1915
Barker, John	14 May 1915
Barker, Stanley Edward	31 July 1917
Barnden, Stanley Evelyn	12 December 1914
Barnes, Arthur	
Bartram, Reginald James	27 September 1918
Barton, William Joseph (DCM)	27 October 1917
Berry, Thomas Arthur	26 September 1915
Birt, Lightly Harold	5 January 1915
Bly, Harold A.E.	17 November 1918
Botteler, Henry Edward	10 August 1918
Carter, Alfred	18 August 1916
Christmas, J. Alfred	4 September 1916
Clancy, C. Patrick	
Cobb, Frederick Walter	6 October 1916
Coles, William Henry	26 March 1917
Coleman, G.E.	20 May 1918
Cook, E.W.	28 April 1918
Columbine, Herbert (MM)	
Craven, Harry Lees Dacre	4 July 1917
Cutter, James	3 July 1916
Davis, William Richard	27/29 September 1916
Fairbrother, Alfred	
Fairbrother, John	15 October 1916
Fishingdon	1915
Gardiner, William M.	12 November 1915
Gladwell, C. Charles	
Gladwell, Osmond Ernest	8 November 1918
Gooding, S. James	

Griggs, Arthur	9 April 1917
Harland, George Thomas Walter	24 May 1916
Harrison, Arthur F.	
Hughes, Owen	30 November 1915
James, C. Thomas	
Johnson, Cecil Noble	30 March 1918
Kitching, Cecil	19 January 1919
Lee, Frederick	30 July 1915
Lilley, Roger Arthur	4 June 1919
Ling, Herbert Mark	18 November 1916
Lockwood, Stanley C.	
Long, Percy	
Moss, A. George	20 September 1917
Newcombe, Henry	27 May 1915
Page, John Stanley	3 May 1917
Potter, York Briggs	24 September 1916
Procter, Cecil Herbert	15 April 1918
Riches, George William	7 October 1917
Rose, Frederick William	26 September 1915
Sab(h)an, Jack A.	25 January 1915
Sadler, John	4 December 1917
Salzmann, Russell Bernhard	9 April 1917
Scholl, Claude	15 September 1916
Sharman, R.	20 May 1918
Smith, J. Bertie	
Smith, Thomas F.	
Summers, Walter	
Sweeney, Arthur George	27 February 1918
Turner, J.E.	13 July 1918
Wade, William Swift	27 August 1921
Webb, Albert Ernest	19 August 1917
Wiffen, Ernest	23 October 1918
Wightman, Francis L.	
Williams, Bertie	6 June 1915

Wood, William George	2 January 1916
Wright, Cecil George	25 August 1918
Wyatt, Clifford Charles	27 May 1916

The following Roll of Honour is the names of those that appear on a memorial in Great Clacton Church but I am unable to find them or establish their connection to the Clacton and Holland-on-Sea area. It is possible that their names have been spelt incorrectly.

Name	Died
Aldous, S.	
Anes, W.R.L.	
Bridges, F.	
Britton, S.	
Gregg, C.	
Hammond, E.	
Hatcher, L.	
Hooper, H.J.E.	
Hooper, W.	
Hughes, E.J.W.	
Ingarfield, P.	
Jenkins, F.W.	
Kittle, J.	
Levy, A.E.	
Nicholson, H.H.	
Randle, P.	
Seaman, M.A.	
Valentine, H.E.	
Watling, P.	
Watton, P.	
Wright, E.W.G.	

After the war a bronze plaque and scrolls were produced to commemorate those who gave that gave their lives and to acknowledge their sacrifice. They were intended to give to the next of kin as a tangible memorial of their lost loved ones. Some 1,355,000 were issued to the relatives of British and Empire service personnel: it became known as the 'Dead Man's Penny'.

It has been said that the Great War marked the beginning of the modern age. Countries of our empire were beginning to look for independence and one cannot blame them: they came to our aid in their thousands. India for one supplied nearly a million men to fight for our cause. For many it was going to be well after the Second World War before they actually became independent. However, the majority have stayed our friends and work closely together in the Commonwealth.

Two Minutes

TWO MINUTES- TWO – that was all,
All the King's subjects answered the Call;
Hats held in hand, hearts deep in thought,
Thinking of those who for Country fought.

TWO MINUES – then all was still,
As if the stream had ceased turning the mill;
Thinking of those as we paused in our toil,
Our 'Glorious Dead' that lay under the soil.

TWO MINUTES – Before a Nation's Shrine,
Surmounted by HIM our Maker Divine;
Mothers and Sisters kneel reverently in prayer
For those who gave their lives 'over there,'
Gone – but not forgotten,
To realms of Glory up in Heaven;
With Him – who for our souls, was slain,
Through Him, we hope to meet again
R.I.P.

By Private A. A. Brown (Royal Sussex Regiment)

Sources

⁓⁓

100 Years of the Parish of St. James Clacton-on-Sea by Jo Jellis
A History of the Town of Brightlingsea, member of the Cinque Ports by Edward P. Dickin.
AGE UK Essex memories project 1966.
AIF Project 2015.
Ancestry.com (on line).
Brightlingsea Museum.
British Newspapers Archive.
Chelmsford Chronicle.
Clacton Past by Norman Jacobs.
Commonwealth War Graves Commission.
Daily Mail.
Defending Essex by Mike Osborne.
Essex Countryside magazine.
Essex in the First World War by Michael Foley.
Essex Newsman (British Newspaper Archives).
Essex Record Office (SEAX).
Find My Past (on line).
Firstworldwar.com.
Forces War Records.co.uk (on line).
Geoff's Search Engine (www.hmt-six.co.uk).
Great War Forum (on line).
Herbert Columbine VC by Carole McEntee-Taylor.
Hold the Torch High by Phyllis M. Hendy.
Maldon, Essex Museum.
Men of Essex Volume 7, 8, 11 – Essex/Western Front Association.
National Archives.
St Osyth – Wikipedia.
The Clacton Roll of Honour 1914-1919 – Cann Hall Primary School.
The English & their History by Robert Tombs.

The Great War Book by Dawn Knox.
The History of Clacton by Kenneth Walker.
The History of the Lincolnshire Regiment 1914-1918 by Major General
    Simpson.
The Tank Museum.
The Victoria History of the Counties of England – Essex Vol. XI.
True Blue Magazine – October 1916.
VCs of the First World War – Spring Offensive 1918 by Gerald Gliddon.
Wartime Memories Project (online).
www.bbc.co.uk/essex/content/articles.
www.brightlingsea-town.co.uk/history.
www.pglcornwall.org.uk.
www.roll-of-honour.com.
www.stosyth.gov.uk.

Index